STUDY GUIDE

Individual Income Taxes

2000 Edition

General Editors

William H. Hoffman, Jr., J.D., Ph.D., C.P.A.
University of Houston

James E. Smith, Ph.D., C.P.A.
College of William and Mary

Eugene Willis, Ph.D., C.P.A.
University of Illinios-Urbana

Prepared by

Gerald E. Whittenburg, Ph.D., C.P.A.
San Diego State University

South-Western College Publishing
an International Thomson Publishing company I(T)P®

Cincinnati • Albany • Boston • Detroit • Johannesburg • London • Madrid • Melbourne • Mexico City
New York • Pacific Grove • San Francisco • Scottsdale • Singapore • Tokyo • Toronto

Accounting Team Director: Richard K. Lindgren
Acquisitions Editor: Maureen Riopelle
Developmental Editor: Esther Craig
Production Editor: Rebecca Glaab
Marketing Manager: Jennifer Codner
Manufacturing Coordinator: Doug Wilke

ISBN: 0-324-00908-9

1 2 3 4 5 6 7 GP 5 4 3 2 1 0 9

Printed in the United States of America

I(T)P®

International Thomson Publishing
South-Western College Publishing is an ITP Company.
The ITP trademark is used under license.

CONTENTS

PREFACE

This Study Guide has been designed to be used as a supplement to the 2000 Edition of *West's Federal Taxation: Individual Income Taxes*. Its purpose is to help you master the material presented in the text.

This Study Guide contains two features to help you understand income taxes.

> *Chapter Highlights*– This section provides statements about key concepts presented in the text.
>
> *Tests for Self-Evaluation*– Hundreds of questions and problems are presented (with answers) so that you may evaluate how well you understand the material in the text. The answers are keyed to the page numbers in the text.

I recommend the following approach as a method to use this Study Guide effectively:

- ✔ Study the textbook chapter.
- ✔ Review the *Chapter Highlights* section of the Study Guide. If something is not clear to you, review the chapter in the textbook.
- ✔ Mark the *Test for Self-Evaluation* and resolve your missed answers by referring to the solutions and to the textbook.

It is important that you use this Study Guide as an aid to mastering the material in the textbook, and not as a replacement for it. I suggest that you incorporate (as outlined above) the Study Guide into your regular study routine.

I would like to express my appreciation to Martha Altus for her help in preparing this edition of the Study Guide.

G. E. Whittenburg, March 1999

CHAPTER 1
AN INTRODUCTION TO TAXATION AND UNDERSTANDING THE FEDERAL TAX LAW

CHAPTER HIGHLIGHTS

A review of the history of the U.S. Federal tax system is helpful for the student to gain an understanding of the principles which have shaped the development of the system. This chapter introduces the student to the structure of the U.S. Federal tax system, the major types of taxes, and the organizational aspects of administering the tax law.

I. HISTORY OF U.S. TAXATION

A. There have been several income taxes in the past. The first North American income tax was enacted in 1634 in the Massachusetts Bay Colony. The first U.S. income tax was passed in 1861 to help finance the Civil War. In 1894, the Supreme Court, in *Pollock v. Farmers' Loan and Trust Co.*, held that an early version of the individual income tax was unconstitutional. In response to this Supreme Court decision, a constitutional amendment was passed to authorize the individual income tax. The Sixteenth Amendment, which was ratified in 1913, gave Congress the power to impose and collect an income tax. Before the Sixteenth Amendment, the corporate income tax was held to be an excise tax, and therefore deemed to be constitutional by the Supreme Court.

B. Various Revenue Acts were passed between 1913 and 1939. In 1939 these Acts were codified into the Internal Revenue Code of 1939, which was later recodified in 1954 and renamed in 1986 as the *Internal Revenue Code of 1986.*

C. Over the years the income tax has become the major source of revenue for the Federal government. During World War II, the tax went from a select tax to a mass tax. The individual and corporate income taxes constitute 57 percent (1999) of all Federal budget receipts. Social Security taxes represent 34 percent (1999) of Federal receipts.

II. CRITERIA USED IN THE SELECTION OF A TAX STRUCTURE

Adam Smith listed certain criteria with which to evaluate a particular tax or tax structure. These "canons of taxation" are *equality, convenience, certainty,* and *economy.*

III. THE TAX STRUCTURE

A. Tax Base. The tax base is the amount to which the tax rate is applied.

B. Tax Rates. Tax rates are the percentage applied to the tax base.

A *progressive tax* is one in which the tax rates increase as the tax base increases. The Federal income, gift, and estate taxes and most state income taxes are progressive taxes.

A *proportional tax* is one in which the rate of tax remains constant despite the size of the tax base.

C. The *incidence of taxation* is the degree to which each segment of society shares the total tax burden.

IV. MAJOR TYPES OF TAXES

A. Property taxes or *ad valorem* taxes are taxes that are based on value. The tax is usually imposed on realty or personalty. Realty taxes are a major source of revenue for local government, while personalty taxes generally have low compliance by taxpayers, except personal property taxes on items such as inventory, automobiles, boats, etc.

B. Transaction taxes impose a tax on transfers of property and are normally computed as a straight percentage of the value of the property involved.

Excise taxes are taxes on products such as gasoline, telephone usage, air travel, alcohol and tobacco. Both the Federal and state governments usually impose some form of excise tax.

Sales taxes differ from excise taxes in that sales taxes are applied to many different transactions, while excise taxes are applied to one product or transaction. A use tax is designed to prevent circumvention of the sales tax, such as where a resident of a state with a sales tax buys products in another state in an attempt to avoid the sales tax. Many states allow local sales taxes by cities, counties, etc., besides the general sales tax.

C. Death taxes are taxes imposed on either the right to transfer property at death (estate tax) or the right to receive property from a decedent (inheritance tax).

The Federal estate tax is designed to prevent large concentrations of wealth from being kept within the same family. The unified transfer credit eliminates or reduces the estate tax liability for small estates. For deaths in 1999, estate tax on a taxable estate up to $650,000 is eliminated by a credit of $211,300. The Federal government does not impose an inheritance tax.

Most states levy some form of death tax. If the death tax is an inheritance tax, the rates are generally lower for close family members and get larger the more distant the heir.

D. The Federal gift tax was enacted into law to complement the estate tax because without it, it would be possible to avoid the estate tax by making lifetime gifts and eliminating the gross estate. In 1999, taxable gifts are those gifts that exceed $10,000 per year per donee, reduced by any marital deduction. The Federal gift tax is determined by taking into account prior taxable gifts so that the tax rate is based on cumulative taxable gifts.

E. In the United States, income taxes are levied by the Federal government and most state governments and are the most popular forms of tax. Income taxes are imposed on individuals, corporations, and certain estates and trusts. The tax formula for individuals is shown as follows:

Income broadly conceived
(Exclusions)
Gross income
(Certain business deductions)
Adjusted gross income
(Greater of itemized deductions or the standard deduction)
(Exemptions)
Taxable income

Tax on taxable income
(Credits and withholding)
Tax due or refund

For individual taxpayers a standard deduction amount is available to taxpayers who do not itemize deductions.

The Federal income tax applies to corporations. The taxable income of a corporation is the difference between gross income and deductions.

Nearly all the states impose a state income tax on individuals and corporations. Most states pattern their income tax after the Federal income tax and use an adjusted Federal taxable income figure as a base, on which to apply the tax. Most states have some form of withholding procedures. The states taxing authorities work closely with the IRS and share information about audits and other changes in tax returns.

F. Employment taxes such as the FICA (Federal Insurance Contributions Act) tax are collected by the Federal government. The FICA tax consists of the old age, survivors, and disability insurance tax and the hospital insurance tax.

FICA taxes fund the Social Security system and are levied on both the employee and the employer. For 1999, an employee's FICA tax is equal to the sum of the old age, survivors, and disability insurance tax of 6.2% of the first $72,600 of wages and the Medicare tax of 1.45% of all wages. The employer must match the employee's contribution. If an employee pays too much FICA tax because he or she worked two or more jobs, a credit for the excess amount may be claimed.

The FUTA tax is levied only on the employer, with the purpose of providing the states with funds to administer the unemployment program. For 1999, the FUTA tax is equal to 6.2% of the first $7,000 of covered wages. A credit is allowed (up to 5.4%) for any FUTA paid to a state government so that the amount paid to the IRS could be as little as 0.8 percent.

G. Other U. S. Taxes. Federal Customs Duties are tariffs on certain imported goods. In recent years Customs Duties are used more to protect U.S. industries from foreign competition than to raise revenue to run the government.

There are several miscellaneous state and local taxes such as franchise taxes, occupational taxes, etc.

H. Proposed U.S. Taxes. There are several proposed changes to the U.S. tax system. These changes include The Flat Tax, The Value Added Tax, and a national sales tax. The Flat Tax would keep the income tax with substantial changes. The other two taxes would replace the U.S. income tax with a different system of taxation altogether.

V. TAX ADMINISTRATION

A. The Internal Revenue Service (IRS), which is part of the Treasury Department, has responsibility for administering the Federal tax law. The IRS uses statistical sampling techniques to select tax returns for an audit.

B. IRS audits are classified as "office audits" or "field audits." Office audits are restricted in scope and are conducted in the IRS office. A field audit is comprehensive and is conducted on the premises of the taxpayer or the taxpayer's representative.

C. The general statute of limitations for an IRS assessment is three years from the date the return is filed, unless the return is filed early in which case the limitation period runs from the date the return is due. There is no statute of limitations if no return or a fraudulent return is filed.

D. The interest rate used by the federal government is adjusted quarterly. Besides interest, various penalties are applied for noncompliance. For "failure to file" a tax return a penalty of 5 percent per month, or fraction thereof, is charged up to a 25 percent maximum. The penalty for "failure to pay" is one-half percent per month, or fraction thereof, up to a maximum of 25 percent. If both penalties apply to the same return, the failure to file penalty is reduced by the failure to pay penalty. Penalties also apply where the underpayment is due to negligence or fraud.

VI. UNDERSTANDING THE FEDERAL TAX LAW

A. Revenue Needs

Raising revenue is a major function of taxation. However, there are several other functions of the U.S. tax law. The tax law is also used to control the economy. Attempts at stimulation or temperance of the national economy have led to many amendments to the Internal Revenue Code.

B. Economic Considerations

The tax law contains many provisions to encourage investment and capital formation.

Lowering the tax rates gives taxpayers more income to spend, and is another method used to stimulate the economy. An increase in tax rates would have the opposite effect.

Another economic consideration of the tax law is to encourage certain activities. The favorable incentives granted research and development expenditures, the rapid amortization of pollution control facilities, and Foreign Sales Corporations (FSC) are examples of these types of provisions in the tax law. IRAs and other pension plans are examples of using the tax law to help the economic problem of capital formation.

The encouragement of certain industries is another economic consideration of the tax law. Agriculture, for example, is an industry that has special tax benefits.

Small businesses are generally considered good for the economy as a whole. Therefore, certain provisions of the tax law are designed to help small businesses. The S Corporation election is an example of the methods Congress uses to help small businesses through tax law provisions.

C. Social Considerations

The U.S. tax law contains many provisions intended to achieve social objectives. Examples of such social provisions are:

Nontaxability of employer-sponsored accident and health plans

Nontaxability of employer paid premiums for group-term insurance

Qualified pension and profit sharing plans

Deductions for contributions to charitable organizations

Credit for child care expenditures

Disallowance of deductions for expenditures that are against public policy (fines, penalties, etc.)

D. Equity Considerations

The Federal tax law attempts to alleviate the effect of multiple taxation in several areas. Examples include the deduction for state, local, and foreign income tax and the foreign tax credit.

The wherewithal to pay concept recognizes the inequity of taxing a transaction where the taxpayer lacks the means with which to pay the tax. Sometimes the Federal tax rules, such as those applicable where a taxpayer reinvests the proceeds from an involuntary conversion (e.g., a casualty loss) in similar property, allow the taxpayer to defer recognition of gain when his or her economic situation has not changed significantly.

Mitigating the effect of the concept of an annual accounting period is an equity consideration that deals with the inequities which arise from the arbitrary use of the annual accounting period to divide the taxpayer's life into taxable segments. The annual accounting period concept could lead to different treatment of two individuals who are, from a long-range standpoint, in the same economic position. Measures to alleviate this inequity include the carryover procedure for net operating losses, excess capital losses and excess charitable contributions, and the installment method of recognizing gain.

One major problem in recent years has been bracket creep which was caused by inflation. Taxpayers were pushed into higher tax brackets without a real increase in income. This problem is addressed by indexing. Each year, beginning in 1989, the tax brackets and the standard deduction are indexed upward by the amount of inflation. The personal and dependency exemptions are also indexed based on inflation.

E. Political Considerations

Special interest legislation includes tax provisions sponsored because of the instigation of influential constituents. Such legislation is inevitable in our political system and can sometimes be justified on economic, social or utilitarian grounds.

Political expediency is responsible for the passage of tax provisions which have popular appeal such as measures that insure wealthy taxpayers pay their "fair" share of tax, the lowering of individual income tax rates and increasing the exemption amount.

State and local influences explain the nontaxability of interest received on state and local obligations, and the extension under Federal tax law of community property tax advantages to residents of common law states.

F. Influence of the IRS

As protector of the revenue, the IRS has a great deal of influence on shaping the tax law. In this role the IRS tries to close what it sees as loopholes in the tax law.

Many provisions of the tax law are for administrative feasibility, and exist because they simplify the work of the IRS in collecting the revenue or administering the tax law. Withholding procedures place taxpayers on a pay-as-you-go basis and so aid the IRS in the collection of revenue. Interest and penalties imposed for noncompliance with tax laws are also of considerable help to the IRS.

G. Influences of the Courts

The Federal courts have influenced the tax law. Some court decisions have been of such consequence that Congress has incorporated them into the Internal Revenue Code. The rule that allows tax-free stock dividends is an example of a court decision being codified.

KEY TERMS:

Tax Rate Structure

Property Tax

Sales Tax

Excise Tax

Estate and Gift Tax

Income Tax

Tax Administration

Revenue/Economic Consideration

Social/Equity/Political Considerations

TEST FOR SELF-EVALUATION

True or False

Indicate which of the following statements are true or false by circling the correct answer.

T F 1. The first U.S. Federal income tax was enacted to provide revenues for the Civil War.

T F 2. The Supreme Court held that the 1894 income tax law was constitutional since it was a direct tax.

T F 3. The Sixteenth Amendment was necessary to enact the corporate income tax of 1909.

T F 4. The first Internal Revenue Code was the Internal Revenue Code of 1939.

T F 5. The current tax law is the Internal Revenue Code of 1986, as amended.

T F 6. The corporate income tax provides the largest percentage of Federal tax revenues.

T F 7. During World War II, the income tax was converted from being a select tax to being a mass tax.

T F 8. The responsibility for administering the Federal tax law rests with the Treasury Department.

T F 9. The Internal Revenue Service openly reveals its audit selection techniques.

T F 10. The purpose of the gift tax is to prevent widespread avoidance of the estate tax.

T F 11. For 1999, the maximum amount of salary to which the old age, survivors, and disability insurance (OASDI) portion of the FICA tax will be applied is $72,600.

T F 12. Tax rates are applied to a tax base to determine a taxpayer's liability.

T F 13. For 1999, tax collections from individual income taxes account for 46 percent of the Federal government's budget receipts.

T F 14. Ad valorem taxes are taxes that are based on income derived from property.

T F 15. Property taxes on personalty have a high rate of compliance, while taxes on realty have a low rate of compliance.

T F 16. Excise taxes are levied on specific transactions or products, while sales taxes are collected on transactions involving a wide range of products.

T F 17. Excise taxes are sometimes used to influence social behavior.

T F 18. The Federal government is the only government allowed to impose excise taxes on products.

T F 19. The primary purpose of the estate tax is to generate revenue with which to operate the Federal government.

T F 20. For deaths after 1999, the unified transfer tax credit is $211,300.

T F 21. State inheritance taxes usually tax all heirs at the same rate.

T F 22. The annual exclusion for Federal gift tax purposes is $47,000 per year per donee.

T F 23. A taxpayer can minimize his Federal gift tax liability by making several small taxable gifts rather than a single large taxable gift.

T F 24. All states impose some form of income tax on individuals who reside in that state.

T F 25. Some cities impose an income tax along with the federal and state income taxes.

T F 26. In recent years, tariffs have served the nation more as an instrument for carrying out protectionist policies than for generating revenue.

T F 27. The interest rates applicable to underpayments and overpayments of federal income taxes used by the Internal Revenue Service are determined every quarter.

T F 28. The progressiveness of the U.S. Federal income tax rate structure for individuals has varied over time.

T F 29. Certain provisions of the U.S. income tax law are designed to help small businesses.

T F 30. An example of a social consideration in the tax law is the nontaxability of health plan benefits.

T F 31. The wherewithal to pay concept states that a taxpayer should pay the tax on all gains, even when his economic position has not changed.

T F 32. Many provisions of the tax law can be explained by looking at the influence of pressure groups on Congress.

T F 33. One role assumed by the Internal Revenue Service is that of "protector of the revenue."

T F 34. Some of the tax law is justified because it complicates the Internal Revenue Service's task of collecting revenue.

T F 35. The courts have established the rule that the relief provisions of the Code are to be broadly interpreted.

T F 36. Some court decisions have been of such consequence that Congress has written them into the tax laws.

T F 37. The tax law attempts to encourage technological progress.

T F 38. Economic considerations in the tax law help regulate the economy.

T F 39. One equity consideration of the tax law is the alleviation of multiple taxation.

T F 40. Carryback and carryover procedures help mitigate the effect of limiting a loss or deduction to the accounting period in which it was realized.

T F 41. The amounts of the standard deduction, exemptions, and tax brackets will be indexed for inflation in the future.

T F 42. In future years, budget deficit problems will probably influence many new tax provisions passed by Congress.

T F 43. For purposes of the gift tax, a special election applicable to married persons allows 75 percent of a gift made by a donor spouse to be treated as made by the nondonor spouse.

T F 44. In addition to the Federal gift tax, several states impose a state gift tax on their residents.

T F 45. A piggyback state tax is a state income tax based on a federal tax number (such as calculating the state income tax on based federal adjusted gross income).

Fill-in-the-Blanks

Complete the following statements with the appropriate word(s) or amount(s).

1. Adam Smith's "canons of taxation" are __________, __________, __________, and __________.

2. Tax rates applied to a taxpayer's tax base may be __________ or __________.

3. Taxes imposed on luxury items such as alcoholic beverages, tobacco products, and highway fuels are called __________ taxes.

4. Property transferred at death is subject to the Federal __________ tax based on the value of the property.

5. The Internal Revenue Service is part of the Department of __________.

6. Audits other than those settled through correspondence between the taxpayer and the Internal Revenue Service, are classified as __________ audits or __________ audits.

7. The usual statute of limitations is __________ years, but if no return is filed the statute of limitations period is __________.

8. The penalty for failure to file a tax return is __________ percent per month, up to a maximum of _______ percent.

9. An ______________ tax is a tax on the right to receive property from a decedent.

10. The funds provided by the _______ tax system are used by the states to provide unemployment benefits to workers.

Multiple Choice

Choose the best answer for each of the following questions.

1. Which of the following is an employment tax?
   a. The Gift Tax
   b. FICA Tax
   c. Customs duties
   d. Excise taxes
   e. None of the above

2. Which of the following items will not be subject to indexing under the tax law?
   a. The standard deduction
   b. Personal and dependency exemptions
   c. The child care credit
   d. The individual tax brackets
   e. All of the above are indexed

3. For 1999, the tax rate for the old age, survivors, and disability insurance portion of the Social Security tax imposed on employees' wages up to $72,600 is:
   a. 1.45%
   b. 6.06%
   c. 6.20%
   d. 7.65%
   e. Some other amount

4. The installment method of reporting gains is justified on the basis of:
   a. Mitigation of the annual accounting period
   b. Wherewithal to pay
   c. Social consideration
   d. Both a and b
   e. None of the above

5. Jack's gross income for 1999 is $60,000 and he has business deductions of $6,000. His itemized deductions are $7,000 and he has one personal exemption worth $2,750. For 1999 Jack's taxable income is:
   a. $54,000
   b. $53,000
   c. $47,000
   d. $44,250
   e. Some other amount

6. For 1999, Jeanne earned wages of $81,000. The total amount of FICA tax due from Jeanne and her employer is:
   a. $5,675.70
   b. $11,351.40
   c. $5,553.90
   d. $11,107.80
   e. Some other amount

7. During 1999, Steve earned $4,000 and Lynne earned $12,000 from Red Inc. The total FUTA tax payable by their employer before any state credits is:
   a. $420
   b. $240
   c. $682
   d. $660
   e. Some other amount

8. Byron files his tax return 45 days late. Along with the return he remits a check for $6,000 which is the balance of the tax owed. Disregarding interest, what is Byron's penalty for failure to file?
   a. -0-
   b. $60
   c. $540
   d. $600
   e. Some other amount

9. The value added tax is:
   a. used by several European Union countries.
   b. a form of income tax on corporations.
   c. a tax on consumption.
   d. Both a and c are correct.
   e. Answers a, b, and c, are correct.

10. John received $140,000 when the state condemned his house for a new freeway. The house cost John $84,000. John immediately purchased a new home for $140,000. From this sale John should report a taxable gain of:
    a. $-0-
    b. $56,000
    c. $140,000
    d. $84,000
    e. Some other amount

11. If the quarterly rate charged by the IRS for taxpayer assessments (underpayments) is 8%, then the rate paid for tax refunds (overpayments) is:
    a. 6%
    b. 7%
    c. 8%
    d. 9%
    e. 10%

12. Vicky filed her 19X3 individual tax return on January 15, 19X4. The return was properly signed and filed. The statute of limitations for Vicky's 19X3 return expires on:
    a. January 15, 19X7
    b. April 15, 19X7
    c. January 15, 19X0
    d. April 15, 19X0

13. Mike had two jobs during 1999. He earned $50,000 from his first employer and $30,000 from his second employer. All of the wages were subject to the FICA tax. When Mike files his tax return he can claim a credit for excess FICA of how much?
    a. -0-
    b. $458.90
    c. $4,501.20
    d. $4,960.00
    e. Some other amount

14. Which of the following is not an economic consideration of the tax law?
    a. Encouragement of small business
    b. Encouragement of certain industries
    c. The wherewithal to pay concept
    d. Encouragement of certain activities
    e. None of the above

15. The net operating loss provision of the tax law is an example of:
    a. An economic consideration
    b. A social consideration
    c. A political consideration
    d. An equity consideration
    e. None of the above

16. Which of the following is not a social consideration in the tax law?
    a. Qualified pension and profit-sharing plan
    b. Expensing soil and water conservation costs
    c. Child care credit
    d. A speeding ticket paid by a truck driver is nondeductible
    e. All of the above are social considerations

17. Which of the following is the best example of a tax law provision designed to aid in controlling the economy?
    a. Depreciation deduction
    b. Child care credit
    c. Personal exemption
    d. Net operating loss carryover
    e. None of the above

18. Smith Corporation pays $2,000 per month rent on a building to Mary Smith, its sole shareholder. The fair market value of the rent determined at "arm's length" would be $900 per month. Smith Corporation will be allowed a monthly rental deduction of:
    a. -0-
    b. $900
    c. $1,000
    d. $2,000
    e. None of the above

19. A father rents property to his daughter for $10,000 a year. If the IRS wants to examine this transaction it will be interested in:
    a. The tax benefit rule

b. Installment sales rules
c. The arm's length concept
d. Public policy limitations
e. None of the above

20. Several years ago, Fran entered an agreement to rent a building to Meg for 20 years. During the first year of the lease, Meg made $60,000 in capital improvements to the building. This year the lease is terminated and Fran takes possession of the building. The fair market value of the capital improvements in the year of termination is $75,000. In the year of the termination of the lease, Fran must recognize taxable gain of?
a. $-0-
b. $15,000
c. $60,000
d. $75,000
e. Some other amount

21. On a tax return that is filed 45 days late, Christy pays $33,000 in additional taxes. Of this amount $10,000 is attributable to Christy's negligence. What is Christy's negligence penalty?
a. $-0-
b. $500
c. $2,000
d. $6,600
e. Some other amount

22. When a tax base is $20,000, the tax liability is $6,000 and when the tax base is $200,000 the tax liability is $60,000. This tax rate structure is:
a. Progressive
b. Regressive
c. Proportional
d. Parallel
e. VAT

23. When a tax base is $20,000, the tax liability is $6,000 and when the tax base is $200,000 the tax liability is $80,000. This tax rate structure is:
a. Progressive
b. Regressive
c. Proportional
d. Parallel
e. VAT

24. For 1913 individual tax returns filed on March 1, 1914, the maximum marginal tax rate was?
a. 6%
b. 10%
c. 12%
d. 15%
e. 18%

25. The pay-as-you-go system of withholding used by the United States Government was passed into law in?
a. 1913

b. 1925
c. 1943
d. 1954
e. 1961

26. Jim, a single taxpayer, died in 1999. He had made no taxable gifts before his death. Jim's taxable estate is $750,000. What part of his taxable estate will be subject to the Federal estate tax?
a. $-0-
b. $100,000
c. $650,000
d. $750,000

27. A(n) _________ tax is an ad valorem tax (usually at the same rate as the sales tax) on the utilization, consumption, or storage of tangible property.
a. Excise
b. Severance
c. Luxury
d. Use
e. Property

28. Which of the following states does not impose an income tax on individuals?
a. Virginia
b. Nevada
c. Vermont
d. Alabama
e. North Dakota

SOLUTIONS TO CHAPTER 1

True or False

1. True (p. 1-2)
2. False The income tax was unconstitutional because it was not apportioned. (p. 1-3)
3. False The 1909 corporate income tax was held to be constitutional. (p. 1-3)
4. True (p. 1-3)
5. True (p. 1-3)
6. False The individual income tax provides the largest percent. (p. 1-4)
7. True (p. 1-4)
8. True (p. 1-18)
9. False The IRS does not disclose its audit selection techniques. (p. 1-18)
10. True (p. 1-12)
11. True (p. 1-16)
12. True (p. 1-5)
13. True (p. 1-4)
14. False Ad valorem taxes are based on the value of the property. (p.1-6)
15. False The tax on realty has a high compliance rate. (p. 1-7)
16. True (p. 1-9)
17. True (p. 1-9)
18. False State and local governments can also impose excise taxes. (p. 1-9)
19. False The estate tax is intended to prevent concentrations of wealth. (p. 1-11)
20. True (p. 1-11)
21. False Inheritance taxes generally are imposed on distant heirs at a higher rate. (p. 1-11)
22. False The exclusion is $10,000 per year. (p. 1-12)
23. False The gift tax is based on the taxpayer's cumulative taxable gifts. (p. 1-12)
24. False Several states do not have a state income tax. (p. 1-13)
25. True (p. 1-15)
26. True (p. 1-16)
27. True (p. 1-21)
28. True (p. 1-6)
29. True (p. 1-25)
30. True (p. 1-25)
31. False The wherewithal to pay concept recognizes that under some circumstances, even though a gain has been realized by the taxpayer, the taxpayer's economic position may not have changed. (p. 1-27)
32. True (p. 1-29)
33. True (p. 1-30)
34. False Some of the law is justified because it simplifies the work of the IRS. (p. 1-30)
35. False The relief provisions are narrowly interpreted. (p. 1-31)
36. True (p. 1-32)
37. True (p. 1-24)
38. True (p. 1-24)
39. True (p. 1-26)
40. True (p. 1-28)
41. True (p. 1-28)
42. True (p. 1-24)
43. False The gift is split 50-50. (p. 1-12)
44. True (p. 1-13)
45. True (p. 1-14)

Fill-in-the-Blanks

1. equality, convenience, certainty, economy (p. 1-4)
2. proportional, progressive (p. 1-5)
3. excise (p. 1-9)
4. estate (p. 1-11)
5. the Treasury (p. 1-18)
6. office, field (p. 1-19)
7. three, indefinite (p. 1-20)
8. five, 25 (p. 1-21)
9. Inheritance (p. 1-10)
10. FUTA (p. 1-16)

Multiple Choice

1. B (p. 1-15)
2. C (p. 1-28)
3. C (p. 1-16)
4. D (p. 1-27)
5. D \$60,000 - 6,000 - 7,000 - 2,750 = \$44,250. [1999] (p. 1-14)
6. B [(6.2% x \$72,600) + (1.45% x \$81,000)] x 2 = \$11,351.40 [1999] (p. 1-16)
7. C [\$4,000 + \$7,000 (maximum)] x 6.2% = \$682.00. [1999] (p. 1-16)
8. C 5% per month or fraction thereof, or 10% x \$6,000 = \$600, less failure to pay penalty of .5% per month or fraction thereof, (1% x \$6,000 = \$60), which equals \$540. (p. 1-21)
9. D (p. 1-17)
10. A (p. 1-27)
11. B (p. 1-21)
12. B (p. 1-20)

13. B

\$3,100.00 =	(\$50,000 x 6.2%) employer 1 (non-Medicare)
1,860.00 =	(\$30,000 x 6.2%) employer 2 (non-Medicare)
\$4,960.00	Amount paid
-4,501.20 =	(\$72,600 x 6.2%) maximum non-Medicare FICA due
\$458.80	Credit [1999] (p. 1-16)

14. C This is an equity consideration. (p. 1-27)
15. D (p. 1-28)
16. B (p. 1-25)
17. A (p. 1-24)
18. B (p. 1-32)
19. C (p. 1-31)
20. A (p. 1-31)
21. C \$2,000 = 20% x \$10,000. (p. 1-22)
22. C (p. 1-5)
23. A (p. 1-5)
24. A (p. 1-3)
25. C (p. 1-4)

26. B $750,000 - $650,000 = $100,000 [1999]. (p. 1-11)
27. D (p. 1-10)
28. B (p. 1-13)

CHAPTER 2
WORKING WITH THE TAX LAW

CHAPTER HIGHLIGHTS

Familiarity with the statutory, administrative, and judicial sources of the tax law is essential in learning to work with tax legislation. This chapter considers the sources of the tax law, the application of research techniques to tax problems, and the effective use of tax planning procedures.

I. TAX SOURCES

A. Statutory Sources of Tax Law. The Internal Revenue Code of 1939 was the first codification of all Federal tax provisions into a logical sequence. The 1939 Code was recodified into the 1954 Code, which was renamed the Internal Revenue Code of 1986. New tax laws are integrated into the 1986 Code.

For a tax bill to become law, it must be passed by both houses of Congress and signed by the President. Tax legislation is first considered in the House by the Ways and Means Committee. Legislation, once approved by the House of Representatives, is then considered by the Senate Finance Committee, and finally the entire Senate. When the House and Senate cannot agree on the tax bill, the differences are worked out by the Joint Conference Committee.

The Code is arranged by Subtitles, Chapters, Subchapters, Parts, and Sections. However, to identify any part of the Code, it is only necessary to know the Section number because these numbers are not repeated. The normal progression for a citation is Section, Subsection, Paragraph, and Subparagraph.

Tax Treaties are negotiated with most foreign countries. If a treaty comes in conflict with the Code, the most recent item will take precedence. A taxpayer must disclose (subject to penalties for non-disclosure) on a tax return if a treaty overrides a provision of the tax law.

B. Administrative sources of Tax Law. There are numerous administrative sources of Federal tax law. These can be grouped as Treasury Department Regulations, Revenue Rulings and Procedures, and other pronouncements. All are issued by the U.S. Treasury Department or one of its instrumentalities such as the Internal Revenue Service or a District Director.

Treasury Department Regulations is the Internal Revenue Service's official interpretation of the Code. They are arranged in Code section sequence with a prefix to designate the type of regulation.

Revenue Rulings and Procedures are official pronouncements of the National Office of the IRS. They do not, however, carry the same legal force as Regulations. Revenue Rulings are usually concerned with a restrictive problem or area, while Revenue Procedures are concerned with internal management practices of the IRS. Both Revenue Rulings and Procedures are published weekly by the U.S. government in the *Internal Revenue Bulletin*. Every six months the weekly bulletins are published in a bound volume entitled the *Cumulative Bulletin*.

Individual Letter Rulings are issued by the National Office of the IRS in response to a taxpayer's request and describe how the IRS will treat a proposed transaction. Individual Letter Rulings are available for public inspection after identifying details are removed.

Determination Letters are rulings that generally deal with completed transactions, and are issued by District Directors, instead of the National Office of the IRS.

The IRS also makes the following administrative communications:

Treasury Decisions (TDs) are issued by the Treasury Department to promulgate new Regulations, amend or change existing Regulations, or to announce the government's position on selected court decisions.

Technical Advice Memoranda, released by the National Office of the IRS, are private rulings initiated by the IRS during its audit activities.

Other pronouncements (e.g., Announcements and Notices) that allow the IRS to communicate necessary information to taxpayers.

C. Judicial Sources of Tax Law. After a taxpayer has exhausted the remedies available with the IRS, a dispute can be taken to the Federal courts. The dispute is first heard by a trial court (the court of original jurisdiction) with any appeal taken to the appropriate appellate court. A description of the various courts is as follows:

District Courts. *The Federal District Courts are organized into geographical regions, and will hear cases involving any Federal matter, both tax and nontax issues. Taxpayers cannot choose a particular District Court but must use the one having jurisdiction over the case. Each District Court has only one judge and it is the only court in which the taxpayer may have a jury trial.*

U.S. Claims Court. *The U.S. Claims Court has sixteen judges and meets in Washington, D.C. The purpose of this court is to hear any case involving a monetary claim against the Federal government.*

U.S. Tax Court. *The U.S. Tax Court is a national court with nineteen judges. However, only one judge hears a case unless it is unusual. The Tax Court hears only cases involving tax matters. The Tax Court will follow decisions of the Court of Appeals in the jurisdiction in which the case is being heard. The Tax Court is the only court in which the taxpayer need not pay the deficiency before taking the dispute to court. Before 1943, the Tax Court was called the Board of Tax Appeals (BTA).*

Small Claims Division of U.S. Tax Court. *The small claims division of the U.S. Tax Court will hear matters involving amounts up to $50,000. The decisions of the small claims division are final and cannot be appealed.*

U.S. Court of Appeals. *There are eleven numbered Court of Appeals plus one for the District of Columbia, and one for the Federal District. Each Court of Appeals has jurisdiction in a specific geographical region of the country, except the Federal District, which hears cases only from the U.S. Claims Court.*

U.S. Supreme Court. *The Supreme Court, a nine-judge panel, has final say in all tax matters. Appeal to the Supreme Court is by Writ of Certiorari, and acceptance is not automatic.*

Court decisions are reported in a variety of publications. Decisions of the District Court, U.S. Claims Court, Court of Appeals, and Supreme Court that deal with tax matters are reported in both the CCH *U.S. Tax Cases* (USTC) and the RIA (formerly P-H) *American Federal Tax Reports* (AFTR) series. All District Court decisions are published by West Publishing Company in their *Federal Supplement Series* (F.Supp.). All decisions of the U.S. Claims Court beginning October 1982 are published in the *Claims Court Reporter* (Cl.Ct.), by West Publishing Company. All decisions of the Courts of Appeals and U.S. Claims Court decisions prior to October 1982, are published by West in a reporter designated as the *Federal Second Series* (F.2d). Supreme Court decisions are published by West in its *Supreme Court Reporter* (S.Ct.), by the U.S. Government Printing Office in the *United States Supreme Court Reports* (U.S.), and by the Lawyer's Cooperative Publishing Company in its *United States Reports, Lawyer's Edition* (L.Ed.).

The Tax Court issues two kinds of decisions, Regular and Memorandum. Generally, Regular decisions deal with a new or unusual point of law, while Memorandum decisions deal with an established point of law. The Regular decisions of the Tax Court are published by the U.S. Government Printing Office (GPO) in a series designated *Tax Court of the United States Reports* (T.C.). Memorandum decisions are published by CCH in *Tax Court Memorandum Decisions* (TCM) and by RIA in *T.C. Memorandum Decisions*.

Citations of a court decision generally consist of two parts: (1) the name of the case and the abbreviated title of the report volume and (2) the number or page of the report that contains the text of the decision. After each citation, a parenthetical reference identifies the court rendering the decision and the year the decision was reached.

If the IRS loses at the trial court level and does not appeal the decision this does not indicate that the IRS agrees with the result or that it will not litigate similar situations in the future.

II. WORKING WITH THE TAX LAW-- TAX RESEARCH

A. Identifying and refining the Problem. The first step in tax research is to identify and define the problem. All facts having a bearing on the problem must be gathered since any omission could have a substantial impact on the conclusion reached. Once a problem has been identified, it should be refined. New facts may lead to a faster problem solving or lead to the discovery of new problem areas.

B. Locating the Appropriate Tax Law Sources. The second step in tax research involves locating the appropriate sources of tax law. Most tax research begins with the index volume of a tax service. A tax service is a comprehensive set of books on Internal Revenue law. The major tax services are arranged by Code section number or topic. When using any tax service one should always check for current developments. Besides the tax services there are many tax periodicals that are indexed in CCH's *Federal Tax Articles*.

C. Assessing the Validity of the Tax Law Sources. The third step in tax research, once a source of tax information has been located, is to assess the source in relation to the problem at hand. Some of the characteristics of sources that need to be assessed would include conflicting Code provisions, the relative importance of Treasury Regulations, Revenue Rulings, and court decisions.

The language of the Code can be extremely difficult to comprehend, with extremely long sentences and many cross references between interrelated provisions. Also, occasional conflicts between old and new Code provisions arise. For these and other reasons, great care should be exercised when interpreting the Code.

The Treasury Regulations are not the law, but have the force and effect of law if they are reasonable interpretations of the Code. The burden of proof rests with the taxpayer to show that a Regulation is wrong. Certain "legislative regulations" are virtually impossible to overturn.

Revenue Rulings carry less weight than the Regulations, but are important reflections of the IRS's position on certain tax matters.

The validity of a court decision depends on the level of the court, the residence of the taxpayer, and the status of the decision.

D. Arriving at the Solution or at Alternative Solutions. The fourth step of the tax research process is arriving at a solution based on the information gathered. Often a clear-cut answer is impossible to obtain, and a guarded judgment is the best solution that can be given.

E. Communicate Tax Research. Once a conclusion has been reached, it is necessary to communicate the findings to the client. This is normally done by preparing a memo that explains the findings and how the conclusions were reached. The contents of a Tax Memo are as follows:

A clear statement of the issue(s).

A short review of the factual pattern.

A review of the tax law.
Any assumptions.

The solution recommended and the logic supporting the conclusion.

References consulted while doing the research.

After the memo is prepared a letter based on the memo is written and sent to the client.

The tax practitioner should follow-up, where necessary, on the solution reached during the research process. Developments could occur that might alter the conclusion reached at the end of the research project.

F. Follow up. The tax researcher should follow up on the solution (where appropriate) in light of any new developments.

III. WORKING WITH THE TAX LAW-- TAX PLANNING

A. Nontax Consideration. In tax planning, it is necessary to take into account many nontax considerations. What may produce the best tax result may not be an acceptable alternative to the taxpayer. Generally, tax planning involves producing the smallest tax within the nontax and legal constraints. Tax considerations should not impair the exercise of sound business judgment by the taxpayer.

B. Tax Avoidance and Tax Evasion. There is a difference between tax avoidance and tax evasion. Tax avoidance is merely minimization through legal means, while evasion is illegal tax planning.

C. Follow-up Procedures. A change in the tax law could alter a conclusion. Additional research may be necessary to test any solution in light of current developments.

D. Electronic Tax Research. Computer tax research is part of the day-to-day tax practice for many tax professionals. The computer data bases provide the tax practitioner instant access to the entire legal data base. The four major CD-ROM tax research data bases are WESTLAW, RIA OnPoint, CCH ACCESS, and Kleinrock's. These data bases are searched by using a system of key words. The document(s) that meet the search criteria are then displayed on the computer screen for the tax researcher.

LEXIS/NEXIS, WESTLAW, RIA Checkpoint, and CCH ACCESS provide online tax research services. These services are very up-to-date and are expensive because of their real time ability. The Internet (World Wide Web) provides many sites with tax information. See text for site addresses.

KEY TERMS:

Administrative Sources

Judicial Sources

Statutory Sources
Court of Appeals

Court of Federal Claims

District Court

Regulations

Revenue Ruling

Supreme Court

Tax Court

Tax Research

Tax Planning

TEST FOR SELF-EVALUATION

True or False

Indicate which of the following statements are true or false by circling the correct answer.

T F 1. Both Revenue Rulings and Revenue Procedures are published weekly by the U.S. Government in the *Internal Revenue Bulletin*.

T F 2. There is only one U.S. Court of Federal Claims and it meets most often in Washington, D.C.

T F 3. The U.S. Claims Court has seven judges and the Tax Court has nineteen judges.

T F 4. Regulation Sec. 1.61 refers to Internal Revenue Code Sec. 61.

T F 5. Appeal to the Supreme Court is by Writ of Certiorari.

T F 6. Revenue Ruling 87-61 relates to Sec. 61 of the Internal Revenue Code.

T F 7. In general, a U.S. Tax Court Regular decision deals with a new or unusual point of law.

T F 8. The Internal Revenue Service usually acquiesces or nonacquiesces to all regular Tax Court decisions.

T F 9. To go to the Tax Court, a taxpayer must pay the tax and sue for a refund.

T F 10. A jury trial may be obtained in the Tax Court.

T F 11. *Bradford v. Comm.*, 56-1 USTC Para.9552 (CA-6, 1956) is an example of a citation from Commerce Clearing House's *United States Tax Cases*.

T F 12. RIA publishes Revenue Rulings in its *American Federal Tax Reports* (AFTR).

T F 13. The United States Tax Court is one of the federal trial courts that is a court of original jurisdiction.

T F 14. When confronted with a particularly troublesome problem, the taxpayer may always obtain an Individual Letter Ruling.

T F 15. *Morris Alexander v. Comm.*, 61 T.C. 278 is an example of a citation from Commerce Clearing House's *Tax Court of the United States Reports*.

T F 16. Temporary Regulations are also issued as Proposed Regulations and automatically expire within three years after the date of issuance.

T F 17. In a challenge by the IRS, the burden of proof is on the taxpayer to show that a Regulation is wrong.

T F 18. Tax avoidance is illegal tax planning while tax evasion is legal tax planning.

T F 19. A case is appealed from the U.S. Claims Court to the Court of Appeals for the Federal Circuit and then to the Supreme Court.

T F 20. *John Smith*, T.C. Memo 1980-32 is the thirty-second Tax Court Memorandum decision of 1980.

T F 21. The Tax Court follows the decisions of the Court of Appeals for the appropriate jurisdiction of the case being heard.

T F 22. The District Courts hear cases involving both tax and nontax litigation.

T F 23. The appellate courts are the Supreme Court, Courts of Appeals, and the U.S. Claims Court.

T F 24. The *Cumulative Bulletins* contain the IRBs for a semiannual period.

T F 25. The prefix "1" designates an income tax Regulation when referring to a Treasury Department Regulation.

T F 26. Tax legislation originates in the House of Representatives Ways and Means Committee.

T F 27. Technical Advice Memoranda are not available for public inspection.

T F 28. A taxpayer must pay any tax deficiency assessed by the IRS and then sue for a refund in the U.S. Claims Court.

T F 29. The phrase *Cert. Granted* indicates that the Supreme Court will hear the tax case.

T F 30. For a taxpayer residing in California, a decision of the Ninth Circuit Court of Appeals has more precedence than one rendered by the Eleventh Circuit Court of Appeals.

T F 31. If a taxpayer loses in the Tax Court Small Claims Division, he or she may not appeal to the regular U.S. Tax Court.

T F 32. Since Letter Rulings apply to only one taxpayer, the IRS is not required to make Letter Rulings public.

T F 33. *Technical Advice Memoranda* (TAMs) are only issued on proposed transactions while Letter Rulings are only issued on completed transactions.

T F 34. Under the doctrine of *stare decisis*, each case (except in the Small Claims Division) has precedential value for future cases with the same set of controlling facts.

T F 35. Research Institute of America (RIA) publishes a tax research CD-ROM service called RIA OnPoint.

T F 36. Tax forms and publications can be downloaded from the IRS site on the Internet.

T F 37. Many large accounting firms (e.g., Ernst & Young) maintain home pages on the World Wide Web.

Fill-in-the-Blanks

Complete the following statements with the appropriate word(s) or amount(s).

1. Federal tax legislation generally originates in the House of Representatives where it is first considered by the __________ __________ and __________ Committee.

2. When the Senate version of a tax bill differs from that passed by the House, the __________________ ______________ Committee resolves the differences.

3. To locate a provision in the Code, all that is necessary is the _________ number of that provision.

4. The Treasury Department Regulations are arranged in Code _________ sequence.

5. Every six months the *Internal Revenue Bulletins* are published in a bound volume designated as the ____________ _____________.

6. The ___________ Office of the Internal Revenue Service issues Individual Letter Rulings, while a _________ _________ issues determination letters.

Multiple Choice

Choose the best answer for each of the following questions.

1. Appeal from the Tax Court is to the:
   a. Court of Appeals
   b. District Court
   c. U.S. Claims Court
   d. Supreme Court
   e. None of the above

2. If taxpayers choose not to pay a tax deficiency, then they must petition which court?
   a. District Court
   b. U.S. Claims Court
   c. Tax Court
   d. Court of Appeals
   e. None of the above

3. Which of the following court(s) would have jurisdiction if a taxpayer paid a tax deficiency and sued for a refund (instead of petitioning the court)?
   a. Tax Court
   b. District Court and U.S. Claims Court
   c. Tax Court and District Court
   d. U.S. Claims Court

e. None of the above

4. A decision of which of the following courts could not be found in CCH's *U.S. Tax Cases*?
   a. District Court
   b. Court of Appeals
   c. Supreme Court
   d. U.S. Claims Court
   e. None of the above

5. Which of the following does not publish a tax service?
   a. Commerce Clearing House
   b. Matthew Bender
   c. Research Institute of America
   d. Government Printing Office
   e. None of the above

6. The *Federal Tax Articles* index is a three-volume service published by:
   a. Government Printing Office
   b. BNA
   c. Commerce Clearing House
   d. Matthew Bender, Inc.
   e. None of the above

7. Tax evasion is:
   a. Legally minimizing taxes
   b. Illegally minimizing taxes
   c. The same as tax avoidance
   d. None of the above

8. In *Walter H. Johnson*, 34 TCM 1056, 34 stands for:
   a. The year of decision
   b. The page number
   c. The volume number
   d. The paragraph number
   e. None of the above

9. Decisions by which court are published by West Publishing Company in its *Federal Supplement Series* (F.Supp.)?
   a. District Court
   b. Tax Court
   c. U.S. Claims Court
   d. Court of Appeals
   e. None of the above

10. The largest subdivision of material in the Internal Revenue Code is the:
   a. Subtitle
   b. Chapter
   c. Part
   d. Subchapter

e. None of the above

11. The annual maximum dollar amount that is within the jurisdiction of the Small Claims Division of the United States Tax Court is:
a. $5,000
b. $10,000
c. $25,000
d. $50,000
e. None of the above

12. Which of the following Federal courts has limited geographical jurisdiction within the United States?
a. Supreme Court
b. District Court
c. U.S. Claims Court
d. United States Tax Court
e. None of the above

13. The United States Tax Court:
a. Has nineteen judges
b. Will hear any Federal case
c. Is an appeals court
d. Has jurisdiction over the District Courts
e. None of the above

14. The *Standard Federal Tax Reporter* is published by:
a. BNA
b. Commerce Clearing House
c. Research Institute of America
d. Bureau of National Affairs
e. None of the above

15. According to the text, the primary purpose of effective tax planning is:
a. Eradicating the tax entirely
b. Deferring the receipt of income
c. Converting ordinary income into capital gain
d. Eliminating tax in the current year
e. None of the above

16. Which of the following best describes WESTLAW, LEXIS, and ACCESS?
a New computer tax services
b. Computerized legal data bases that can be used (among other things) for tax research
c. Electronic spreadsheets for tax planning
d. Computer programs that can be used for estate planning for wealthy taxpayers
e. Tax return preparation computer programs

17. At the completion of the tax research process the results are generally set forth in which of the following ways?
a. A phone call to the client
b. A note to the IRS

c. Preparing a tax research memo
d. Adding the results to the LEXIS data base
e. Nothing is done formally

18. Which of the following is not a tax periodical?
a. *The Journal of Taxation*
b. *Taxation for Accountants*
c. *TAXES-the Tax Magazine*
d. *The American Tax Journal*
e. *Estate Planning*

19. Which of the following is a primary source of tax law?
a. Tax treaties
b. Legal journals
c. Technical Advice Memoranda (TAM)
d. Tax textbooks
e. General Counsel Memoranda (GCM)

20. In Letter Ruling 8515087, the 087 refers to the:
a. Year of the Letter Ruling
b. Issue of the Bulletin in which the Letter Ruling appears
c. Day of the year the Letter Ruling was issued
d. The number of the Letter Ruling issued during the week

21. Which of the following is a "secondary" source of tax law?
a. A Tax Court case
b. A Revenue Ruling
c. A tax treaty between the U.S. and Mexico
d. An article on partnership tax in the *Tax Advisor*
e. All of the above are secondary sources

22. According to the textbook, which of the following trial court decisions is sometimes believed to have the "highest" authority in a tax matter?
a. Tax Court Memorandum decisions
b. Tax Court Regular decisions
c. Tax Court Small Claims decisions
d. Tax Court Annotation decisions

23. What statement is true of a Temporary Regulation?
a. It is issued simultaneously as a Revenue Ruling.
b. It may be cited as precedent.
c. It is first found in the *Internal Revenue Bulletin*.
d. It automatically expires after two years from the date of issuance.
e. All of the above are true.

24. Which of the following has the lowest tax validity?
a. Letter Ruling
b. Regulation
c. Revenue Ruling

d. Revenue Procedure
e. Tax treaty

25. Which of the following courts has the lowest tax validity?
a. Supreme Court
b. Court of Appeals for the 9th Circuit
c. Tax Court
d. Court of Appeals for the Federal Circuit
e. All of the above are of equal validity

26. Which of the following is a secondary source of tax law?
a. Revenue Ruling
b. Internal Revenue Code
c. Tax treaty
d. Regulations
e. *Taxation for Accountants*

27. Which of the following would be considered "authority" for purposes of the accuracy-related penalty under Sec. 6662?
a. Legal opinion of an attorney who is a tax specialist
b. *Harvard Law Review*
c. IRS Letter Ruling
d. *West's Federal Taxation* (a widely used tax textbook)
e. All of the above are authority

28. In general, when a provision of a tax treaty comes in conflict with a provision of the Internal Revenue Code, which has precedence?
a. The Treaty provision
b. The Code provision
c. The provision that was passed earliest.
d. The provision that was passed latest.

29. In which of the following states would a taxpayer appeal a decision of a U.S. District Court to the Ninth Court of Appeals?
a. Texas
b. Colorado
c. North Dakota
d. Arizona
e. Utah

30. In which of the following court reporters could be found a decision of the Small Case division of the United States Tax Court?
a. TCM
b. USTC
c. AFTR2d
d. T.C.
e. None of the above

31. A tax research memo should contain which of the following elements?

a. a clear statement of the issue(s)
b. a review of the tax law sources
c. any assumptions made
d. only a and c are elements of a tax research memo
e. a, b, and c, are all elements of a tax research memo

32. At the end of a tax research project, which of the following is usually sent to the taxpayer by the tax practitioner?
a. a client letter
b. a copy of the tax research memo
c. copies of the tax research material found by the researcher
d. nothing is sent, a phone call is made to the taxpayer
e. Both b and c are sent to the taxpayer

33. Which of the following is not an online tax research service?
a. WESTLAW
b. LEXIS/NEXIS
c. CCH ACCESS
d. Kleinrock's

34. The IRS's Internet newsletter is called?
a. Taxes Today
b. The Digital Daily
c. Taxes on Parade
d. The IRS Weekly
e. Internet Tax Review

Using the legend provided, classify each of the following courts for questions #35 to #41:

Legend
A = Tax Court
B = District Court
C = U.S. Court of Federal Claims

____ 35. Has 19 judges (not counting Special and Senior judges).

____ 36. A jury trial is available in this court.

____ 37. General Trial Court.

____ 38. Hears only tax cases.

____ 39. Appeal is to the U.S. Court of Appeals for the Federal Circuit.

____ 40. Hears mostly criminal and civil cases.

____ 41. A taxpayer does not have to pay a tax deficiency before going to trial in this court.

SOLUTIONS TO CHAPTER 2

True or False

1. True (p. 2-10)
2. True (p. 2-14)
3. False The U.S. Claims Court has sixteen judges. (p. 2-13)
4. True (p. 2-8)
5. True (p. 2-17)
6. False It is the 61st Revenue Ruling of 1987. (p. 2-10)
7. True (p. 2-18)
8. False IRS acquiesces or nonacquiesces to decisions it loses. (p. 2-19)
9. False The taxpayer generally does not have to pay the tax in order for the Tax Court to have jurisdiction. (p. 2-15)
10. False A jury trial is available only in the District Courts. (p. 2-15)
11. True (p. 2-20)
12. False Court decisions are published in the AFTR. (p. 2-20)
13. True (p. 2-13)
14. False There are many issues on which the IRS will not rule. (p. 2-11)
15. False *Tax Court of the United States Reports* is published by the U.S. Government. (p. 2-19)
16. True (p. 2-9)
17. True (p. 2-27)
18. False Tax planning (avoidance) is legal while tax evasion is illegal. (p. 2-32)
19. True (p. 2-13)
20. True (p. 2-20)
21. True (p. 2-16)
22. True (p. 2-14)
23. False The U.S. Claims Court is a court of original jurisdiction. (p. 2-13)
24. True (p. 2-10)
25. True (p. 2-8)
26. True (p. 2-4)
27. False They must be made available to the public. (p. 2-12)
28. True (p. 2-15)
29. True (p. 2-17)
30. True (p. 2-16)
31. True (p. 2-12)
32. False Letter Rulings are public information. (p. 2-11)
33. False TAMs are on completed transactions, while Letter Rulings are on proposed transactions. (p. 2-12)
34. True (p. 2-13)
35. True (p. 2-36)
36. True (p. 2-37)
37. True (p. 2-39)

Fill-in-the-Blanks

1. House Ways, Means (p. 2-4)
2. Joint Conference (p. 2-4)
3. Section (p. 2-6)

4. Section (p. 2-8)
5. *Cumulative Bulletin* (p. 2-10)
6. National, District Director (p. 2-11)

Multiple Choice

1. A (p. 2-15)
2. C (p. 2-15)
3. B (p. 2-15)
4. E (p. 2-20)
5. D (p. 2-24)
6. C (p. 2-25)
7. B (p. 2-32)
8. C (p. 2-20)
9. A (p. 2-20)
10. A (p. 2-6)
11. D (p. 2-12)
12. B (p. 2-14)
13. A (p. 2-13)
14. B (p. 2-24)
15. E (p. 2-31)
16. B (p. 2-36)
17. C (p. 2-30)
18. D (p. 2-25)
19. A (p. 2-29)
20. D (p. 2-11)
21. D (p. 2-29)
22. B (p. 2-29)
23. B (p. 2-9)
24. A (p. 2-11)
25. C (p. 2-29)
26. E (p. 2-29)
27. C (p. 2-29)
28. D (p. 2-7)
29. D (p. 2-17)
30. E Small Case decisions are not published. (p. 2-13)
31. E (p. 2-30)
32. A (p. 2-30)
33. D Kleinrock's is CD-ROM only. (p. 2-36)
34. B (p. 2-37)
35. A (p. 2-13)
36. B (p. 2-14)
37. B (p. 2-14)
38. A (p. 2-14)
39. C (p. 2-15)
40. B (p. 2-14)
41. A (p. 2-15)

CHAPTER 3
TAX DETERMINATION; PERSONAL AND DEPENDENCY EXEMPTIONS; AN OVERVIEW OF PROPERTY TRANSACTIONS

CHAPTER HIGHLIGHTS

This chapter continues to develop the components of the individual income tax formula. To determine a taxpayer's Federal tax liability, an amount known as taxable income must be computed. Taxable income includes all realized income less deductions specifically provided in the tax law. The standard deduction and personal exemption are available for most taxpayers. An overview of property transactions is helpful at this point, although the subject will be covered in greater detail in later chapters.

I. THE TAX FORMULA

A. Components of the Tax Formula. Taxable income is calculated based on the following formula:

Income (broadly conceived)	$xxxx
Less: Exclusions	xxxx
Gross Income	xxxx
Less: Deductions for AGI	xxxx
Adjusted Gross Income (AGI)	$xxxx
Less: the greater of	
Itemized Deductions, or	
the Standard Deduction	xxxx
Exemptions	xxxx
Taxable Income	$xxxx

The tax formula can be broken down as follows.

1) Income includes all taxable and nontaxable income of the taxpayer.

2) Exclusions are items of income which Congress has chosen to exclude from the tax base due to various social, economic, equity, and other considerations.

3) Gross income is defined in the Code as "all income from whatever source derived," but does not include unrealized gains.

4) Deductions for adjusted gross income include ordinary and necessary expenses incurred in a trade or business, alimony paid, and deductible IRA contributions, among others.

5) Adjusted gross income (AGI) is an important subtotal which serves as a basis for calculating limitations on certain itemized deductions.

6) Itemized deductions are expenses, personal in nature, for which Congress has specifically allowed a deduction. Taxpayers are allowed to use a standard deduction in lieu of itemizing deductions. The base standard deduction amounts are shown below.

Filing Status	1998	1999
Single	$4,250	$4,300
Married, filing jointly	7,100	7,200
Surviving spouse	7,100	7,200
Head of Household	6,250	6,350
Married, filing separately	3,550	3,600

For 1999 blind and aged (65 years old) taxpayers are given additional standard deduction amounts of either $1,050 or $850, depending on their filing status.

B. Individuals Not Eligible for the Standard Deduction. Certain taxpayers are not allowed to use the standard deduction. These taxpayers are:

1) a married taxpayer filing a separate return when either spouse itemizes deductions

2) a nonresident alien; and

3) an individual with a short tax year, resulting from a change in the annual accounting period

C. Special limitations for Individuals Who can be Claimed as Dependents. The calculation of taxable income for an individual who can be claimed as a dependent is subject to special provisions. Dependents cannot claim a personal exemption for themselves on their own tax returns. Also, a dependent's standard deduction is limited to the greater of $700 (for 1999) or the individual's earned income for the year plus $250. However, if the individual's standard deduction based on earned income exceeds the normal standard deduction amount, then the standard deduction is limited to the normal amount shown in the text.

II. PERSONAL AND DEPENDENCY EXEMPTIONS

A. Personal Exemptions. The law provides for a personal exemption for the taxpayer and an additional exemption for the spouse if a joint return is filed. The determination of marital status is made at the end of the taxable year. If spouses enter a legal separation agreement before the end of the taxable year, they are considered unmarried at the end of the taxable year. For 1999 the exemption amount is $2,750.

B. Dependency Exemptions. For an individual to qualify as a dependent, five tests must be met. These tests are:

1) support

2) relationship or member of the household

3) gross income

4) joint return

5) citizenship or residency

For the *support test* to be met, over one-half of the dependent's support must be furnished by the taxpayer. The term "support" generally includes expenditures for food, shelter, clothing, medical care, and education.

The *relationship test* requires that the dependent be a relative as specified in the Code or an individual who has a principal place of residence in the taxpayer's household for the entire year.

The dependent's *gross income* must be less than $2,750 (the 1999 exemption amount) unless the dependent is the taxpayer's child under 19, or the taxpayer's child who is a full-time student under the age of 24.

If the dependent is married, the supporting taxpayer is not permitted a dependency exemption if the person being supported files a *joint return* with his or her spouse, unless neither the dependent nor the dependent's spouse is required to file a return.

A dependent must be a *U.S. citizen* or a resident of the U.S. or a country which is contiguous to the U.S.

Multiple Support Agreements. Under a multiple support agreement, one member of a group of taxpayers who together furnish over one-half of the support of a dependent can claim a dependency exemption even when no one person provides more than 50 percent of the support. Any person who contributed more than 10 percent of the support is entitled to claim the exemption if each person in the group who contributed more than 10 percent files a written consent.

Divorced Parents. For divorced parents, the Code has established rules to help settle disputes as to who is eligible to claim the children as dependents. For divorce decrees after 1984, the parent with custody is allowed to claim the exemption except where the parents agree in writing that the noncustodial parent can claim the exemption (providing the other conditions for dependency are met).

Exemptions Phase-out. The personal and dependency exemptions are phased out when adjusted gross income reaches a certain level. The exemptions are phased out at the rate of 2 percent for each $2,500 ($1,250 for married filing separately), or fraction thereof, of adjusted gross income above the threshold amount. The threshold amount varies based on the taxpayer's filing status. The 1999 amounts are as follows:

Filing Status	**Threshold**
Married-joint/Surviving Spouse	$189,950
Head of Household	$158,300
Single	$126,600
Married-separate	$94,975

Child Tax Credit. In addition to a dependency exemption, a child of a taxpayer may be allowed tax credit. The credit is $500 for each child under the age of 17. The credit is phased out as family income increases from $110,000 to $120,000. Taxpayers filing joint returns lose $50 credit for every $1,000 or portion thereof, of AGI over $110,000.

III. TAX DETERMINATION

A Tax Table Method. Most taxpayers compute their tax using a Tax Table. Taxpayers who cannot use the tax tables include estates and trusts, individuals filing a short period return, and individuals with taxable income larger than the maximum amounts in the tables.

B. Tax Rate Schedules. All other taxpayers use the Tax Rate Schedules (X, Y, & Z). For 1999, a taxpayer's income may be subject to tax at rates of 15 percent, 28 percent, 31 percent, 36 percent, and 39.6 percent.

C. Computation of Net Taxes Payable or Refund Due. The pay-as-you-go feature of the Federal income tax system requires payments of all or part of a taxpayer's tax liability during the year. These prepayments (along with certain credits discussed in Chapter 13) are applied against the tax from the Tax Table or Tax Rate Schedule to determine if the taxpayer will get a refund or pay additional tax.

D. Unearned Income of Children Under Age 14 Taxed at Parents' Rate. The "unearned income" of minor children is taxed at their parent's marginal rate. The provision applies to any child if the child:

1) has not reached age 14 by the close of the tax year, and

2) has at least one living parent, and

3) has net unearned income for the tax year.

In 1999, net unearned income is unearned income less $700 and less the greater of a $700 standard deduction or the amount of allowable itemized deductions directly connected with the production of the unearned income.

For a child under age 14 the parents may elect to report the child's unearned income on the parent's tax return if the following conditions are met:

1) gross income is from dividends and interest only

2) gross income is over $700 and less than $7,000

3) no estimated tax has been paid by the child

4) there is no backup withholding on the child

IV. FILING CONSIDERATIONS

A. Filing Requirements. An individual taxpayer must file a tax return if certain minimum amounts of gross income have been received (See text for the current dollar amounts).

A self-employed individual with net earnings from self-employment of $400 or more must file a tax return whatever the dollar amount of gross income.

Special filing requirements apply to individuals who can be claimed as dependents on another taxpayer's return. See table in text.

Individual taxpayers file either a Form 1040 (long form), Form 1040A (short form), or 1040EZ (certain single taxpayers).

B. Filing Status. There are five different statuses under which a taxpayer can file. These are single, married filing jointly, married filing separately, head of household, and qualifying widow(er). The tax liability will vary with the filing status. The filing statuses are:

Single (Schedule X). Taxpayers who are unmarried on December 31, are single unless they qualify as head of household.

Married (Schedule Y-1 or Y-2). Taxpayers who are married on December 31, are married and must use married filing jointly or married filing separately tax rates.

Head of Household (Schedule Z). Taxpayers may file as head of household if the following conditions are met:

1) They are unmarried on December 31,

2) They provide over one-half the cost of a household, and

3) They have a dependent relative as defined in the Code living in the household (certain unmarried relatives such as a child need not qualify as a dependent and a dependent parent of the taxpayer need not live in the taxpayer's home).

Surviving Spouse (Schedule Y). A taxpayer who maintains a household for a dependent child may file as a surviving spouse (joint return rates apply) for the two years immediately following the death of one spouse

V. GAINS AND LOSSES FROM PROPERTY TRANSACTIONS– IN GENERAL

A. The sale or other disposition of property may result in gain or loss. Realized gain or loss is the *amount realized less the adjusted basis of the property.* In general, the adjusted basis is the cost of the property plus capital additions, less depreciation (if any). The calculation is as follows:

Amount realized from sale	$xxxxx
Adjusted basis	-xxxxx
Realized gain or loss	$xxxxx

B. All realized gains are recognized for tax purposes unless some provision of the tax law provides otherwise. Realized losses may or may not be recognized as a deduction for tax purposes. Losses on personal use property are generally not recognized.

VI. GAINS & LOSSES FROM PROPERTY TRANSACTIONS– CAPITAL GAINS

A. Definition of a Capital Asset. The Code defines a capital asset as property owned by the taxpayer other than items such as inventory, accounts receivable, depreciable property, or real estate used in a business.

The principal capital assets held by individuals for personal (nonbusiness) use include automobiles, a personal residence, and assets held for investment (such as stocks, bonds, and land).

For 1999, capital gains are taxed at the following maximum rates:

Short-term Gains (held for 12 months or less)	39.6%
Long-term Gains (held over 12 months)	20.0%

Collectibles (e.g., art, gems, metals, etc.) over 12 months are tax at a maximum of 28% and certain real estate recapture is tax at 25%. Further, if a taxpayer has long-term gain and his or her regular tax bracket for the year is 15 percent, the 20 percent capital gains rate is reduced to 10 percent.

B. Computation of Net Capital Gains and Losses. Gains and losses from capital assets must be classified as long-term or short-term. After such classification, long-term and short-term gains and losses are netted against one another. If an excess loss results, it is shifted to the category with the highest tax rate.

C. Capital Loss limitations. Capital losses are first offset against capital gains. For individuals, net capital losses are deductible against other income up to a maximum of $3,000 per year. Any loss more than $3,000 annually carries forward for an unlimited period.

KEY TERMS:

Adjusted Basis

Adjusted Gross Income

Capital gains and losses

Exemptions

Filing Requirements

Filing Status

Kiddie Tax

Standard Deduction

Tax Determination

TEST FOR SELF-EVALUATION

True or False

Indicate which of the following statements are true or false by circling the correct answer.

T F 1. For divorce decrees after 1984, the mother is always eligible to claim the dependency exemption for any child of divorced parents.

T F 2. The standard deduction amount for 1999 is $4,300 for single taxpayers, $7,200 for married individuals filing jointly, and $3,600 for married individuals filing separately.

T F 3. Itemized deductions are deductible even if they do not exceed the standard deduction amount.

T F 4. If married individuals file separate returns and one spouse itemizes, both must itemize.

T F 5. For 1999, the personal and dependency exemption amount is $2,750.

T F 6. Taxpayers are allowed additional standard deduction amounts for old age and blindness.

T F 7. If taxpayers are married at the end of the taxable year, they are considered married for the entire year.

T F 8. The additional standard deduction amount for old age or blindness can apply to a dependent of the taxpayer who is not the taxpayer's spouse.

T F 9. For the support test to be met, a taxpayer must furnish over one-half of the support of the dependent.

T F 10. Amounts received by a taxpayer, but not spent, are not considered in determining whether or not the support test for the dependency exemption has been met.

T F 11. An adopted child qualifies as the taxpayer's child for purposes of determining an exemption allowance.

T F 12. For 1999, all individuals whose gross income is $2,750 or more cannot be a dependent of another taxpayer.

T F 13. If an individual is married and files a joint return with her spouse, she generally cannot qualify as a dependent of another taxpayer.

T F 14. A person who lives in Mexico or Canada could qualify as a dependent of a taxpayer.

T F 15. To qualify for a multiple support agreement, a group of taxpayers must supply over 50 percent of the support of an individual.

T F 16. In order for a taxpayer's dependent parents to qualify him or her for head of household filing status, the parents must live in the taxpayer's home.

T F 17. All realized gains are recognized for tax purposes unless some specific provision of the tax law provides otherwise.

T F 18. For individual taxpayers, net long-term capital losses carry forward for five years and carries back for three years.

T F 19. In general, for 1999, net (long-term) capital gains of an individual taxpayer are taxed at a maximum rate of 20 percent.

T F 20. Capital assets must be held for over 12 months in order for realized gains to be considered long-term capital gains.

T F 21. Parents may elect to include their 10-year-old child's interest income of $7,750 on their tax return to prevent the child from having to file a tax return.

T F 22. For the tax year 1999, the additional standard deduction amount for a single taxpayer is $850.

T F 23. A nonresident alien taxpayer is allowed a standard deduction of $4,300 (in 1999) if he or she is single.

T F 24. In 1999, when filing his or her own tax return, a dependent's basic standard deduction is limited to the greater of $700 or the individual's earned plus $250 income for the year.

T F 25. A father-in-law and a mother-in-law meet the relationship test for claiming a dependency exemption.

Fill-in-the-Blanks

Complete the following statements with the appropriate word(s) or amount(s).

1. A parent who provides over one-half of the support of a __________ who is under 19 or who is a full-time student under 24 may claim a dependency exemption, without regard to the gross income test.

2. A dependent must be a U.S. citizen or a resident of the United States, __________, or __________.

3. The tax rate schedules are mainly used by __________ income taxpayers while the tax tables are used by low and middle income taxpayers.

4. In calculating their tax liability, taxpayers with income over the ceiling amount will be required to use the tax _______ schedule method in calculating their tax liability.

5. The determination of marital status is generally made at the __________ of the tax year, except where a spouse dies during the year.

6. Form 1040A, 1040EZ, or 1040 is due on or before the 15th day of the _________ month following the close of the tax year.

7. The joint return rate schedule was originally enacted to establish equity for married taxpayers in common law states, because married taxpayers in __________ property states could split their income.

8. Unmarried individuals who maintain a household for dependents are entitled to use the Head of ___________ tax rate schedule.

9. A taxpayer is required to file a tax return if his or her self-employment income is $_________ or more.

10. In order to meet the dependent support test, over ________% of the support must be furnished by the taxpayer.

11. If a child reaches _________ years of age the *kiddie tax* no longer applies.

Multiple Choice

Choose the best answer for each of the following questions.

1. For 1999, the standard deduction amount for a single taxpayer is:
   a. -0-
   b. $3,600
   c. $4,300
   d. $7,200
   e. None of the above

2. During 1999, Gail, a single taxpayer with no dependents, has adjusted gross income of $20,000. She has itemized deductions of $7,500. What is Gail's taxable income?
   a. $17,250
   b. $10,100
   c. $9,750
   d. $12,450
   e. None of the above

3. Jimmy is 10 years old and during 1999 has interest earnings of $1,900 from a savings account at a local bank. If Jimmy is claimed as a dependent on his parent's tax return, what is Jimmy's "net unearned income?"
   a. -0-
   b. $1,900
   c. $1,400
   d. $500
   e. None of the above

4. For 1999, the maximum tax rate applicable to capital gains on collectibles of individual taxpayers is:
   a. 39.6%
   b. 33%
   c. 28%
   d. 20%
   e. None of the above

5. A head of household taxpayer uses which of the following tax rate schedules?
   a. Schedule X
   b. Schedule Y
   c. Schedule Z
   d. Schedule G
   e. None of the above

6. A taxpayer's child who is under 19 or who is a full-time student under 24 does not have to meet which of the following dependency tests?
   a. Support test
   b. Relationship test
   c. Joint return test
   d. Gross income test
   e. Citizenship test

7. Walter is a divorced individual. He has a dependent son, age six, who is in the custody of his ex-wife. In addition, Walter supports his dependent mother who does not live in Walter's home. Walter's filing status would be:
   a. Head of household
   b. Married filing jointly
   c. Married filing separately
   d. Single

8. Which of the following is subtracted from the original basis to obtain the adjusted basis of an asset?
   a. Capital improvements
   b. The gain realized
   c. The gain recognized
   d. Depreciation
   e. None of the above

9. During the current year, Tim sells his truck for $8,000 (adjusted basis of $7,000) and Exxon stock for $20,000 (adjusted basis of $10,000). What is Tim's recognized gain?
   a. $11,000
   b. $10,000
   c. $8,000
   d. $1,000
   e. None of the above

10. Dee is 66 years old and files as a single taxpayer. For 1999 her standard deduction amount is:
    a. $4,300
    b. $5,050
    c. $5,150
    d. $5,350
    e. Some other amount

11. Which of the following is a capital asset?
    a. Inventory
    b. Accounts receivable

c. Stock held as an investment by an individual taxpayer
d. Real estate used in a business
e. None of the above

12. The maximum deduction for capital losses against an individual taxpayer's ordinary income in 1999 is:
a. $6,000
b. $5,000
c. $4,000
d. $3,000
e. None of the above

13. Which of the following is not a deduction for adjusted gross income?
a. Deductible IRA contributions
b. Trade or business expenses
c. Alimony
d. Medical expenses
e. None of the above

14. For individual taxpayers, unused capital losses can be carried forward:
a. 3 years
b. 4 years
c. 5 years
d. 7 years
e. None of the above

15. During 1999 Trudy had a long-term capital gain of $8,000 and a short-term capital loss of $2,000. What is the net amount included in income for Trudy?
a. $8,000
b. $6,000
c. $5,000
d. -0-
e. None of the above

16. Mike owns machinery, with an adjusted basis of $50,000, for use in his car-washing business. In addition, Mike owns his personal residence and furniture, which together cost him $100,000. The capital assets amount to:
a. $-0-
b. $50,000
c. $100,000
d. $150,000
e. Some other amount

17. The highest individual tax rate in the United States for 1999 is:
a. 15.0%
b. 36.4%
c. 39.6%
d. 28.0%
e. 31.5%

18. In 1999, for single taxpayers the 31 percent tax bracket starts at taxable income levels over:
    a. $34,550
    b. $25,750
    c. $62,450
    d. $130,250

19. Mr. and Mrs. Gold, both age 48, file a joint tax return for 1999. They provide all the support for their son who is 20 years old and has no income. Their daughter, age 22, is a full-time student at a local college. She had $5,300 of income and provided 60% of her own support. How many exemptions should Mr. and Mrs. Gold claim on their 1999 joint tax return?
    a. 2
    b. 3
    c. 4
    d. 5
    e. None of the above

20. Felix, age 20 is a full-time student at Big State University (BSU) and is claimed as a dependent on his parents' tax return. During the summer of 1999, Felix earned $1,800 from a part-time job. His only other income was $1,200 interest on his savings account. What is Felix's taxable income?
    a. $1,800
    b. $950
    c. $3,000
    d. $1,200
    e. Some other amount.

21. Hank, a widower, maintains a home in which he and his unmarried 17-year-old daughter reside. His daughter does not qualify as Hank's dependent. Hank's wife died in 1995. What is Hank's filing status for 1999?
    a. Head of household
    b. Surviving spouse
    c. Married filing jointly
    d. Single
    e. None of the above

22. For 1999, Kyle's adjusted gross income is $96,000, and his taxable income is $80,000. Kyle is single. Using the tax rate schedules (not the tax tables), what is Kyle's income tax liability before any credits for 1999?
    a. $22,400
    b. $24,800
    c. $19,579
    d. $24,800
    e. Some other amount

23. For 1999, exemptions are phased out as adjusted gross income exceeds specified amounts. For taxpayers who are married filing jointly, the phase-out starts at?
    a. $189,950
    b. $158,300
    c. $126,600
    d. $94,975

e. Some other amount

24. Fred is retired and lives with his son Andy. Fred's total support is provided as follows:

Son Andy	$4,000
Son Bob	2,000
Daughter Cathy	1,000
Social Security	4,300

Which of Fred's children can file a multiple support agreement and claim Fred as a dependent?
a. Andy, Bob, or Cathy
b. Andy or Cathy
c. Andy or Bob
d. Bob or Cathy
e. None of the above

25. For 1999, Sue, a single taxpayer, had adjusted gross income of $190,000. She has one exemption. What is Sue's allowable exemption for 1999?
a. $-0-
b. $1,320
c. $1,430
d. $2,750
e. Some other amount

26. Waldo is 66 years old and he is single. For 1999, what is the minimum amount of gross income required for Waldo to be required to file a tax return?
a. $400-
b. $4,300
c. $7,050
d. $8,100
e. Some other amount

27. Sam is 67 years old and files a joint tax return with his wife, Zelda, who is 66 years old. They have the following income and expense items for the current year:

Salary	$20,000
Interest income	5,000
Alimony from ex-wife	15,000
Gift from Uncle George	12,000

Using the above information what is Sam and Zelda's *gross income* for the year?
a. $52,000
b. $25,000
c. $35,000
d. $40,000
e. Some other amount

28. Sara had the following items of income and expenses during the current year:

Salary	$32,000
Interest	2,000
STCG	2,000
LTCL	2,500
Itemized deductions	7,300

Sara also paid $625 in state income tax during the year. What is Sara's *adjusted gross income* for the year?

a. $32,000
b. $34,000
c. $33,500
d. $36,000
e. Some other amount

29. Which of the following taxpayers are required to file a tax return for 1999?
   a. Able and Abby are married and both are 66 years old. Their total gross income is $12,275.
   b. Betty is 27 years old and single. She received $7,100 in wages from a part-time job and interest income of $2,500.
   c. Charles is single and 70 years old. His gross income is $7,200.
   d. Darlene is a self-employed single taxpayer with gross income of $4,300 from an unincorporated business. Business expenses amounted to $4,600.
   e. None of the above taxpayers must file a tax return

30. Carrie earned a salary of $70,000 in 1999. She sold common stock she had owned for eight months for a $2,000 loss and she sold her jet-ski for a loss of $1,800. Carrie also sold a painting for a gain of $8,000. The painting was acquired in 1960. What is Carrie's AGI for 1999?
   a. $76,000
   b. $78,000
   c. $74,200
   d. $70,000
   e. Some other amount

31. In 1999, Jan is in the 15 percent tax bracket and has the following capital gains for the year:

Red Corporation stock (held 24 months)	$2,000
Blue Corporation stock (held 8 months)	1,000

   What is Jan's tax on these transactions?
   a. $400
   b. $450
   c. $600
   d. $350
   e. Some other amount

32. In 1999, Bruce is in the 31% tax bracket and has the following capital transactions for the year:

Gold Corporation stock (held 7 months)	$2,000.
Green Corporation stock (held 10 months)	(6,000.)
Coin Collection (held 5 years)	5,000.
Land (held three years)	8,000.

What is the tax on these transactions?
a. $1,800
b. $2,600
c. $1,880
d. $2,790

33. John and Marsha file a joint tax return. The have three dependent children. Able, age 13, and Bea, age 17, live at home. Charles, age 21, is a college student at Football State University (FSU), where he lives in the dormitory. If their AGI is $95,000, what is John and Marsha Child credit for 1999?
a. $500
b. $1,000
c. $1,500
d. $2,000
e. Some other amount

Use the legend provided below to indicate for each item (#34 to #45) if it would be included, excluded, or sometimes included in gross income of an individual taxpayer:

Legend
A = Never Included in Gross Income
B = Always Included in Gross Income
C = Sometimes Included (in whole or part) in Gross Income

34. Alimony

35. Dividends

36. Child support payments

37. Embezzled funds

38. Social Security Benefits

39. Welfare payments

40. Pensions

41. Jury duty payments

42. Inheritances

43. Severance pay

44. Meals and lodging

45. Military pay

Problems

1. In each of the independent cases below, indicate the total number of exemptions for the taxpayer, T. Assume any test not mentioned has been met.

   a. T is age 70, his wife is age 64, and they file a joint return.

   b. T is age 73, blind, and has adjusted gross income of $10,000. His wife is 66 and they file a joint return.

   c. T is age 66 and his wife is age 34. During the year, Mrs. T gave birth to a son.

   d. T is unmarried and supports her 10-year-old sister who does not live with her. The sister had income of $3,865 from interest on a savings account.

   e. T and his wife, W, have a foster child who lived with them the entire year. They provide over one-half the support of the foster child.

   f. T and his wife furnish all the support of F, T's father. F is 80 years old and blind. T and W file a joint return claiming F as a dependent.

2. Cathy is a secretary, and for 1999 her salary was $28,630. Cathy is single, lives in an apartment and cannot itemize deductions. During the year her employer withheld $3,610 of Federal income taxes from her salary. River Bank paid Cathy $750 of interest on her savings account. Determine the following amounts for Cathy for 1999.

Adjusted Gross Income	____________
Standard Deduction	____________
Exemption	____________
Taxable Income	____________
Tax Liability	____________
Withholding	____________
Tax Due or (Refund)	____________

SOLUTIONS TO CHAPTER 3

True or False

1. False Exemptions are generally based on which parent has custody. (p. 3-13)
2. True (p. 3-8)
3. False If itemized deductions do not exceed the standard deduction, the taxpayer will compute taxable income using the standard deduction amount. (p. 3-7)
4. True (p. 3-9)
5. True (p. 3-11)
6. True (p. 3-7)
7. True (p. 3-24)
8. True (p. 3-9)
9. True (p. 3-11)
10. True (p. 3-12)
11. True (p. 3-14)
12. False Certain children of the taxpayer do not have to meet the gross income test. (p. 3-14)
13. True (p. 3-15)
14. True (p. 3-15)
15. True (p. 3-12)
16. False Dependent parents do not have to live in the taxpayer's home. (p. 3-27)
17. True (p. 3-28)
18. False Net capital losses of individual taxpayers carry forward indefinitely. (p. 3-30)
19. True (p. 3-29)
20. True (p. 3-28)
21. False The child's gross income must be less than $7,000. [1999] (p. 3-21)
22. False The amount is $1,050. (p. 3-8)
23. False Nonresident aliens are not allowed any standard deduction. (p. 3-9)
24 True (p. 3-10)
25. True (p. 3-14)

Fill-in-the-Blanks

1. child (p. 3-14)
2. Mexico, Canada (p. 3-15)
3. upper (p. 3-17)
4. rate (p. 3-16)
5. end (p. 3-24)
6. fourth (p. 3-23)
7. community (p. 3-25)
8. household (p. 3-26)
9. $400 (p. 3-22)
10. 50% (p. 3-11)
11. 14 (p. 3-19)

Multiple Choice

1. C (p. 3-8)
2. C $20,000 - 7,500 - 2,750 = $9,750. [1999] (p. 3-9)
3. D $1,900 - 1,400 = $500. [1999] (p. 3-20)
4. C (p. 3-29)
5. C (Appendix)
6. D (p. 3-14)
7. A (p. 3-26)
8. D (p. 3-28)
9. A (p. 3-28)
10. D $4,300 + 1,050 = $5,350. [1999] (p. 3-8)
11. C (p. 3-28)
12. D (p. 3-30)
13. D (p. 3-7)
14. E There is no time limit on the carryforward period. (p. 3-30)
15. B $8,000 - 2,000 = $6,000. (p. 3-30)
16. C (p. 3-28)
17. C (p. 3-2)
18. C [1999] (p. 3-17)
19. B The daughter does not meet the support test. (p. 3-11)
20. B ($1,800 + 1,200) - ($1,800 + $250) (max standard deduction) = $950. (p. 3-10)
21. A A taxpayer's child does not have to be a dependent to use head of household rates. (p. 3-26)
22. C [$14,138.50 + 31% ($80,000 - 62,450)] = $19,579. [1999] (p. 3-16)
23. A (p. 3-15)
24. C Daughter C does not supply at least 10% of the total support, therefore she is not eligible to claim the exemption. (p. 3-12)
25. B
    1. $190,000 - 126,600 = $63,400 excess amount
    2. $63,400/$2,500 = 26 x 2 = 52% (phase-out percentage)
    3. 52% x $2,750 = $1,430 amount of exemption phased out
    4. $2,750 - 1,430 = $1,320 allowable exemption deduction [1999] (p. 3-15)
26. D See table in the text. (p. 3-22)
27. D $20,000 + $5,000 + $15,000 = $40,000. (p. 3-4)
28. C $32,000 + $2,000 - $500 = $33,500 (p. 3-5)
29. B (p. 3-22)
30. A $70,000 + $8,000 - $2,000 = $76,000. The jet-ski is not deductible. (p. 3-29)
31. D (10% x $2,000) + (15% x $1,000) = $350 (p. 3-28)

32. C

1. Net short-term loss $2,000 + ($6,000)	-$4,000
2. Short-term loss applied against coin gain (28% tax rate)	1,000
3. Long-term gain (land) taxed at 20%	8,000
4. Total tax (20% x $8,000) + (28% x $1,000) =	$1,880

(p. 3-29)

33. A ($500 x 1) Only Able counts for the child credit, Bea and Charles are too old. (p. 3-16)
34. B (p. 3-4)
35. B (p. 3-4)
36. A (p. 3-4)
37. B (p. 3-4)
38. C (p. 3-4)
39. A (p. 3-4)

40.	B	(p. 3-4)
41.	B	(p. 3-4)
42.	A	(p. 3-4)
43.	B	(p. 3-4)
44	C	(p. 3-4)
45.	C	(p. 3-4)

Problems

1. a. 2; 2 personal (p. 3-11)
   b. 2; 2 personal (p. 3-11)
   c. 3; 2 personal, 1 dependency (p. 3-11)
   d. 1; 1 personal, sister fails the gross income test (p. 3-14)
   e. 3; 2 personal, 1 dependency (p. 3-14)
   f. 3; 2 personal, 1 dependency (p. 3-14)

2.

AGI: ($28,630 + $750)	$29,380
Standard Deduction:	-4,300
Exemption:	-2,750
Taxable Income:	$22,330
Tax Liability: (15% of Tax Inc.)	$3,350
Withholding:	-3,610
Refund:	$260

(Tax formula on page 3-2) [1999]

CHAPTER 4
GROSS INCOME: CONCEPTS AND INCLUSIONS

CHAPTER HIGHLIGHTS

The calculation of gross income is the first computation needed in the formula for taxable income. This chapter defines gross income and describes certain sources of gross income. The effect of the cash and accrual methods of accounting on the calculation of gross income is also discussed.

I. GROSS INCOME

A. Section 61(a) of the tax law defines gross income as "all income from whatever source derived." However, this definition is rather broad so the courts have established the principle that for income to be recognized for tax purposes, it must be realized. Therefore, increases in value (economic income) would not be taxed as income until the property is sold or exchanged.

B. Although financial accounting and tax accounting measurement concepts are frequently parallel, they have different purposes. The primary goal of financial accounting is to provide useful information to management, shareholders, creditors, and other interested parties, while the goal of tax accounting is the equitable collection of revenue.

C. Gross income is not limited to cash received. Income can be realized as money, property, or services received by the taxpayer.

D. Under the "recovery of capital doctrine" the proceeds from the sale or disposition of property are reduced by the basis of the property sold to determine gross income. This is to ensure that income is not taxed until the capital initially invested is recovered.

II. YEAR OF INCLUSION

A. As a rule, taxpayers are required to use a calendar year to report income. However, taxpayers who keep adequate books and records (and meet certain other tests) may use a fiscal year.

B. The three major methods of accounting used in computing taxable income are the cash method, the accrual method, and the hybrid method.

The cash method of accounting is used by most individuals and many small businesses. Under the cash method, property or services are included in the taxpayer's gross income in the "year of actual or constructive receipt."

The accrual method of accounting is used by many corporations. Under this method, income is recognized "in the year it is earned," no matter when it is collected. Income is considered earned when (1) all events have occurred which fix the right to receive such income and (2) the amount of the income can be determined with reasonable accuracy.

The hybrid method is a combination of cash and accrual accounting concepts.

Chapter 18 discusses the limitations applicable to accounting periods and methods.

C. Exceptions applicable to the cash method include the following:

1) The "doctrine of constructive receipt" limits an individual's ability to shift income arbitrarily to a later taxable year. If a taxpayer is entitled to receive income and the income is made available to him, it must be included in gross income.

2) Income set apart or made available is not constructively received if it is subject to substantial restrictions. For example, the increase in cash surrender value on ordinary life insurance is not taxed as the policy increases in value.

3) When a lender makes a loan with an original issue discount, the accrued interest must be reported each year, despite the taxpayer's accounting method. Interest on long-term bonds issued at a discount must also be accrued.

4) Interest on U.S. Series E or EE Savings Bonds is usually deferred until the bonds mature; however, a taxpayer may make an election to use the accrual method which requires that the annual increase in the bond's redemption value be included in gross income. By making the accrual election, the taxpayer prevents the bunching of income in a future year.

5) No income is realized when money is borrowed. Receipt of funds under an obligation to repay is not a taxable event.

D. Exceptions to the accrual method include the following:

1) "Prepaid income" is generally taxed in the year of receipt. Many court cases have been brought against the IRS by taxpayers arguing that the proper matching of revenue and expenses requires that income is recognized only when it is earned (e.g., the accrual method). The IRS has modified its position in several areas.

2) Generally, a taxpayer can elect to defer "advance payments for goods" if the taxpayer's method of accounting for the sale is the same for tax and financial reporting purposes.

3) A taxpayer can defer "advance payments for services" to be performed by the end of the tax year following the year of receipt. Such "services" do not include prepaid interest, amounts received under guarantee or warranty contracts, or prepaid rent.

III. INCOME SOURCES

A. Income from personal services must be included in the gross income of the person who "performs the services." A mere assignment of income will not shift the tax liability.

B. Income from property (e.g., interest, dividends, rent) must be included in the gross income of the "owner of the property."

When property is sold with accrued interest, part of the selling price is treated as interest and taxed to the seller in the year of sale. Under IRS rules, interest accrues daily.

Dividends, unlike interest, do not accrue on a daily basis. Dividends are normally taxed to the taxpayer who is entitled to receive them, the holder of the stock on the corporation's record date.

C. Income received by a taxpayer's agent is considered received by the taxpayer, thus a cash basis taxpayer must recognize income at the time it is received by his or her agent.

D. A partner in a partnership or a shareholder in an S Corporation must "include his or her share of income" from these entities on his or her individual tax return. The income must be included in the partner's or shareholder's return for the year with or within which the entity's tax year ends. Beneficiaries of estates and trusts are generally taxed on income earned by the estate or trust that is actually distributed or required to be distributed to them. Any excess income is taxed to the estate or trust.

E. In nine states -- Louisiana, Texas, New Mexico, Arizona, California, Washington, Idaho, Nevada, and Wisconsin -- marital rights to the ownership of property are controlled by community property laws. Income from personal services (e.g., salaries and wages) is treated as earned equally by both spouses. Income from community property is taxable as community income, one-half to each spouse. Income from separate property is taxable to the person who owns the property, except in Texas, Louisiana, Wisconsin, and Idaho, where the income from separate property is community income.

F. Under Sec. 66, spouses living apart in community property states will be taxed only on their separate earnings from personal services if certain conditions occur. These conditions are:

1) The individuals live apart for the entire year.

2) They do not file a joint return with each other.

3) No portion of the income is transferred between the individuals.

IV. ITEMS SPECIFICALLY INCLUDED IN GROSS INCOME

A. Post-1984 Alimony and Separate Maintenance Payments. For divorces after 1984, alimony is cash payments meeting the following three conditions:

1) The decree does not specify the cash payments are not alimony.

2) The payor and payee are not members of the same household.

3) There is no liability for payments after the death of the payee.

If the payment meets the definition of alimony, the amount is deductible by the payor and included in the gross income of the payee.

If the divorce decree is executed after 1986, special recapture rules apply if the payments exceed \$15,000 in the first or second year. In the third year, the payor must include the excess alimony payments for the first and second years in gross income and the payee is allowed a deduction for the excess alimony payments. The recaptured amount is computed as shown as follows:

$$R = D + E$$
$$D = B - (C + \$15{,}000)$$
$$E = A - [(B - D + C)/2 + \$15{,}000]$$

Where,

R = amount of recapture in Year 3.
D = recapture from Year 2.
E = recapture from Year 1.
A, B, C are the alimony payments in Years 1, 2, and 3, respectively.

For post-1984 decrees, if cash payments would be reduced by a "contingency related to a child," then the amount of the potential reduction in the payments is considered child support. The amount of the payment which is considered child support under this provision is not deductible by the payor or income to the payee.

Under post-1984 rules, transfers of appreciated property to a former spouse under a divorce decree are not taxable events.

B. Imputed Interest on Below-Market Loans. If a taxpayer makes a "below-market interest rate" loan to a related party, there can be imputed interest. The imputed interest is income to the lender and deductible to the borrower. The rate of imputed interest is the rate the Federal government pays on new borrowing, compounded semiannually. This rate is adjusted monthly and published by the IRS. These rules apply to the following types of loans:
1) Gift loans

2) Compensation-related loans

3) Corporation-shareholder loans

4) Tax avoidance loans

The below-market rules do not normally apply to gift loans between individuals where the total loans between the related parties are $10,000 or less, unless income producing property is purchased. On loans between individuals of $100,000 or less, the imputed interest cannot be greater than the net investment income earned by the borrower in that year, unless there is evidence of tax avoidance. Interest is not imputed on loans of $100,000 or less if the borrower's net investment income is $1,000 or less, unless there is evidence of tax avoidance.

C. Income From Annuities. Amounts received as annuity payments are included in gross income subject to the following rules:

For collections on or after the annuity starting date, the recipient may exclude part of the payment that represents a recovery of his or her investment. The formula is as follows:

$$\textit{Percent Excluded} = \frac{\textit{Investment in the contract}}{\textit{Total expected return}}$$

The exclusion ratio applies until the annuitant has recovered his or her investment in the contract. Once the investment is recovered, all subsequent payments are fully taxable. If the annuitant dies before recovering his or her investment, the unrecovered cost is deductible in the year the payments cease.

D. Prizes and Awards. Under Sec. 74, the fair market value of "prizes and awards" (other than qualified scholarships) is included in gross income. If the award is for recognition of religious, charitable, scientific, educational, artistic, literary, or civic achievement, the recipient transfers the prize to a qualified governmental unit or nonprofit organization, the recipient is selected with no action on his or her part, and if no substantial future services are required, then the award may be excluded from gross income. Certain employee achievement awards can be excluded from gross income. The maximum amount of such an employee award is $400 ($1,600 for qualified plan awards).

E. Group Term Life Insurance. There is an exclusion for premiums on up to $50,000 of "group-term" life insurance provided to employees. An amount, based on a Uniform Premium table supplied by the Internal Revenue Service, must be included in the employee's gross income for each $1,000 of coverage more than $50,000. If the group-term insurance plan discriminates in favor of certain key employees, the Sec. 79 exclusion does not apply and special rules apply in determining the amount to be included in the employee's gross income.

F. Unemployment Compensation. All unemployment compensation benefits are included in gross income.

G. Social Security Benefits. Part of a taxpayer's Social Security benefits may be included in gross income. The amount included is the lesser of the amount calculated under two different formulas.

The first set of base amounts is as follows:

1) $32,000 for married taxpayers filing jointly
2) $0 for married taxpayers who did not live apart for the entire year but filed separate returns
3) $25,000 for all other taxpayers

The second set of base amounts is as follows:

1) $44,000 for married taxpayers filing jointly
2) $0 for married taxpayers who did not live apart for the entire year but filed separate returns
3) $34,000 for all other taxpayers

If modified adjusted gross income (MAGI) plus one-half of Social Security benefits exceeds the first set of base amounts, but not the second set, the taxable amount of Social Security benefits is the lesser of the following:

.50(Social Security benefits)

.50[MAGI + .50(Social Security benefits) - base amount]

If MAGI plus one-half of Social Security benefits exceeds the second set of base amounts, the taxable amount of Social Security benefits is the lesser of the following:

.85(Social Security benefits), or
Sum of:
  .85[MAGI + .50(Social Security benefits) - base amount]
  lesser of:
    Amount included by the first formula, or
    $4,500 ($6,000 for married filing jointly)

KEY TERMS:

Alimony/Child Support

Annuities

Cash/Accrual

Community Property

Gross Income

Group term Life Insurance

Prizes/Awards

Social Security Benefits

Year of Inclusion

TEST FOR SELF-EVALUATION

True or False

Indicate which of the following statements are true or false by circling the correct answer.

T F 1. The general definition of gross income is found in Sec. 161(a) of the Internal Revenue Code.

T F 2. The term "income" is used in the Code but is not separately defined.

T F 3. Economic income is the sum of the taxpayer's change in net worth and the actual consumption of goods and services during the tax period.

T F 4. An accountant's concept of income is based on the recognition principle.

T F 5. For any individual taxpayer, financial income and taxable income are always the same amount.

T F 6. For post-1984 divorce decrees, payments must be made in cash to qualify as deductible alimony.

T F 7. Under the *recovery of capital doctrine,* sellers can reduce their gross receipts (selling price) by the adjusted basis of the property sold.

T F 8. Corporate taxpayers must always use the cash method of accounting.

T F 9. A cash basis taxpayer defers income recognition on an accounts receivable until it is collected.

T F 10. The benefits of the group-term life insurance premium exclusion are not available to proprietors and partners.

T F 11. The interest on U.S. "Series EE" savings bonds must always be reported using the cash method of accounting.

T F 12. Prepaid income is always income in the year payment is received.

T F 13. Taxable income from personal services can be shifted to other taxpayers such as family members.

T F 14. In all community property states (Texas, California, etc.), income derived from separate property is separate income.

T F 15. On the sale of stock, dividends are generally taxed to the person who is entitled to receive the dividends.

T F 16. Income from property must be included in the gross income of the owner of the property.

T F 17. If a taxpayer is entitled to receive income, which is made available to him, he cannot "turn his back" on it and refuse the income.

T F 18. Most individual taxpayers use the cash method of accounting.

T F 19. The recovery of capital doctrine means that the amount received from a sale of property is reduced by the adjusted basis in arriving at the taxable gain on the property sold.

T F 20. For 1999, the maximum amount of Social Security benefits that can be included in the taxable income of an individual taxpayer is 85%.

T F 21. The premiums on the first $50,000 worth of nondiscriminatory group-term life insurance provided to an employee can generally be excluded from gross income.

T F 22. If the interest charged on a loan is less than the Federal rate, the imputed interest is the difference between the amount that would have been charged at the Federal rate and the amount actually charged.

T F 23. If a group-term life insurance plan discriminates in favor of key employees, the key employees must include in gross income the lesser of the actual premiums paid by the employer or the amount calculated from the Uniform Premiums table.

T F 24. A cash basis taxpayer must recognize income when a check is received, even if the check is received after banking hours.

T F 25. A taxpayer includes funds received from an agent (such as an auctioneer) in the year the funds are received from the agent, not in the year the agent collected the funds.

Fill-in-the-Blanks

Complete the following statements with the appropriate word(s).

1. Income from property belongs to the __________ of the property.

2. Every partner in a partnership must report his or her __________ share of partnership income.

3. Income from personal services is treated as being earned equally by both spouses in a __________ property state.

4. The Supreme Court in *Eisner v. Macomber* added the ______________ requirement to the judicial definition of income.

5. The primary goal of __________ accounting is to provide useful information to interested parties, while the goal of ____________ accounting is the equitable collection of revenue.

6. The __________ accounting period is a basic component of the U.S. tax system.

7. The Regulations require that the __________ method be used for determining purchases and sales when a taxpayer maintains an inventory.

8. Dividends are generally taxed to the person who owns the stock as of the corporation's __________ date.

9. Property may be held as ___________ property in a community property state if it is acquired before marriage or by gift or inheritance following marriage.

Multiple Choice

Choose the best answer for each of the following questions.

1. A bank deposits $500 in interest in a savings account on December 31, 1999. The depositor withdraws $2,000 on January 3, 2000 How much income must be recognized for 1999?
   a. $2,000
   b. $500
   c. $1,500
   d. None of the above

2. On December 1, 1999, Drew receives $3,000 for three months rent (December, January, and February) of an office building. Drew is an accrual basis taxpayer. How much income must be recognized for 1999?
   a. $-0-
   b. $1,000
   c. $2,000
   d. $3,000
   e. None of the above

3. Chris is a 30-year-old single taxpayer. He has one dependent child living with him. During 1999 Chris received the following items:

Salary	$25,000
Child support	6,000
Alimony	9,000
Unemployment compensation	4,000
Interest on U.S. Treasury bonds	400
Net Lotto Winnings	600

   Of the above amounts, how much must Chris include in his gross income for the year?
   a. $45,000
   b. $39,000
   c. $34,600
   d. $38,000
   e. $38,400

4. Dan and his wife live in Texas. During the year, Dan earned a salary of $20,000 and his wife earned a salary of $10,000. If they file separate income tax returns, Dan would report how much income?
   a. $-0-

b. $10,000
c. $15,000
d. $20,000
e. None of the above

5. Which of the following is not a community property state?
a. Texas
b. New York
c. California
d. New Mexico
e. Washington

6. Dave, a calendar year taxpayer, owns 30% of Red Corporation, an S Corporation. For the year ended December 31, 1999, Red Corporation had taxable income of $100,000. During the year the corporation made distributions of $20,000. Dave's dividend income from other corporations was $25,000. What is Dave's taxable income from the corporations for 1999?
a. $25,000
b. $45,000
c. $55,000
d. $125,000
e. None of the above

7. For 1999, Jill, a single taxpayer, received $10,000 in Social Security benefits. Her adjusted gross income was $31,000 and she had no tax-free interest income. How much of the Social Security benefits should Jill include in her income?
a. $-0-
b. $5,000
c. $10,000
d. $7,500
e. Some other amount.

8. Same as number 7 above except Jill's adjusted gross income is $70,000. How much Social Security benefits should Jill include in her income?
a. $-0-
b. $5,000
c. $8,500
d. $10,000
e. Some other amount

9. Judy has savings bonds (Series EE) which increase in redemption value by $600 during 1999. In addition, Judy has $1,000 in interest on her savings account at Big Town Savings & Loan. If Judy has not made any elections and she is a cash basis taxpayer, she should report taxable interest income of:
a. $-0-
b. $600
c. $1,000
d. $1,600
e. Some other amount

10. A lawyer drafts a will for a dentist in exchange for dental work. The dentist would normally have charged $400 for this work. Since the attorney normally charges $300 for drafting a will, he paid the dentist $100 in cash. Based on this transaction, how much should the dentist include in his gross income?
    a. $-0-
    b. $100
    c. $300
    d. $400
    e. Some other amount

11. Erin, a cash basis calendar year taxpayer, received the following from her employer during 1999:

Salary	$50,000
Bonus	6,000
Travel advance ($1,800 of which was used for business travel)	2,000
Rental value of company car used for vacation (Erin paid for the gasoline)	$700

    What is Erin's gross income from the above Items?
    a. $56,000
    b. $56,700
    c. $56,200
    d. $56,900
    e. Some other amount

12. Lisa owned stock in X Corporation, which originally cost $100,000. She sold the stock for $75,000 plus 10% of X's income in the year of sale plus 10% of five additional years of income. The value of the future income cannot be determined in the year of sale. In the first year, Lisa received payments of $84,000 from the purchaser. What is Lisa's taxable gain in the first year?
    a. $-0-
    b. $9,000
    c. $25,000
    d. $16,000
    e. None of the above

13. In November 1999, John entered a contract to deliver goods to a customer in March 2000 for $12,000. John uses the *accrual method* of accounting for both financial and tax purposes. He collected $8,000 in 1999 and the balance in 2000. John did not have the goods in stock on December 31, 1999. The cost of the goods to him is $9,000. How much net income must John report in 1999?
    a. $-0-
    b. $1,000
    c. $5,000
    d. $8,000
    e. None of the above

14. Sky Corporation sells service contracts for 12 and 24 month periods. In September 1999, the company sold $8,000 of the 12-month contracts and $10,000 of the 24-month contracts. If the company services each customer each month (October, November, and December 1999), how much income should be reported for 1999 if Sky Corporation follows Rev. Proc. 71-21?
    a. $2,000

b. $6,000
c. $8,000
d. $12,000
e. None of the above

15. Vicki owns 25 percent of K&A Partnership. For the 1999 tax year the partnership had net income of $200,000. During the year Vicki withdrew $35,000 from her capital account. What is Vicki's reported share of net income from K&A?
a. $-0-
b. $35,000
c. $50,000
d. $200,000
e. None of the above

16. On July 15 the Board of Directors of Blue Corporation declared a $1 per share dividend payable July 30 to shareholders of record on July 25. As of July 15, Norman owned 1,000 shares. On July 16 he sold 700 shares to Sam for the fair market value, and he gave 300 shares to his son. How much dividend income must Norman report?
a. $-0-
b. $300
c. $700
d. $1,000
e. None of the above

17. Dave, an employee of Purple, Inc., is covered by a group-term life insurance policy that has a face amount of $60,000. The company pays all the policy premiums which amount to $500 per year. According to Reg. Sec. 1.79-3, the cost of a policy for a man Dave's age is 48 cents per $1,000 per month. How much income should Dave report on his tax return?
a. $-0-
b. $57.60
c. $500.00
d. $345.60
e. Some other amount

18. Robert is divorced in the current year. He makes cash payments to his ex-wife of $1,000 per month. When their son, who is in the wife's custody, turns 18 years old, the payments are reduced to $600 per month. How much can Robert deduct as alimony each month?
a. $-0-
b. $400
c. $600
d. $1,000
e. Some other amount

19. Nicky goes on the T.V. game show, Wheel of a Deal. She wins cash of $15,000 and a new car with a fair market value of $20,000. How much income must Nicky report from these winnings?
a. $-0-
b. $15,000
c. $20,000
d. $35,000

e. Some other amount

20. In the current year Dave receives stock from his employer worth $25,000. The stock cannot be sold by Dave for seven years. Dave estimates that the stock will be worth $60,000 after the seven years. In the current year how much income must Dave recognize?
a. $-0-
b. $25,000
c. $35,000
d. $60,000
e. Some other amount

21. Hank retired last year after investing $100,000 in an annuity which pays $12,000 per year. Hank had a life expectancy of 10 years at the annuity starting date. What is Hank's income for the current year, assuming Hank receives $12,000 during the current year?
a. $-0-
b. $2,000
c. $10,000
d. $12,000
e. None of the above

22. Larry, a cash basis taxpayer, paid $42,000 for an 18-month certificate-of-deposit with a maturity value of $50,000. The effective interest rate on the certificate was 12 percent. If Larry bought the certificate on June 30 of the current year, how much interest income should he report?
a. $2,520
b. $3,000
c. $5,040
d. $6,000
e. Some other amount

23. Under a current year's divorce decree, Oliver has to pay his ex-wife alimony. The cash payments are as follows:

Year 1	32,000
Year 2	25,000
Year 3	-0-

What is Oliver's alimony deduction for Year 1?
a. $-0-
b. $32,000
c. $22,000
d. $12,000
e. Some other amount

24. Assume the same facts as question 23. What is the amount of alimony that Oliver will have to recapture in Year 3?
a. $-0-
b. $10,000
c. $19,500
d. $9,500

e. Some other amount

25. Under a current year's divorce decree, Van transfers appreciated property to his ex-wife. The property has a fair market value of $150,000 and an adjusted basis to Van of $60,000. From the transaction Van should report a taxable gain of:
a. $-0-
b. $60,000
c. $90,000
d. $150,000
e. Some other amount

26. If Van's wife in question 24 above were to sell the property three years later for $160,000, how much gain should she report?
a. $-0-
b. $90,000
c. $100,000
d. $10,000
e. Some other amount.

27. Assume during the first six months of the current year the Federal imputed interest rate is 9 percent and during the second six months it is 10 percent. On January 1, a father gives his son an interest-free loan of $50,000. The son has $5,000 of investment income for the year. For the current year, what is interest income that the father must recognize and what amount of interest expense is the son treated as incurring?
a. $-0-
b. $4,863
c. $4,750
d. $5,000
e. Some other amount

28. Assume the same facts as in question 27. How much of a "gift" has the father made to his son?
a. $-0-
b. $4,863
c. $4,750
d. $5,000
e. Some other amount

29. Kathy, a cash basis taxpayer, gave away Green, Inc. bonds with a face amount of $10,000 to her son Bill. The bonds have a stated annual interest rate of 9%. The gift was made on February 10, 1999 and interest was paid to Bill on December 31, 1999. How much interest income must Kathy recognize in 1999?
a. $-0-
b. $101
c. $799
d. $900
e. Some other amount

30. Mabel owned the following stock on January 1, 1999:

	Basis	FMV
Red Corp.	$200	$220
Yellow Corp.	$175	$170

During the year Mabel sold the Red stock for $215 and the Yellow stock for $180. Mabel's income under the *economic* concept of income is:
a. $-0-
b. $5
c. $20
d. $35
e. Some other amount

31. On June 30, 1999, Wendy purchased for $7,500 a 30-month, $10,000 certificate of deposit from Shakie Bank & Trust. The yield to maturity on the certificate was 12%, interest compounded semiannually. What is Wendy's interest income for the six months ended on December 31, 1999?
a. $-0-
b. $600
c. $500
d. $450
e. Some other amount

32. Gold Corporation purchased a group-term life insurance plan which covered only management and officers of the company. Mr. Gold received $250,000 of life insurance under this plan. The cost to Gold Corporation for the premiums of Mr. Gold's insurance was $3,100. The Uniform Premium amount for each $1,000 of insurance for a man Gold's age is $9 annually. Mr. Gold must include in gross income:
a. $-0-
b. $2,250
c. $2,575
d. $3,100
e. Some other amount

33. Peg owns a life insurance policy with a face amount of $100,000. On January 1, 1999, the policy had a cash surrender value of $15,000 and on December 31, 1999 the cash surrender value was $16,500. During the year, Peg paid premiums on the policy of $2,500. What amount of income must Peg report from this insurance policy for 1999?
a. $-0-
b. $1,000
c. $1,500
d. $2,500
e. None of the above

34. Devona, age 54, purchased and annuity for $100,000 under which she is to receive $600 per month for life. Her life expectance is 29.5 years at the annuity starting date. Thus, her expected return is $600 x 12 x 29.5 = $212,400 and the annual exclusion amount is $3,390 [($100,000/$212,400 x $7,200)]. If Devona dies after four years, how much is the deduction (if any) from the annuity on her final return?
a. $-0-
b. $13,560
c. $86,440
d. $212,400

e. Some other amount

35. Bill, age 57, receives an annuity distribution of $600 per month for life from a qualified retirement plan. His investment in the contract is $139,500. How much of each payment is excluded from Bill's income using the Simplified Method of Annuity Distributions from Qualified plans?

a. $-0-
b. $150
c. $450
d. $600
e. Some other amount

SOLUTIONS TO CHAPTER 4

True or False

1. False The definition of gross income is found in Sec. 61. (p. 4-3)
2. True (p. 4-3)
3. True (p. 4-3)
4. False The accountant's concept is based on the realization principle. (p. 4-4)
5. False Financial income concepts may differ from those used in determining taxable income. (p. 4-4)
6. True (p. 4-20)
7. True (p. 4-6)
8. False Most corporations use the accrual method. (p. 4-7)
9. True (p. 4-8)
10. True (p. 4-32)
11. False Taxpayers may elect the accrual method. (p. 4-12)
12. False In some cases an accrual basis taxpayer may be able to defer recognition of the income under Rev. Proc. 71-21. (p. 4-13)
13. False The assignment of income does not shift the tax liability. (p. 4-14)
14. False In Texas, Louisiana, Wisconsin, and Idaho income derived from separate property is community income. (p. 4-18)
15. True (p. 4-16)
16. True (p. 4-15)
17. True (p. 4-10)
18. True (p. 4-7)
19. True (p. 4-6)
20. True (p. 4-33)
21. True (p. 4-32)
22. True (p. 4-23)
23. False The *greater* of the actual premiums paid by the employer or the amount calculated from the Uniform Premiums table must be included in the employee's gross income. (p. 4-33)
24. True (p. 4-8)
25. False It is taxable in the year collected by the agent. (p. 4-16)

Fill-in-the-Blanks

1. owner (p. 4-15)
2. distributive (p. 4-17)
3. community (p. 4-18)
4. realization (p. 4-4)
5. financial, tax (p. 4-5)
6. annual (p. 4-7)
7. accrual (p. 4-7)
8. record (p. 4-16)
9. separate (p. 4-18)

Multiple Choice

1. B (p. 4-8)
2. D The entire $3,000 is taxable when received. (p. 4-14)
3. B $25,000 + $9,000 + $4,000 + $400 + $600 = $39,000 (various pages)
4. C 50% ($20,000 + 10,000) = $15,000. (p. 4-18)
5. B New York (p. 4-17)
6. C 30% ($100,000) + $25,000 = $55,000. (p. 4-17)

7. B Lesser of:
   (1) 50% x $10,000 = $5,000, or
   (2) 50% x [$31,000 + 50%($10,000) - $25,000] = $5,500. (p. 4-34)

8. C Lesser of:
   (1) 85%($10,000) = $8,500, or
   (2) Sum of:
      85%[$70,000 + 50%(10,000) - $34,000] = $34,850, plus
      Lesser of:
         amount from first formula (question #7) = $5,000, or
         $4,500 (p. 4-34)

9. C (p. 4-12)
10. D $300 + 100 = $400. (p. 4-5)
11. D $50,000 + $6,000 + $200 + $700 = $56,900 (various pages)
12. A The $84,000 is a recovery of capital. (p. 4-6)
13. A The income is reported in 2000. (p. 4-13)
14. D 3/12 ($8,000) + $10,000 = $12,000. (p. 4-13)
15. C 25% ($200,000) = $50,000. (p. 4-17)
16. B Norman is taxed on the dividends related to 300 shares because the gift was made after the declaration date. He is not taxed on the shares sold. (p. 4-16)
17. B $.48 x [($60,000 - 50,000)/$1,000] x 12 months = $57.60. (p. 4-32)
18. C The contingent amount is "disguised child support." (p. 4-22)
19. D (p. 4-30)
20. A (p. 4-11)
21. B $100,000/($12,000 x 10 years) x $12,000 = $10,000 excluded
    $12,000 - 10,000 = $2,000 included. (p. 4-28)
22. A (.12 x $42,000) x ½ year = $2,520. (p. 4-11)
23. B (p. 4-20)
24. C D = $25,000 - ($0 + 15,000) = $10,000
    E = $32,000 - [($25,000 - 10,000 + 0)/2 +$15,000] = $9,500
    R = $10,000 + 9,500 = $19,500. (p. 4-21)
25. A (p. 4-20)
26. C $160,000 - 60,000 = $100,000. (p. 4-20)

27. B

Jan. 1 to June 30: 9% x $50,000 x ½ year =	$2,250	
July 1 to Dec. 31: 10% x $52,250 x ½ year =	2,613	
	$4,863	(p. 4-23)

28. B (p. 4-23)
29. B 9% x $10,000 x (41 days/365 days) = $101. (p. 4-15)

30. B Economic income is the change in the FMV of the taxpayer's assets. ($215 - $220) + ($180 - $170) = $5 (p. 4-3)

31. D Wendy must use the current interest method, $7,500 x .12 x (6/12) = $450. (p. 4-11)

32. D The plan is discriminatory, therefore the greater of the actual premiums paid or the Uniform Premium amount is included in income. (p. 4-33)

33. A The increase in value is not taxed because of "substantial restrictions" on the life insurance policy. (p. 4-10)

34. C $100,000 - (4 x $3,390) = $86,440. (p. 4-29)

35. C $139,500 / 310 months = $450. (p. 4-30)

CHAPTER 5
GROSS INCOME: EXCLUSIONS

CHAPTER HIGHLIGHTS

This chapter focuses on those items which are specifically excluded from gross income by Congress. Exclusions are not deductions, they are items that are by definition not income. Deductions are items that are subtracted from income.

I. EXCLUSIONS FROM GROSS INCOME– STATUTORY AUTHORITY

Generally, everything received by a taxpayer is income unless a "specific statutory exclusion" can be found. Congress has chosen to exclude certain items from gross income for various social, economic, and equity purposes.

II. GIFTS AND INHERITANCES

A. In General. The value of property received by gift or inheritance is excluded from gross income under Sec. 102. A gift is "a voluntary transfer of property by one taxpayer to another without any valuable consideration or compensation therefrom." The payment must be made "out of affection, respect, admiration, charity, or like impulses."

Gifts made in a business setting often represent compensation for past, present, or future services and are not gifts. In most cases, transfers from employers to employees may not be treated as gifts.

B. Gifts to Employees. Cash or property received by an employee cannot be excluded from the employee's income unless it fits into one of the statutory provisions.

C. Employee Death Benefits. In certain circumstances employer payments (death benefits) to a deceased employee's surviving spouse, children, or other beneficiaries can be excluded from income by the recipient. However, if the deceased employee had any claim to the payments the IRS will consider the payments as income to the recipient.

III. LIFE INSURANCE PROCEEDS

A. In General. The proceeds of life insurance are excluded from the income of the beneficiary of the policy.

B. Accelerated Death Benefits. If an insured is terminally or chronically ill, then he or she may take advanced payments or assign the policy to a qualified third party and not be taxed on the proceeds. Taxpayers who are not terminally or chronically ill are taxed on any gain from accelerated life insurance death benefits.

C. Transfers for Valuable Consideration. If a life insurance policy is transferred for valuable consideration or is an amount due from the decedent, the net proceeds of the policy will be included in income. The net proceeds will not be included if the policy is transferred to the following:

- a partner of the insured
- a partnership in which the insured is a partner
- a corporation in which the insured is an officer or a shareholder
- a transferee whose basis in the policy is determined by reference to the transferor's basis

The first three exceptions facilitate the use of life insurance to fund buy-sell agreements.

IV. SCHOLARSHIPS

A. In General. For tax purposes a scholarship is defined as "an amount paid or allowed to, or for the benefit of, an individual . . . to aid such individual in the pursuit of study or research." The recipient must be a candidate for a degree at an educational institution. Scholarship grants for tuition and related expenses are excluded from income under Sec. 117 of the Code. Other scholarship amounts received (e.g., room and board) are included in the taxable income of the recipient.

B. Timing Issues. The amount eligible for exclusion may not be known at the time a scholarship is received. In this case, the transaction is held open until the education expenses are paid.

C. Disguised Compensation. Employer-sponsored scholarships made available solely to the children of key employees are generally includible in the income of the parent-employee.

D. Qualified Tuition Reduction Plans. Employees of nonprofit education institutions are allowed to exclude a tuition waiver from gross income. Generally the exclusion is limited to undergraduate tuition waivers.

V. COMPENSATION FOR INJURIES AND SICKNESS

A. Damages. A person who suffers harm caused by another is often paid damages. Generally, the reimbursement for loss of income is taxed in the same manner as the income being replaced by the damages. If the damages represent a recovery of a previously deducted expense, income may arise under the tax benefit rule. Payments for personal injury are specifically excluded from the gross income of the person receiving the payment.

Punitive damages arising from a claim of physical injury or physical sickness are excluded from gross income, while all other punitive damages are fully taxable.

B. Workers' Compensation. Payments received by a taxpayer from workers' compensation and benefits from accident and health insurance policies purchased by the taxpayer are specifically excluded from gross income under Sec. 104.

C. Accident and health Insurance Benefits. The income tax treatment of accident and health insurance benefits depends on whether the policy providing the benefits was purchased by the taxpayer or the taxpayer's employer. Benefits under policies purchased by the taxpayer are excludible, see below for employer plan rules.

VI. EMPLOYER-SPONSORED ACCIDENT AND HEALTH PLANS

Premiums paid on "employer sponsored" accident and health plans are excluded from the income of the employee and are deductible by the employer. When the employee collects the insurance benefits, such benefits are considered taxable income with the following exceptions:

- Payments received for the medical care of the employee, spouse, and dependents are excluded except to the extent the payments are reimbursements for medical expenses which were deducted in the previous year or the payments are reimbursements of expenses that do not meet the test for deduction as a medical expense under the Code.

- Payments for the permanent loss or the loss of the use of a member or function of the body or the permanent disfigurement of the employee, spouse, or dependent are also excluded.

A. Medical Reimbursement Plans. Amounts received under employer medical reimbursement plans are excluded from gross income unless the plan discriminates in favor of certain groups of employees (e.g., management level). Benefits which are paid only to a particular group of employees must be included in income.

B. Long-term Care Benefits. Generally long-term care insurance is treated the same as accident and health insurance. Thus, premiums paid by an employer are not income to an employee. The maximum exclusion for benefits is the greater of $175 per day or actual cost of the care.

VII. MEALS AND LODGING

A. Furnished for the Convenience of the Employer. The value of meals and lodging provided to an employee, the employee's spouse, and the employee's dependents is excluded from gross income if certain conditions are met. To qualify for the exclusion, meals must be furnished by the employer on the business premises of the employer and be for the convenience of the employer. In addition to these tests, lodging must be a condition of employment for an employee to be able to exclude it.

B. Other Housing Exclusions. Under certain conditions, an employee of an educational institution can exclude the value of campus housing provided by the employer. Generally, the employee does not recognize income if he or she makes annual rent payments equal to or greater than 5 percent of the value of the facility; however, if the rent payments are less than 5% of the value of the facility, the difference must be included in gross income. A "minister of the gospel" can exclude the rental value of a home furnished as compensation. Military personnel are allowed exclusions under various circumstances.

VIII. OTHER EMPLOYEE FRINGE BENEFITS

A. Specific Benefits. Certain employee benefits that are excluded from the gross income of an employee by special provisions in the tax law. These are:

The value of child care services paid by an employer, enabling the employee to work, limited to the lesser of $5,000 annually ($2,250 if married, filing separately), or the taxpayer's earned income. For married taxpayers, the earned income of the spouse with the lesser amount of earned income is used for the limitation.

The value of gymnasium and athletic facilities.

Qualified employer provided educational assistance, limited to $5,250 annual amount.

Adoption Assistance Tax Provisions

B. Cafeteria Plans. A cafeteria plan is an employee plan that offers an employee a choice between cash and some other form of compensation (i.e., a benefit). If a plan meets the requirements under the tax law, then the employee can choose between nontaxable benefits (e.g., health insurance) or taxable income in the form of a cash payment.

C. Flexible Spending Plans. Under these plans, an employee accepts lower cash compensation in return for the employer agreeing to pay certain costs the employer (e.g., dental expenses) can pay without the employee recognizing gross income.

D. General Classes of Excluded Benefits. The tax law establishes four broad classes of nontaxable employee benefits. These benefits are:

- No-additional cost services (e.g., an employee of an airline can fly for free if the seat would otherwise be empty).

* Qualified employee discounts. In the case of services, employees do not have to report as income employee discounts up to 20 percent. In the case of property, employees do not have to report as income employee discounts provided the discount does not exceed the employer's gross profit margin. The exclusion is not available for real property.

* Working condition fringes. Employees can exclude those items from gross income that would be deductible if the employees had paid them. In addition, certain nondeductible items such as free parking do not have to be included as income.

* *De minimis* fringes. Small benefits, such as using the company copy machine, do not have to be reported as income.

* Qualified transportation fringe benefits.

* Qualified moving expense reimbursements.

E. Taxable Fringe Benefits. Employee fringe benefits that do not qualify for specific exclusions must be recognized as gross income equal to the fair market value of the benefit(s).

IX. FOREIGN EARNED INCOME

A U.S. citizen is generally subject to U.S. tax on total worldwide income. However, qualified U.S. citizens working abroad can exclude up to $74,000 per year in 1999 of earned income. In addition, an exclusion is allowed for a reasonable amount of housing costs in the foreign country in excess of a base amount. The base amount of "housing allowance " is 16 percent of the pay for a GS-14 (Step 1) Federal employee.

To qualify for the exclusion the taxpayer must either be a resident of the foreign country, or present in the country for 330 days during any 12 consecutive months.

The taxpayer may include the foreign income in gross income and elect to claim a credit for foreign taxes paid as an alternative to the credit.

X. INTEREST ON CERTAIN STATE AND LOCAL GOVERNMENT OBLIGATIONS

Taxpayers can exclude interest on the "obligations of state and local governments" from their gross income. However, the interest on certain types of state and local government bonds is taxable.

XI. DIVIDENDS

A. In General. A dividend payment to a shareholder with respect to the ownership of stock is normally included in income to the extent of the corporation's earnings and profits. Distributions in excess of earnings and profits are a nontaxable recovery of capital to the extent of the taxpayer's basis in the corporation's stock and any distributions in excess of basis are taxed as capital gains.
The following items are not considered regular dividends for tax purposes:

* payments received on savings and loan association deposits,

* patronage dividends from cooperatives,

* mutual life insurance dividends, and

* capital gain distributions from mutual funds.

B. Stock Dividends. Generally, no income is recognized on the receipt of stock dividends on stock.

XII. EDUCATIONAL SAVINGS BONDS

A. For certain savings bonds issued after 1989, an exclusion is available with respect to bonds redeemed to provide funding for higher education. Taxpayers may exclude interest on Series EE savings bonds that are redeemed to pay for qualified higher education expenses. To qualify, the following requirements must be met:

* The bonds must be issued after December 31, 1989, and

* The bonds must be issued to an individual who is at least 24 years old at the time of issuance.

B. Once modified adjusted gross income exceeds $53,100 ($79,650 on a joint return) in 1999 the exclusion begins to be phased out. Thus, the exclusion is phased out entirely when modified adjusted gross income reaches certain levels. See text for the exclusion calculation.

XIII. QUALIFIED STATE TUITION PROGRAMS

Several states have plans to allow parents to prepay tuition for the child's future college education. Under a qualified state tuition program, the amounts contributed must be used for qualified higher education expenses. Amounts spent on higher education in excess of the prepaid amount is income to the student (not the parent).

If the child does not attend college, the excess refunded to the parents is income to the parents.

XIV. TAX BENEFIT RULE

Under the tax benefit rule, if a taxpayer obtains a deduction for an item in one tax year and in a later year recovers a portion of the prior deduction, the recovery is included in taxable income in the year it is received. Examples of items subject to this rule include bad debts, prior taxes, and delinquency amounts.

The recovery of a deduction which did not yield a tax benefit in a prior year is not included in gross income under the tax benefit rule.

XV. INCOME FROM DISCHARGE OF INDEBTEDNESS

The transfer of appreciated property in satisfaction of a debt is treated first as a sale of the property and then as payment of the debt. Any gain on the sale of the property must be recognized as income.

Under the Bankruptcy Act, the discharge of indebtedness is not recognized as income to the taxpayer whose debt is forgiven. The realized gain from the discharge of the debt is applied against the taxpayer's basis in the assets, effectively deferring the gain until the assets are sold.

KEY TERMS:

Exclusions

Gift & Inheritances

Life Insurance

Scholarships

Heath Insurance

Employee Fringe Benefits

Foreign Earned Income

Tax Benefit Rule

TEST FOR SELF-EVALUATION

True or False

Indicate which of the following statements are true or false by circling the correct answer.

T F 1. Public assistance payments (welfare) are generally nontaxable.

T F 2. Gifts in a business setting are always excluded from gross income.

T F 3. In a flexible spending plan, the employee accepts lower cash wages in return for the employer agreeing to pay certain costs of the employee.

T F 4. Life insurance proceeds are always excluded from the gross income of the recipient.

T F 5. The interest element received by a beneficiary on life insurance proceeds taken in installments is excluded from income.

T F 6. A transfer of appreciated property in satisfaction of a debt is a realizable event for income tax purposes.

T F 7. The maximum exclusion for employee child care fringe benefits is $5,000 per year.

T F 8. Under the tax benefit rule if a taxpayer obtains a deduction in one year and later recovers a portion of the prior deduction, the recovery produces taxable income.

T F 9. There are limits on the use of tax-exempt bonds to finance private business activities.

T F 10. A United States citizen is generally subject to U.S. tax on his total income regardless of the geographic origin of the income.

T F 11. To be excluded from gross income, meals furnished by an employer to an employee must be on the business premises and be for the convenience of the employer.

T F 12. Workers' compensation benefits are included in the gross income of the taxpayer receiving the benefits.

T F 13. The maximum foreign earned income exclusion in 1999 is $74,000, plus a limited exclusion for foreign housing costs.

T F 14. To qualify for the foreign earned income exclusion, the taxpayer must be either a bona fide resident of the foreign country or present in the country for 250 days during any 12 consecutive months.

T F 15. Dividends on a mutual life insurance policy are taxable to the owner of the policy only if the policy has a cash surrender value of $5,000 or more.

T F 16. "Cafeteria" plans allow employees to choose nontaxable benefits rather than cash compensation and have the benefits remain nontaxable to the employee.

T F 17. Ministers can exclude from gross income the rental value of a home furnished as compensation or a rental allowance used to provide a home.

T F 18. Professor Gomez's son is enrolled as an undergraduate at the nonprofit university where he teaches. The university waived the tuition of $6,000 for the son. Professor Gomez must include the $6,000 in his income because his son went to school for free.

T F 19. Scholarship income used for expenses of room and board is treated as earned income for purposes of calculating the standard deduction for one who is claimed as a dependent of another taxpayer.

T F 20. If the amount of a scholarship eligible for exclusion is not known at year-end the transaction is held open until the education expenses are paid.

T F 21. Generally, punitive damages are not taxed to the recipient because they represent a penalty to the person causing the damages.

T F 22. Generally, if an employee has an option of taking cash instead of employer-provided housing then the amount is taxable.

T F 23. Employer-paid parking for company officers qualifies as a working condition fringe benefit and would not be income to the officers.

T F 24. The annuity rules are used to apportion an installment payment of life insurance proceeds between the principal and interest on earnings from reinvestment of the life insurance proceeds.

T F 25. Under a cafeteria plan, an employee is permitted to choose between cash and nontaxable benefits (e.g., child care).

T F 26. Leslie is a graduate research assistant. She receives $4,000 for working 400 hours during the semester. Also, she receives a $5,000 tuition waiver from the university. The $5,000 is excluded from Leslie's income.

T F 27. Long-term care benefits received by a taxpayer are excluded to the greater of actual costs or $195 per day.

Fill-in-the-Blanks

Complete the following statements with the appropriate word(s) or amount(s).

1. Amounts received as qualified scholarships to cover the cost of tuition and related expenses are ______________ from gross income.

2. To be excluded from gross income, meals must be on the __________ __________ of the employer and be furnished for the __________ of the employer.

3. U.S. taxpayers are allowed a __________ against U.S. tax for foreign income taxes paid.

4. The interest on __________ and __________ government bonds is usually exempt from the Federal income tax.

5. If a taxpayer obtains a deduction for an item in one year and later recovers a portion of that deduction, the recovery produces income under the tax __________ rule.

Multiple Choice

1. Andrew, a single taxpayer, received $1,100 in dividends on his Texaco Inc. stock and $600 on Harrod stock (a U.K. Corporation). Assuming Andrew is a cash basis, calendar year taxpayer, what amount would be included in his 1999 gross income?
   a. $-0-
   b. $1,100
   c. $1,700
   d. $1,600
   e. Some other amount

2. Bess received gifts of $9,000 in cash and an automobile with a fair market value of $2,000 (cost $12,000). Assuming Bess is a cash basis, calendar year taxpayer, what amount would be included in her 1999 gross income?
   a. $-0-
   b. $2,000
   c. $9,000
   d. $11,000
   e. Some other amount

3. Conrad Corporation sues Amber Corporation and recovers $500,000 lost income damages and $300,000 in punitive damages for loss of income. Assuming Conrad is a cash basis, calendar year taxpayer, what amount would be included in its 1999 gross income?
   a. $-0-
   b. $300,000
   c. $500,000
   d. $800,000
   e. Some other amount.

4. Doris recovered $12,000 of $18,000 that was deducted for tax purposes in 1997. Assuming Doris is a cash basis, calendar year taxpayer, what amount would be included in her 1999 gross income?
   a. $-0-
   b. $12,000
   c. $18,000
   d. $6,000
   e. Some other amount

5. On the death of his father, Edgar received $50,000 (cash value of the policy is $24,000) as the beneficiary of his father's life insurance policy. Assuming Edgar is a cash basis, calendar year taxpayer, what amount would be included in his 1999 gross income?
   a. $-0-
   b. $50,000
   c. $24,000
   d. $26,000
   e. Some other amount

6. Fay inherited several AT&T bonds. The bonds had a fair market value of $70,000 at the date of death. After receiving the bonds, she was also paid $2,000 in interest. Assuming Fay is a cash basis, calendar year taxpayer, what amount would be included in her 1999 gross income?
   a. $-0-
   b. $72,000
   c. $70,000
   d. $2,000
   e. Some other amount

7. As the result of an accident on the job Garth is disabled. Under workers' compensation insurance, he received $7,200. Assuming Garth is a cash basis, calendar year taxpayer, what amount would be included in his 1999 gross income?
   a. $-0-
   b. $2,000
   c. $7,200
   d. Some other amount

8. Pat (a single taxpayer) received the following income for 1999:

Salary	$30,000
Dividends from G.M. stock	1,000
Interest on City of Houston bonds	2,000
Life insurance proceeds	10,000
Dividends on Mexican stock	1,600

   What is Pat's gross income for 1999?
   a. $42,600
   b. $31,000
   c. $32,600
   d. $30,000
   e. Some other amount

9. Sam paid $20,000 into a qualified state tuition program for his son, Bill. This amount prepaid $5,000 per year of tuition. When Bill went to college the tuition is $6,500 per year. Bill uses the plan to pay for his current year's college. How much must Bill include in income from utilizing the plan?
   a. $-0-
   b. $1,500
   c. $5,000
   d. $6,500
   e. Some other amount

10. Jill works for a hospital which provides employees free meals in a lunchroom. During 1999 the value of the meals received by Jill are $2,300. If Jill had eaten all the meals available at the hospital, she would have eaten $4,800 worth of meals. The reason the hospital provides the meals is so that employees will be available for emergencies. How much will Jill have to include in her income from the free meals?
    a. $-0-
    b. $2,300
    c. $4,800
    d. $2,500
    e. Some other amount.

11. In the current year Armadillo Airlines covers an employee with a qualified dental plan at a cost of $200. In addition, its employees are allowed to fly for free on a standby basis, and this same employee takes free flights valued at $3,000. The employee is also provided with free parking at the airport worth $400 per year. Of these amounts, how much must the employee include in his gross income for the current year?
    a. $-0-
    b. $200
    c. $3,200
    d. $3,600
    e. Some other amount

12. Chris had adjusted gross income of $5,000 after deducting a bad debt of $2,000. Her itemized deductions and personal exemptions were $6,600. The next year, much to her surprise, Chris collected the bad debt. How much must she include in income for the year of recovery?
    a. $-0-
    b. $200
    c. $400
    d. $1,000
    e. Some other amount

13. Janis owed Friendly Bank and Trust $50,000 on an unsecured note. She paid off the note with stock worth $50,000 (basis of $40,000). How much gain must Janis recognize on the transfer of the stock to the bank?
    a. -0-
    b. $10,000
    c. $40,000
    d. $50,000
    e. Some other amount

14. Mike is an employee of Mega Corporation. As an employee, Mike received the following fringe benefits.

Benefit	Value
Free use of company gym	$200
10% discount on $250 TV (employer's standard gross profit margin, 25%)	25
Free company parking	400
Personal use of copy machine	8

If the plan does not discriminate, what amount of these fringe benefits must Mike report as income on his tax return?

a. $-0-
b. $1,233
c. $600
d. $400
e. Some other amount

15. During the current year Alfred sustained a serious injury while on the job. As a result of his injury, Alfred received the following amounts during the same year:

Workers' compensation payments	$2,400
Reimbursement from employer's accident and health plan for medical expenses paid by Alfred	1,800
Damages for personal injuries	8,000

How much of the above amounts should Alfred include in his gross income for the current year?
a. $12,200
b. $8,000
c. $1,800
d. $-0-
e. Some other amount

16. Lyle and Maria are married and live in Palm Springs. They receive the following distributions from securities during the year:

Lyle:	ATT, cash dividends	$200
	City of Las Vegas Bonds, interest	500
Maria:	Southwest Airlines, cash dividends	50
	Bank of Canada, cash dividends	300
	Citibank, stock dividend on com. stock	75

Lyle and Maria file a joint return. Of the above items, what amount must be included in ordinary income for the year after any exclusions?
a. $250
b. $700
c. $550
d. $625
e. Some other amount

17. Phyllis, a cash basis, calendar year taxpayer, works for the Very Big Corporation of America. Her salary is $75,000 per year. Also, she received the following fringe benefits from Very Big during the current year:

Free parking (provided to all employees)	$480
Personal use of xerox machine	30
Personal long distance calls	70
Personal letters typed	100
Membership in a local health club	600

Personal use of firm's hunting lodge	125

What amount of these fringe benefits must be included in Phyllis's gross income?
a. $-0-
b. $600
c. $725
d. $825
e. $925

18. Kurt received the following interest payments during the year:

Interest on municipal bonds	$700
Interest on Series HH savings bonds	500
Increase in value of Series EE savings bonds	400
Interest on last years federal income tax refund	200
Interest on contract settlement from dispute two years ago	500

If Kurt is a cash basis taxpayer and has made no special elections, what should he include in gross income from the above amounts?
a. $-0-
b. $1,200
c. $1,700
d. $700
e. Some other amount

19. Mary is employed as the manager of an apartment complex. Her employer gave her the option of two compensation schemes:

(1) Cash salary of $40,000 per year, or
(2) Cash salary of $32,000 per year plus a free apartment worth $7,000 per year

If Mary selects option two, what amount should she include in gross income?
a. $40,000
b. $32,000
c. $33,000
d. $39,000
e. Some other amount

Use the following information for Questions 20 through 22.

John, who was 58 at the time of his death on July 1, 1999, received $1,000 of interest in 1999 on municipal bonds. John's wife Emma, age 57, received a $300 television set in 1999 as a "gift" for opening a long-term savings account at a bank. On John's death, Emma received life insurance proceeds of $60,000 under a group policy paid for by John's employer. Emma did not remarry in 1999. Emma is the executrix of John's estate.

20. How much taxable interest was received by John and Emma in 1999?
a. $-0-

b. $300
c. $1,000
d. $1,300
e. Some other amount

21. How much of the group-term life insurance proceeds should be excluded from 1999 taxable income?
a. $-0-
b. $5,000
c. $50,000
d. $60,000
e. Some other amount

22. In 1999, Claire's proceeds from the redemption of qualified educational savings bonds during the taxable year were $10,000 (principal of $6,000 and interest of $4,000). Her qualified higher education expenses were $8,000. How much of the interest is excludible (before any phase-out)?
a. $-0-
b. $4,000
c. $3,200
d. $1,771
e. Some other amount

23. Assume the same facts as in question 22, except Claire's modified adjusted gross income is $60,000 and she files as a single taxpayer. How much interest is excludible after the phase-out?
a. $-0-
b. $3,200
c. $1,472
d. $1,728
e. Some other amount

24. Andy, age 20, is a full-time student at Small State University and is studying for his bachelor's degree. During 1999 he received the following cash payments:

Scholarship:		
Books and tuition	$5,000	
Meals and lodging	2,000	$7,000
Interest income		600
Cash support from a rich uncle		2,000
Loan from financial aid office		$4,000

What is Andy's adjusted gross income for 1999?
a. $-0-
b. $2,600
c. $7,600
d. $11,600
e. Some other amount

25. Pete purchased an insurance policy on his life with his son as the beneficiary. Pete paid $28,000 in premiums. The policy had a cash surrender value of $34,000 when Pete died and his son collected the face amount of $150,000. How much income must the son report as beneficiary of the policy?

a. $-0-
b. $28,000
c. $34,000
d. $150,000
e. Some other amount

26. In 1999, Paula was required to pay $200 of nondeductible interest and $100 of nondeductible penalties because her tax return was filed late. Her tax return was late because her CPA was overworked and did not get a chance to finish the return. The CPA reimbursed Paula $300 for the interest and penalties due the IRS. How much of the reimbursement is income to Paula?
a. $-0-
b. $100
c. $200
d. $300
e. Some other amount

27. During 1999, Jude was reimbursed by his employer-sponsored health insurance plan for the following medical expenses:

Doctor visits	$2,000
Hospital stay for son's illness	5,000
Cost of hair transplant	3,000
Prescription drugs	2,000

How much income (if any) must Jude report from these reimbursements?
a. $-0-
b. $2,000
c. $3,000
d. $12,000
e. Some other amount

28. Silver Corporation's management is allowed to purchase goods from the company for a 20% discount and all other employees are allowed a 10% discount. The employer's usual gross profit margin is 25%. Bill, president of the company, purchased from Silver Corporation goods for $1,600 when the price charged to customers was $2,000. How much income must Bill report from the purchase of the goods?
a. $-0-
b. $400
c. $1,600
d. $200
e. Some other amount

29. Big Private University (BPU) allows the children of employees to attend for a special tuition rate that is 30% of the regular tuition. Joel is an employee of BPU and his child attends the school on a full-time basis (paying the special tuition rate). Regular tuition at BPU is $10,000 per year. How much does Joel have to include in income from the tuition reduction?
a. $-0-
b. $3,000
c. $7,000
d. $10,000

e. Some other amount

30. Lance qualifies for the foreign earned income credit. He was present in Ecuador for 344 days in 1999. Lance's salary for 1999 was $90,000. Assuming a 365-day year, what is Lance's earned income exclusion?
a. $-0-
b. $69,742
c. $74,000
d. $90,000
e. Some other amount

31. Edna owns and operates a profitable onion farm. Determine Edna's gross income from the following receipts for the current year:

Gain on sale of Texas bonds	$1,000
Interest on U.S. Bonds	600
Interest on State tax refund	200
Interest on Texas bonds	800
Patronage dividend from Onion Growers Coop	3,000

The patronage dividend was received in April of the current year for amounts paid and deducted on Edna's schedule F for the previous year.
a. $1,800
b. $1,600
c. $4,800
d. $5,600
e. Some other amount

32. Betty owned a $100,000 term life insurance (total premiums paid of $10,000) policy when she was diagnosed as having a terminal illness. She sold the policy to for $75,000 to Bass Benefits, Inc., a company that is qualified by the state of Texas to purchase such policies. How much income must Betty recognized on the date of the policy?
a. $-0-
b. $10,000
c. $65,000
d. $75,000
e. Some other amount

33. Same as number 32. How much must Bass Benefits recognize upon Betty's death if Bass pays an additional $7,000 in premiums?
a. $-0-
b. $75,000
c. $100,000
d. $18,000
d. Some other amount

Use the legend provided below to indicate for each fringe benefit (questions #34 to #40) if it would be included, partially included, or excluded in an employee's taxable income.

Legend

A = included
B = partially included
C = excluded

____ 34. Employer provided services equal to 30% of the customer price.

____ 35. AICPA dues paid by an employer.

____ 36. Qualified parking with a value of $250 per month.

____ 37. A bus pass worth $50 per month.

____ 38. Occasional use of the employer's Xerox machine for personal copies.

____ 39. The employee's wife flies free on a standby airline ticket.

____ 40. A medical reimbursement that is available only to officers of the company.

SOLUTIONS TO CHAPTER 5

True or False

1. True (p. 5-3)
2. False Gifts in a business setting may be included in gross income. (p. 5-5)
3. True (p. 5-19)
4. False Proceeds may be included in gross income if the policy was transferred for valuable consideration. (p. 5-7)
5. False The interest portion of the installment payment received is generally included in income. (p. 5-8)
6. True (p. 5-32)
7. True (p. 5-18)
8. True (p. 5-31)
9. True (p. 5-28)
10. True (p. 5-25)
11. True (p. 5-15)
12. False Workers' compensation is excluded from gross income. (p. 5-12)
13. True (p. 5-27)
14. False 330 days, not 250 days. (p. 5-25)
15. False The dividends are not dividends. (p.5-29)
16. True (p. 5-18)
17. True (p. 5-17)
18. False The tuition reduction is not income to Professor Gomez. (p. 5-9)
19. True (p. 5-9)
20. True (p. 5-9)
21. False Punitive damages are included in gross income unless they are considered compensation for physical injuries or physical sickness. (p. 5-11)
22. True (p. 5-18)
23. True (p. 5-22)
24. True (p. 5-8)
25. True (p. 5-18)
26. True (p. 5-10)
27. False The daily amount is $175. (p. 5-14)

Fill-in-the-Blanks

1. excluded (p. 5-8)
2. business premises, convenience (p. 5-15)
3. credit (p. 5-25)
4. state, local (p. 5-28)
5. benefit (p. 5-31)

Multiple Choice

1. C $1,100 + 600 = $1,700. (p. 5-3)
2. A (p. 5-3)
3. D $300,000 + 500,000 = $800,000 (p. 5-11)

4.	B	(p. 5-31)
5.	A	(p. 5-6)
6.	D	(p. 5-4)
7.	A	(p. 5-12)
8.	C	$30,000 + 1,000 + 1,600 = $32,600. (pp. 5-6 and 5-25)
9.	B	$6,500 - $5,000 = $1,500 included (p. 5-31)
10.	A	(p. 5-15)
11.	A	(pp. 5-13, 20, 22)
12.	C	$7,000 - 6,600 = $400 tax benefit from deduction. (p. 5-31)
13.	B	$50,000 - 40,000 = $10,000 (p. 5-32)
14.	A	(p. 5-18)
15.	D	(pp. 5-10, 12)
16.	C	$200 + 50 + 300 = $550 (p. 5-28, 29)
17.	C	$600 + 125 = $725 (p. 5-18)
18	B	$500 + 200 + 500 = $1,200 (p. 5-28)
19.	D	$32,000 + 7,000 = $39,000 (p. 5-16)
20.	B	The value of the T.V. set "gift" is interest. (p. 5-4)
21.	D	(p. 5-6)
22.	C	($8,000/$10,000) x $4,000 = $3,200. (p. 5-30)
23.	D	$3,200 - [(($60,000 - $53,100)/$15,000) x $3,200] = $1,728 [1999] (p. 5-30)
24.	B	$2,000 + 600 = $2,600. (p. 5-8)
25.	A	(p. 5-6)
26.	A	Under the tax benefit rule, since the reimbursement is for amounts that are not deductible (personal interest and penalties), none of the reimbursement is included in income. (p. 5-31)
27.	C	Cosmetic surgery is not allowed as a medical deduction; therefore, the reimbursement is included in gross income. (p. 5-13)
28.	B	The plan discriminated therefore the discount is income. (p. 5-22)
29.	A	(p. 5-9)
30.	B	(344 days/365 days) x $74,000 = $69,742. [1999] (p. 5-27)
31.	C	$1,000 + $600 + $200 + $3,000 = $4,800. (p. 5-28)
32.	A	(p. 5-6)
33.	D	$100,000 - $75,000 - $7,000 = $18,000 (p. 5-6)
34.	B	(p. 5-21)
35.	C	(p. 5-22)
36.	B	(p. 5-23)
37.	C	(p. 5-24)
38.	C	(p. 5-22)
39.	C	(p. 5-20)
40.	A	(p. 5-24)

CHAPTER 6
DEDUCTIONS AND LOSSES: IN GENERAL

CHAPTER HIGHLIGHTS

All deductions are a matter of legislative grace. For an expenditure to be deductible, it must be specifically authorized by Congress. This chapter introduces and classifies deductions *for* adjusted gross income and deductions *from* adjusted gross income. Specific provisions in the tax law which disallow or limit certain deductions are discussed in detail.

I. CLASSIFICATION OF DEDUCTIONS

Deductions of individual taxpayers fall into one of two classifications, deductions *for* adjusted gross income or deductions *from* adjusted gross income.

A. Section 62 specifies the expenses which are deductible for adjusted gross income. The common deductions *for* AGI include:

1) trade or business deductions

2) certain reimbursed employee business expenses

3) losses on the sale of property other than personal use property

4) rent and royalty expenses

5) alimony payments (Section 215)

6) contributions to self-employed retirement plans

7) deductions for retirement savings (Section 219)

8) the deduction for moving expenses

9) penalties on premature withdrawal of funds from savings accounts

10) interest on student loans

B. The more common deductions *from* AGI (itemized) include:

1) expenses for the production or collection of income

2) expenses for the management, conservation, or maintenance of property held for the production of income

3) expenses for the determination, collection, or refund of any tax

4) charitable contributions

5) medical expenses in excess of 7.5 percent of adjusted gross income

6) certain state and local taxes (e.g., real estate, state and local income taxes)

7) personal casualty losses

8) certain personal interest

9) certain miscellaneous deductions (in excess of 2% of AGI).

Deductions related to the production of rent and royalty income are referred to as deductions *for* adjusted gross income.

C. Trade or business expenses are deductible *for* AGI. For any business expenditure to be deductible it must be "ordinary and necessary." An ordinary expense is one that is normal, usual, or customary in the type of business being conducted by the taxpayer. A necessary expense is one that is appropriate and helpful in furthering the taxpayer's trade or business. Certain payments such as charitable contributions, illegal bribes and kickbacks, and fines and penalties are excluded as trade or business deductions.

Reasonableness Requirement. Besides being ordinary and necessary, the Code specifies that salaries must be "reasonable." The courts have expanded this requirement to cover all business expenses.

D. Business and Nonbusiness Losses. Section 165 provides that losses not covered by insurance are deductible. In general, deductible losses of individual taxpayers are limited to losses in a trade or business, investment losses, and casualty losses.

E. Itemized deductions are reported on Schedule A (and various supporting schedules) of Form 1040. Deductions for AGI are reported primarily on Schedules C (trade or business income), E (rent, royalty, S corporation, and partnership income), F (farm and ranch income), and directly on page one (traditional IRAs and alimony) of Form 1040.

II. TIMING OF EXPENSE RECOGNITION

A. Timing of Expense Recognition. In general, the taxpayer's method of accounting (cash or accrual) will determine the period in which a deduction can be taken. There are limitations on the use of the cash method of accounting by certain taxpayers.

B. The expenses of cash basis taxpayers must be paid in cash before they can be deducted. The issuance of a note or other promise to pay does not qualify as a cash payment. Cash basis taxpayers and accrual basis taxpayers cannot deduct capital expenditures.

C. Accrual basis taxpayers can deduct an expense by meeting the "economic performance test." This test is met only when the service, property, or use of property giving rise to the liability is actually performed for, provided to, or used by the taxpayer.

II. DISALLOWANCE POSSIBILITIES

A. Public Policy Limitation. The Code denies a deduction for an expenditure that is against public policy. Expenses that are against public policy include bribes, kickbacks, fines, and penalties. In general, legal expenses are deductible if incurred in the taxpayer's trade or business.

The usual expenses relating to the operation of illegal business, other than those contrary to public policy, are deductible. However, under the tax law illegal drug traffickers are not allowed a deduction for the ordinary and necessary expenses incurred in their business. They are only allowed a deduction for cost of goods sold.

B. Political Contributions and Lobbying Activities. Generally, no business deduction is allowed for political contributions. A taxpayer may deduct certain lobbying expenditures if he has a direct interest in the proposed legislation. Dues or expenses paid to an organization of individuals with a common direct interest in proposed legislation are also deductible. Expenses which are incurred to influence the public on political matters may not be deducted.

C. Excessive Executive Compensation. Publicly traded corporations cannot deduct executive compensation over $1,000,000 annually. This rule applies to the chief executive officer and the four most highly compensated officers. The following are not subject to the $1,000,000 annual limit:

1) Commissions based on individual performance

2) Performance-based compensation based on a formula approved by the board of directors

3) Payments to tax-qualified retirement plans

4) Payments that are excludible from the employee's gross income (e.g., certain fringe benefits)

D. Investigation expenses for determining the feasibility of entering a new business or expanding an existing business are deductible if the taxpayer is already engaged in a similar business. If the taxpayer is not engaged in a similar business, and a new business is acquired, such expenses are capitalized and may be amortized over 60 months or more. In the event the new business is not acquired, investigation expenses are usually nondeductible.

E. Hobby Losses. Under Sec. 183, if a taxpayer can show that an activity was entered with the intent of making a profit, and not for personal pleasure, then any losses are fully deductible.

The hobby loss rules apply when the taxpayer cannot show that the activity was engaged in for profit. Hobby expenses are only deductible up to the amount of hobby income. The expenses are deductible in the following order:

1) amounts deductible under other Code sections (e.g., property taxes).

2) amounts deductible as if the activity is engaged in for profit, but only if those amounts do not affect the basis of property (e.g., maintenance).

3) amounts deductible as if the activity is engaged in for profit which affect the basis of property (e.g., depreciation).

The tax law states that if a profit is made for "three of five consecutive years" (two of seven years for activities involving horses) then the activity is presumed to be engaged in for profit, and the hobby loss rules do not apply.

If the above presumption is not met, the activity may still qualify as a business if the taxpayer can show a profit-making intent. The Regulations stipulate nine relevant factors in distinguishing between profit-seeking activities and hobbies. The relevant factors are:

1) whether the activity is conducted in a business like manner

2) the expertise of the taxpayers

3) time and effort expended

4) expectation that the assets will appreciate

5) the previous success of the taxpayer in similar activities

6) the history of income and loss from the activity

7) the relationship of profits to losses

8) the financial status of the taxpayer

9) elements of personal pleasure in the activity

F. Vacation homes have loss rules similar to the hobby loss provisions. If the home is rented for 15 days or more and is used for personal purposes for more than the greater of 14 days or 10 percent of the days actually rented, then the deductions for depreciation, maintenance, etc., will be limited to the revenue generated. If the home is rented for 15 days or more, but personal use is not more than the greater of 14 days or 10 percent of the days rented, the home is considered rental property. Finally, if the vacation home is rented for less than 15 days, all rental income is excluded and all rental expenses, other than mortgage interest and property taxes, are disallowed.

Expenses must be allocated between personal and rental days. Expenses, other than property taxes and interest, are allocated on the basis of the total days of use. The IRS and the courts disagree on the allocation of taxes and interest. According to the courts, taxes and interest are to be allocated on the basis of 365 days; however, according to the IRS, taxes and interest should be allocated in the same manner as other expenses, on the basis of total days of use.

G. Expenditures Incurred for the Taxpayer's Benefit or Obligation. For an expenditure to be deductible, it must be incurred for the taxpayer's "benefit or be the taxpayer's obligation." Thus, a taxpayer cannot claim a deduction for paying the expenses of another individual.

H. Disallowance of Personal Expenditures. No deduction is allowed for personal, living, or family expenses unless specifically provided in the Code. Exceptions provided in the Code include:

1) charitable expenses

2) medical expenses

3) expenses for the determination, collection, or refund of tax

4) tax advice in divorce proceedings

I. Disallowance of Deductions for Capital Expenditures. Capital expenditures related to depreciable or amortizable property are added to the basis of the property and may be written off over the life of the property. Often it is difficult to distinguish repairs and maintenance from capital expenditures. The Code defines a capital expenditure as "any amount paid out for new buildings or for permanent improvements or betterments made to increase the value of any property or estate." Other expenditures are considered repairs and maintenance.

Sometimes, taxpayers are permitted an election to capitalize certain expenditures, such as property taxes, which would otherwise be currently expensed.

Exceptions in the Code regarding the deductibility of capital expenditures include the election to expense certain mineral development costs, intangible drilling costs, qualified farm land clearing expenditures, and research expenditures.

J. Transactions Between Related Parties. The tax law places restrictions on transactions between certain related parties due to the potential for "sham" transactions and tax avoidance schemes. Losses and unpaid expenses and interest are "not deductible" if incurred between related parties. However, any disallowed loss may be used to reduce a future gain on the property.

Related parties (as defined in Sec. 267) are:

1) Siblings, spouses, ancestors, and lineal descendants of the taxpayer

2) A corporation owned more than 50 percent (directly or indirectly) by the taxpayer

3) Two corporations that are members of a controlled group

4) A series of other complex relationships between trusts, corporations, estates, and individual taxpayers

Under the constructive ownership rules, stock owned by certain related parties is deemed to be owned by the taxpayer for the disallowance provisions.

K. Substantiation Requirements. To be deductible, expenses must be substantiated by the taxpayer. Travel, entertainment, and business gifts must satisfy more stringent substantiation requirements.

L. Expenses Related to Tax-Exempt Income. No deduction is allowed for expenses (including interest expense incurred to purchase or carry tax-exempt obligations) related to the production of tax-exempt income.

KEY TERMS

Deduction For/From AGI

Section 162 Trade or Business Expenses

Section 212 Production of Income Expenses

Hobby Losses

Vacation Home

Relate Parties

TEST FOR SELF-EVALUATION

True or False

Indicate which of the following statements are true or false by circling the correct answers.

T F 1. The courts have established the doctrine that an item is not deductible unless a specific Code provision allows the deduction.

T F 2. To be deductible under Sec. 162 or Sec. 212, an item must be ordinary and necessary.

T F 3. Alimony, medical expenses, and state and local taxes are deductions from adjusted gross income.

T F. 4. The term "trade or business" is clearly defined by statute in the Code.

T F 5. Expenses incurred in the determination, collection, or refund of any tax are deductible under Sec. 212.

T F 6. To be deductible, salaries must be reasonable.

T F 7. Generally, taxable income will be computed under the method of accounting that the taxpayer regularly uses to compute income and keep his or her books.

T F 8. Generally, accrual basis taxpayers cannot take a current deduction for capital expenditures except through amortization or depreciation over the life of the asset.

T F 9. Legal expenses are never deductible as ordinary and necessary business expenses if incurred in a trade or business activity.

T F 10. In order for an accrual basis taxpayer to deduct an expense, it must pass the "economic performance test."

T F 11. Investigation expenses are always deductible by a taxpayer entering a new trade or business.

T F 12. If an activity shows a profit for three of five years (two of seven years for activities involving horses), then the Code presumes it is not a hobby.

T F 13. If a residence is rented for 15 days or more, Sec. 280A limits the deductions related to the home if the taxpayer uses the home for personal purposes for more than the greater of 14 days or 10 percent of the days actually rented.

T F 14. A taxpayer can claim a deduction for interest he paid on his son's mortgage. (The son is not the taxpayer's dependent).

T F 15. In general, Sec. 262 disallows deductions for personal, living, and family expenses.

T F 16. The tax law disallows a deduction for expenses incurred in producing tax-exempt income.

T F 17. Due to the voluntary nature of the tax law, upon audit the IRS bears the burden of determining the validity of the expenses deducted on the taxpayer's return.

T F 18. Sec. 267 disallows losses and certain deductions between related parties.

T F 19. In 1999, goodwill is amortizable over 15 years for tax purposes.

T F 20. Personal legal fees are generally deductible by individual taxpayers.

T F 21. Expenses associated with a taxpayer's vacation home are deductible in full.

T F 22. To be deductible, an expense must be incurred for the taxpayer's benefit or arise from the taxpayer's obligation.

T F 23. Most expenses of hobbies (to the extent of income from the hobby) are deductible from AGI subject to the 2 percent of AGI limitation.

T F 24. The courts have held that taxes and interest on a vacation home should be allocated over 365 days a year, while the IRS has determined that taxes and interest should be allocated based on total days of use.

T F 25. Gwen rented her condo in Utah for 180 days. If Gwen used the condo for 20 days of personal use, it would be classified as a "personal/rental" asset.

Fill-in-the-Blanks

Complete the following statements with the appropriate word(s) or amount(s).

1. The items that are disallowed under the related party rules are __________, unpaid interest, and unpaid expenses.

2. The expenses of a residence which is rented for 15 days or more and is used for personal purposes for more than the greater of (1) ______ days or (2) _____ percent of the total days rented, must be limited to the rental income generated by the property.

3. On December 1, 19X1, a taxpayer is required to pay three months rent, $3,000, on a building used in her business. If she is a cash basis taxpayer, her rent deduction for 19X1 is __________.

4. The nondeductibility of bribes, kickbacks, fines, and penalties is justified by being against public ___________.

5. If an activity is deemed to be a hobby, the trade or business expenses are deductible only to the extent of the __________ from the hobby.

6. Section 212 allows a deduction for expenses due to the production or __________ of income.

7. Expenses under the accrual method of accounting are deductible when ________ and under the cash method when _______.

8. Itemized deductions from adjusted gross income are reported by individual taxpayers on ____________ of Form 1040.

Multiple Choice

Choose the best answer for each of the following questions.

1. Which of the following is not a deduction for adjusted gross income?
   a. Alimony
   b. State income tax
   c. Trade or business expenses
   d. Traditional IRA contributions
   e. None of the above

2. Section 212 addresses expenses for the production or collection of income and tax return preparation fees. Which of the following is not a Sec. 212 deduction?
   a. Repair expense on a rental house
   b. A fee paid to a CPA for preparing a tax return
   c. Interest expense on a personal residence
   d. Safe deposit box rental used to store stock certificates
   e. None of the above

3. Elizabeth is a physician. In her spare time she wants to become a famous stock car racer. In the current year Elizabeth incurs the following costs:

Stock car purchases	$40,000
Entry fees	5,000
Driving lessons	10,000
Travel expenses to races	15,000
Total	$70,000

   Of the races entered by Elizabeth this year, her total earnings are $250. Probably, the IRS will allow Elizabeth to deduct what amount of the above expenditures (before any 2% limit)?
   a. -0-
   b. $250
   c. $30,000
   d. $70,000
   e. None of the above

4. Under Sec. 183, if an activity is not engaged in for profit, deductions related to the activity will be limited. Which of the following is likely to be deemed a hobby by the IRS?
   a. A CPA in private practice
   b. A ranch owned by an executive that has shown a profit for four of the last 5years
   c. An individual borrowing money to open a gift shop
   d. A physician who operates a photography studio at a loss for five consecutive years

e. None of the above

5. During the current year, Lee pays $5,000 to an attorney to obtain a divorce. Of this amount, $2,000 is for tax advice about the divorce settlement. How much, if any, of the $5,000 is deductible before considering any limitation based on AGI?
   a. -0-
   b. $2,000
   c. $3,000
   d. $5,000
   e. None of the above

6. David made illegal business kickbacks of $10,000 and paid fines of $8,000 during the current year. How much of the expenses can be deducted on his tax return before considering any limitation based on AGI?
   a. -0-
   b. $8,000
   c. $10,000
   d. $18,000
   e. None of the above

7. If a taxpayer paid $5,000 interest on a note, the proceeds of which were used to purchase Texas state bonds, and the bonds produced interest income of $4,000, how much of an interest deduction would be allowed?
   a. -0-
   b. $1,000
   c. $4,000
   d. $5,000
   e. None of the above

8. Todd owns 33 percent of the stock in Todd Corporation, 33 percent is owned by Todd's mother, and 33 percent by Todd's father. On January 1, 19X1, Todd loans Todd Corporation $100,000 at 9 percent interest annually. Todd Corporation is an "accrual" basis taxpayer while Todd is a cash basis taxpayer. Todd Corporation pays the current interest on December 29, 19X1. How much interest is deductible by Todd Corporation for 19X1?
   a. -0-
   b. $4,500
   c. $9,000
   d. None of the above

9. Tom pays $5,000 interest on his home mortgage, and pays $3,000 on his son's mortgage. The son does not qualify as Tom's dependent. How much of an interest deduction will Tom be allowed (before considering any limitations)?
   a. -0-
   b. $3,000
   c. $5,000
   d. $8,000
   e. None of the above

10. Tammie rents her vacation home for 30 days and lives in it for 10 days during the current year. Her gross income from rent payments was $4,000 and she incurred the following expenses:

Taxes and interest	$3,000
Utilities and maintenance	800
Depreciation	4,000
Total	$7,800

Using the IRS approach, what amount of income or loss must Tammie report from this rental (disregard any passive loss limitations)?
a. -0-
b. $200 income
c. $3,800 loss
d. $1,850 loss
e. Some other amount

11. Refer to the preceding problem. If Tammie uses the home for 20 days (instead of 10 days) for personal purposes, the allowable deduction that may be claimed (disregard any passive loss limitations) is:
a. $-0-
b. $200 income
c. $3,800 loss
d. $680 loss
e. Some other amount

12. Robert owns a chain of motels in California. He flies to Arizona to investigate the possibility of buying an automobile dealership. All of the expenses for the trip are deductible in the current year if:
a. The automobile dealership is purchased
b. The auto dealership is not purchased
c. Would never be deductible
d. Robert already owns an auto dealership and does not purchase the Arizona dealership
e. None of the above

13. During the current year, Mary purchased a lot with an old house on it for $100,000. She immediately had the house demolished at a cost of $15,000. Four months later the lot is sold for $160,000. How much gain should be recognized by Mary?
a. -0-
b. $15,000
c. $45,000
d. $60,000
e. None of the above

14. Under Sec. 267(c), the disallowance between related parties provision, which of the following is not a related family member?
a. Spouse
b. Son or daughter
c. Grandchild
d. Grandparent
e. All of the above are related

15. Which of the following expenses are not deductible under Sec. 212?
a. Trade or business expenses

b. Expenses for the production of income
c. Expenses for the management, conservation, or maintenance of property held for the production of income
d. Expenses for the determination, collection, or refund of any tax
e. None of the above

16. Pancho is in the business of importing certain illegal substances. In this business, Pancho incurs the following expenses:

Cost of goods sold	$200,000
Payoffs to customs agents	100,000
Cost of installing false bottom in trunk of car	10,000
Distribution expenses	50,000
Packaging (baggies)	5,000
Kickbacks to narcotics agents	75,000
	$440,000

Of the total, what amount would be deductible by Pancho?
a. -0-
b. $440,000
c. $340,000
d. $200,000
e. None of the above

17. During 1999 Xavier, a single taxpayer, had a salary of $28,000 and incurred the following expenses:

Alimony paid	$5,000
Charitable contributions	1,000
Interest on home mortgage	6,000
Deductible contribution to an IRA	2,000
Moving expense	2,000
Real estate taxes	1,500

What is Xavier's adjusted gross income for 1999?
a. $28,000
b. $26,000
c. $21,000
d. $19,000
e. Some other amount

18. Using the information from question 17, what is Xavier's taxable income for 1999 (the 1999 exemption amount is $2,750)?
a. $7,750
b. $8,800
c. $10,400
d. $10,500
e. Some other amount

19. Gene owns his own business. He hires his 19-year-old daughter (who has just passed introductory accounting with a D+) as an accountant for the summer at a rate of $35.00 per hour. Gene has a full-time accounting clerk who has worked for Gene for many years and he pays her $12.00 per hour. Gene, most likely, has a deductible business expense as a result of the payments to his daughter of:
   a. $12.00 per hour (or less)
   b. $17.00 per hour
   c. $35.00 per hour
   d. None of the above

20. Bea incurred the following expenses during the current year:

Interest on son's home mortgage	$6,000
Payment of son's property taxes	2,000
Payment of son's state income tax	1,000
Payment of son's gambling debts	3,000

What amount of the above can Bea consider in calculating her itemized deductions for the current year?
   a. $-0-
   b. $1,000
   c. $3,000
   d. $8,000
   e. Some other amount

21. Wendy is the 100% owner of Blue Corporation. During the year, Wendy purchased from Blue Corporation depreciable property with an adjusted basis of $50,000 for $40,000, its fair market value. Blue placed this property in service six years ago. What is the available loss that Blue Corporation can claim for the current year?
   a. $-0-
   b. $10,000 ordinary loss
   c. $10,000 capital loss
   d. $10,000 Sec. 1231 loss
   e. Some other amount

22. Which of the following are deductible as a trade or business expense?
   a. Illegal bribes and kickbacks
   b. Charitable contributions
   c. Travel expense incurred by a self-employed dentist
   d. Home mortgage interest
   e. All of the above are deductible

23. Sam is the chief operating officer (CEO) of Silver Corporation, a publicly traded corporation. Silver pays Sam $2,500,000 compensation during the current year. The compensation consists of the following payments:

Salary	$1,400,000
Individual performance commission	1,070,000
Pension plan contribution	30,000
Total	$2,500,000

From the above payments, what amount can Silver Corporation deduct on its income tax return?
a. $2,500,000
b. $1,000,000
c. $2,100,000
d. $1,100,000
e. Some other amount.

24. Laurie has a brokerage account at Dean Schwab, Inc. She buys stock and bonds on margin through this account. During the current year, she incurs $10,000 in margin interest in the account. Income generated through the brokerage account was:

Taxable dividends and interest	$30,000
Municipal bond interest	$20,000

What is the amount of Laurie's deductible investment interest?
a. $-0-
b. $4,000
c. $6,000
d. $10,000
e. Some other amount

25. The stock ownership of Salmon Corporations is as follows:

Shares owned by Jane	600
Shares owned by Jane's husband	300
Shares owned by Jane's brother-in-law	350
Shares owned by Jane's aunt	400
Shares owned by Jane's brother	250
Shares owned by Jane's grandson	100
Total shares	2,000

What is Jane's constructive ownership under Sec. 267?
a. 30%
b. 45%
c. 62.5%
d. 65%
e. 100%

Using the legend provided, classify each of the following expenditures for an individual taxpayer (disregard any percentage limitations):

Legend
A = Deductible for AGI
B = Deductible from AGI
C = Not deductible

____ 26. Moving expenses

____ 27. Commuting expenses

____ 28. Medical expenses

____ 29. Business interest

____ 30. Business casualty losses

____ 31. State income tax

____ 32. Bad debts

____ 33. Personal interest

____ 34. Reimbursed employee expenses

____ 35. Rent and royalty expenses

____ 36. Real property tax on a home

SOLUTIONS TO CHAPTER 6

1. True (p. 6-2)
2. True (p. 6-4)
3. False Alimony is a deduction for AGI. (p. 6-3)
4. False The term is not defined in the Code. (p. 6-5)
5. True (p. 6-4)
6. True (p. 6-7)
7. True (p. 6-9)
8. True (p. 6-9)
9. False Legal expenses which are incurred in connection with a trade or business are deductible. (p. 6-12)
10. True (p. 6-10)
11. False The expenses are not deductible. (p. 6-15)
12. True (p. 6-16)
13. True (p. 6-20)
14. False The mortgage is not the taxpayer's obligation. (p. 6-23)
15. True (p. 6-24)
16. True (p. 6-27)
17. False The burden of proof for substantiating expenses deducted is on the taxpayer. (p. 6-27)
18. True (p. 6-26)
19. True (p. 6-25)
20. False Personal legal fees, other than those related to tax advice, are not deductible. (p. 6-12)
21. False Vacation home expenses are limited to the income generated. (p. 6-18)
22. True (p. 6-23)
23. True (p. 6-17)
24. True (p. 6-20)
25. True (p. 6-20)

Fill-in-the-Blanks

1. losses (p. 6-25)
2. 14, 10 (p. 6-20)
3. $3,000 (p. 6-9)
4. policy (p. 6-11)
5. income (p. 6-16)
6. collection (p. 6-4)
7. incurred, paid (p. 6-9)
8. Schedule A (p. 6-8)

Multiple Choice

1. B (p. 6-3)
2. C (p. 6-4)
3. B (p. 6-16)
4. D (p. 6-16)
5. B (p. 6-13)

6.	A	(p. 6-11)
7.	A	(p. 6-27)
8.	C	9% ($100,000) = $9,000; the interest is paid. (p. 6-26)
9.	C	(p. 6-23)

10. D Note: this is "rental" property because it is only used 10 days for personal purposes.

Gross income	$4,000	
Less: rental expenses		
Taxes & interest (75%)	-2,250	
Utilities and maintenance (75%)	-600	
Depreciation (75%)	-3,000	
Loss	-$1,850	(p. 6-20)

11. A

Gross income	$4,000	
Less: rental expenses		
Taxes & interest (60%)	-1,800	
Utilities and maintenance (60%)	-480	
Depreciation (60%) (Max allowed)	-1,720	
Loss	$-0-	(p. 6-20)

12.	D	(p. 6-15)
13.	C	The basis of the house is $115,000, therefore the gain is $45,000 ($160,000 - $115,000). (p. 6-25)
14.	E	(p. 6-26)
15.	A	(p. 6-4)
16.	D	$200,000. Drug dealers are allowed cost of goods sold only. (p. 6-13)

17. D

Salary	$28,000	
IRA	-2,000	
Moving	-2,000	
Alimony	-5,000	
AGI	$19,000	(p. 6-3)

18. A

AGI	$19,000	
Mortgage interest	-6,000	
Charitable contributions	-1,000	
Taxes	-1,500	
Exemption [1999]	-2,750	
Taxable income	$ 7,750	(p. 6-3, prior chapter)

19.	A	Wage payments must be reasonable to be deductible. (p. 6-7)
20.	A	The payment must be for Bea's benefit or Bea's obligation. (p. 6-23)
21.	A	Wendy and Blue are related parties, therefore no deduction. (p. 6-25)
22.	C	(p. 6-5)
23.	C	$1,000,000 (maximum) + $1,070,000 + $30,000 = $2,100,000. (p. 6-14)
24.	C	$10,000 x ($30,000/$50,000) = $6,000. (p. 6-27)
25.	C	(600 + 300 + 250 + 100) / 2,000 = 62.5% (p. 6-26)

26.	A	(p. 6-30)
27.	C	(p. 6-30)
28.	B	(p. 6-30)
29.	A	(p. 6-30)
30.	A	(p. 6-30)
31.	B	(p. 6-30)
32.	A	(p. 6-30)
33.	C	(p. 6-30)
34.	A	(p. 6-30)
35.	A	(p. 6-30)
36.	B	(p. 6-30)

CHAPTER 7
DEDUCTIONS AND LOSSES: CERTAIN BUSINESS EXPENSES AND LOSSES

CHAPTER HIGHLIGHTS

This chapter discusses certain business expenses and losses which are deducted from gross income to arrive at the taxpayer's adjusted gross income. Casualty losses are also discussed, although personal casualty losses are considered itemized deductions rather than deductions for adjusted gross income.

I. BAD DEBTS

A. Specific Charge-Off Method. For tax years after 1986, all taxpayers, except for certain financial institutions, must use the specific charge-off method for deducting bad debts. The specific charge-off method allows a deduction when a specific debt becomes partially (business only) or totally worthless (business or nonbusiness).

B. Business Versus Nonbusiness Bad Debts. Bad debts fall into one of two classifications: business bad debts or nonbusiness bad debts. Debts that arise from a taxpayer's trade or business are business bad debts while all other debts are nonbusiness bad debts. The primary difference in the tax treatment is that business bad debts are ordinary deductions while nonbusiness bad debts are treated as short-term capital losses.

C. Loans Between Related Parties. Loans between related parties create problems in determining whether the loan was bona fide or it is a gift. If there is no debtor-creditor relationship established, the debt to a related party may be a gift. If the debt is not repaid, the bad debt deduction will be lost and a gift tax may be incurred.

D. Financial Institutions. Under the tax law, qualified individuals can elect to deduct losses on deposits in qualified financial institutions as personal casualty losses in the year in which the loss can be reasonably estimated.

II. WORTHLESS SECURITIES

A. Losses arising from worthless securities, such as stocks and bonds, are generally treated as capital losses deemed to have occurred on the last day of the tax year.

B. Small Business Stock. Another exception to the capital loss rule on worthless securities is for qualified "small business" or "Sec. 1244 stock." Individual taxpayers are allowed ordinary loss treatment limited to $50,000 ($100,000 for a joint return) per year for losses on stock that qualifies as small business stock. Any losses over the above limits are capital losses.

III. LOSSES OF INDIVIDUAL TAXPAYERS

A. Casualty Losses. An individual taxpayer may deduct losses under Sec. 165(c) in each of the following circumstances:

- the loss was incurred in a trade or business,
- the loss was incurred in a transaction entered into for profit, or
- the loss was caused by casualty or theft.

A casualty loss is "the complete or partial destruction of property resulting from an identifiable event of a sudden, unexpected, or unusual nature." Thus, casualties would include such items as hurricanes, floods, storms, shipwrecks, fires, auto accidents, and mine cave-ins.

B. Events that are not casualties are those due to "progressive deterioration," such as termite damage, rust, and erosion. Such events are not considered casualty losses since they are not "sudden and unexpected."

C. Theft Losses. A theft loss includes larceny, embezzlement, and robbery. It does not include misplaced items. Theft losses are deductible in the year the loss is "discovered," not the year of theft. A partial deduction is allowed if a settlement is arrived at, which is less than the property's adjusted basis.

D. When to Deduct Casualty Losses. Generally, casualty losses are deducted in the year of the casualty. However, if the casualty is in an area designated as a disaster area by the President of the United States, then the taxpayer may elect to treat the loss as having occurred in the previous taxable year. When a "reasonable prospect of full recovery" exists, no deduction for a casualty loss may be taken.

E. Measuring the Amount of the Loss.

In computing the amount of a casualty loss, it is necessary to divide the property into that held for personal use and that held for business use. Property held for "personal use" is subject to a $100 statutory reduction in the otherwise allowable deduction. This $100 reduction does not apply to business use property. Personal casualty losses are deductible only to the extent they exceed 10 percent of AGI after reduction by the $100 floor.

The amount of the gross casualty loss deduction, before the $100 floor amount and before the 10 percent of adjusted gross income limitation applicable to personal casualty losses, is the lesser of (1) the adjusted basis of the property, or (2) the decrease in fair market value of the property.

The only exception to this rule is the complete destruction of business property, in which case, the adjusted basis is used to measure the loss.

F. Statutory Framework. Casualty and theft losses by an individual with a trade or business are deductible for AGI. The $100 per event and 10% of AGI limits do not apply. Investment property casualty losses are not subject to the limits. If the investment losses are rent and royalties related the deduction is for AGI, otherwise the deduction is from AGI.

G. Personal Casualty Gains and Losses. If a taxpayer's personal casualty gains exceed personal casualty losses, the gains and losses will be treated as capital gains and losses. If the personal casualty losses exceed the personal casualty gains, then the gains and losses are netted. In determining whether personal casualty gains exceed personal casualty losses, the casualty losses must first be reduced by the $100 statutory floor. Personal casualty losses in excess of personal casualty gains are deductible subject to the 10 percent of AGI limitation. Casualty gains and losses from business properties are not netted with personal casualty gains and losses.

IV. RESEARCH AND EXPERIMENTAL EXPENDITURES

A. Section 174 of the Code controls the tax treatment of research and experimental expenditures. A taxpayer may elect to expense all such costs in the current year. If the election is made for the first year in which the expenses are incurred, the taxpayer does not need the consent of the IRS.

B. A taxpayer may also elect to defer and amortize research and experimental expenditures over a period of not less than 60 months. If the election to expense or defer is not made, the taxpayer must capitalize such expenses.

V. NET OPERATING LOSSES

A. To remove inequities that may be caused by the requirement that annual tax returns be filed, taxpayers are allowed a deduction for net operating losses (NOL). A NOL deduction is allowed in a given period for a business related loss incurred in another period. In computing an NOL, several adjustments have to be made to reflect a true economic loss.

B. Carryback and Carryover Periods. Once the NOL is calculated, the amount can be carried back or forward. For loss years, the loss is carried "back two years and forward 20 years." Alternatively, the taxpayer may elect to carry the loss forward only.

There is a three-year carry back for any portion of an individual's NOL resulting from a casualty or theft loss. The three-year rule also applies to presidentially declared disasters which are incurred by a small business or a taxpayer engaged in farming.

C. Computation of the NOL. Adjustments must be made to an individual's taxable loss so that it reflects only losses related to the operation of a trade or business since the NOL is intended as a relief provision only for business income and losses. All casualty and theft losses, including personal casualty and theft losses, are also allowed in computing the NOL. Examples of some items that must be added to the taxpayer's taxable income to arrive at the NOL deduction are shown below.

1) The deductions for personal and dependency exemptions.

2) The NOL carryovers and carrybacks from other years.

3) Capital losses and nonbusiness deductions are limited in determining the current year's NOL.

4) The excess of nonbusiness capital losses over nonbusiness capital gains must be added back.

5) The excess of nonbusiness deductions over the sum of nonbusiness income and net nonbusiness capital gains must be added back.

6) The excess of business capital losses over the sum of business capital gains and the excess of nonbusiness income and nonbusiness capital gains over nonbusiness deductions must be added back.

7) The add-back for net nonbusiness capital losses and excess business capital losses does not include net capital losses not included in the current year's taxable income because of any capital loss limitation.

8) The excess of business capital losses over the sum of business capital gains plus the excess of net nonbusiness capital gains and nonbusiness income over nonbusiness deductions.

An NOL is carried back for two years and carried forward for a maximum of twenty years. It is first carried to the second prior year, and then to the immediately preceding year. If the loss is not used up, it is carried forward sequentially until the used up or twenty years have passed.

Taxpayers elect to forgo the carry back and only carry the NOL forward. This is advantageous when a taxpayer was in a low marginal tax bracket in the two prior years.

A taxpayer who does not itemize deductions adds the excess of nonbusiness deductions over nonbusiness income by substituting the standard deduction amount for itemized deductions.

D. When an NOL is carried back to a prior year, the taxable income and tax liability for the year to which the loss is being carried must be recomputed. Deductions based on the amount of adjusted gross income, other than charitable contributions, must be recomputed based on the new adjusted gross income after the NOL. Any tax credits limited by tax liability must also be recomputed based on the reduced amount of tax due.

E. Calculation of Remaining NOL. After computing the refund claim for a carryback year it is necessary to determine the amount of the net operating loss that is left to carry into other years. The amount of the carryover loss is the excess of the NOL over the taxable income of the year to which the loss is being applied. However, the taxable income of the year to which the loss is being applied must be recalculated with certain modifications (see the textbook).

KEY TERMS

Worthless Securities

Casualty Losses

Bad Debts

Theft Losses

Net Operating Loss

TEST FOR SELF-EVALUATION

True or False

Indicate which of the following statements are true or false by circling the correct answer.

T F 1. To be written off as a bad debt, accounts receivable must have been previously included in income.

T F 2. Nonfinancial institutions must use the specific charge-off method for bad debts.

T F 3. Nonbusiness bad debts are deductible in the year of partial or total worthlessness.

T F 4. Qualified insolvent financial institution losses may be deducted by certain individuals as personal casualty losses.

T F 5. Amounts spent for consumer surveys, advertising, or promotions qualify under Sec. 174 as research and experimental expenditures.

T F 6. In certain situations, loans between related parties may be classified as gifts.

T F 7. Worthless securities always generate an ordinary loss.

T F 8. Worthless securities are treated as having become worthless on the last day of the taxable year.

T F 9. Within certain dollar limits, individual taxpayers may recognize an ordinary loss as opposed to a capital loss on the disposition of "Sec. 1244 stock."

T F 10. A taxpayer's loss on property used in a trade or business is not limited to loss caused by fire, storm, shipwreck, or other casualty, or by theft.

T F 11. All casualty and theft loss deductions are subject to a $100 statutory floor.

T F 12. A loss caused by rust will be deductible as a casualty loss under Sec. 165.

T F 13. To be deductible, casualty damage must be to the taxpayer's property.

T F 14. Disaster area casualty losses must be deducted in the year of the casualty.

T F 15. The gross amount of a personal casualty loss is the larger of (1) the adjusted basis of the property, or (2) the decrease in fair market value.

T F 16. The general rule for NOL carrybacks and carryovers is two years back and seven years forward.

T F 17. Personal and dependency exemptions are allowed as deductions in arriving at an individual taxpayer's NOL.

T F 18. A taxpayer may elect to expense research and experimental expenditures.

T F 19. The maximum loss on Sec. 1244 stock that may be treated as an ordinary loss is $50,000 for a joint return.

T F 20. "Small business stock" under Sec. 1244 can only be common stock.

T F 21. Prior year net operating losses are subtracted from taxable income in arriving at the current year net operating loss.

T F 22. In determining the amount of a NOL remaining to be carried to another tax year, modified taxable income for a year into which an NOL is carried must be determined without the deduction for personal and dependency exemptions.

Fill-in-the-Blanks

Complete the following statements with the appropriate word(s) or amount(s).

1. A taxpayer may use the __________ __________ method in taking a deduction for bad debts.

2. A business bad debt is an __________ loss while a nonbusiness bad debt is a short-term capital loss.

3. A theft loss is taken in the year of __________ not in the year of occurrence.

4. The three tax treatments for research and experimental expenditures include capitalization, ____________, and deferment.

5. If the deferral method is chosen for research and experimental costs, they must be written off over a period of not less than __________ months.

6. As a general rule, net operating losses are carried back __________ years and carried forward __________ years.

7. In computing an individual taxpayer's net operating loss, adjustments are required to bring the tax loss to a true __________ loss.

8. When a net operating loss is carried into a nonloss year, the __________ income and income tax must be recomputed.

Multiple Choice

Choose the best answer for each of the following questions.

1. Simon, a calendar year taxpayer, owns stock (not Sec. 1244 stock) in Red Corporation (a publicly-held company). The stock was acquired on May 1st of last year. The cost of the stock was $10,000. On March 1st of the current year the stock became worthless. Simon should report (before any limitations) a:

a. $10,000 short-term capital loss
b. $10,000 long-term capital loss
c. $10,000 ordinary loss
d. No gain or loss

2. Liz owns Sec. 1244 stock in X Corporation with a basis of $120,000. She acquired the stock three years ago. During the current year she sells the stock for $40,000. If Liz is single, as a result of the sale of the stock, she should report (before any $3,000 annual capital loss limitation):
a. $80,000 long-term capital loss
b. $80,000 ordinary loss
c. $50,000 long-term capital loss and $30,000 ordinary loss
d. $50,000 ordinary loss and $30,000 long-term capital loss
e. None of the above

3. For tax purposes, research and experimental expenses may be:
a. Capitalized
b. Expensed in the year paid or incurred
c. Deferred and amortized over 60 months or more
d. All of the above
e. None of the above

4. Robert loaned his friend, Fred, $6,000. Fred used the money to start a business. In the current year Fred went bankrupt and the debt became worthless. Assuming he has no other capital transactions, Robert should report (in the current year):
a. No deduction for the loss
b. $6,000 long-term capital loss
c. $3,000 short-term capital loss
d. $6,000 short-term capital loss
e. None of the above

5. Martha had a deductible casualty loss of $10,000 in 19X1. Her taxable income for 19X1 was $55,000. In 19X2, Martha was reimbursed $7,000 for the casualty loss. How much income must Martha report in 19X2 for the reimbursement?
a. $-0-
b. $3,000
c. $7,000
d. $10,000
e. Some other amount

6. During the current year, Tim's house was robbed. His personal stereo and coin collection were taken. The stereo had a basis of $600 and a FMV of $250, while the coin collection's basis was $400 and its FMV was $500. What is Tim's theft loss deduction before the 10 percent of adjusted gross income limitation?
a. $-0-
b. $550
c. $650
d. $450
e. Some other amount

7. Which of the following would be deductible as a personal casualty loss?
   a. Rust on the panels of an automobile
   b. Decrease in value of a personal residence because of the construction of a new sewer plant nearby
   c. Moth damage to clothes
   d. Damage to the roof of a personal residence when a tree blows over in a storm
   e. None of the above

8. Linda had a casualty gain of $6,000 in the current year and a casualty loss of $4,000 (after deducting the $100 floor). Her adjusted gross income for the year is $25,000. Both the casualties are from long-term capital assets. Linda should report:
   a. $2,000 ordinary income
   b. $1,500 casualty loss and $6,000 ordinary income
   c. $6,000 ordinary gain and $2,000 capital loss
   d. $6,000 capital gain and $4,000 capital loss
   e. No gain or loss should be reported

9. Craig had adjusted income of $70,000. During the year his personal winter home was destroyed by fire. Pertinent data with respect to the winter home is as follows:

Cost basis	$40,000
FMV before casualty	$55,000
FMV after casualty	$13,000

   Craig received a $23,000 insurance settlement for the fire. What is Craig's allowable casualty loss?
   a. $-0-
   b. $16,900
   c. $10,000
   d. $9,900
   e. Some other amount

10. Yellow Corporation incurred the following expenditures in connection with the development of a new product:

Salaries	$50,000
Materials	6,000
Marketing survey	4,000
Sales promotion	10,000

   If the corporation elects to expense research and experimental expenditures, what amount is allowed as a deduction in the current year?
   a. $50,000
   b. $56,000
   c. $60,000
   d. $70,000
   e. Some other amount

11. John has the following tax items for the current year:

Nonbusiness capital gains	$5,000
Nonbusiness capital losses	3,000
Dividend income	6,000
Itemized deductions (no casualty losses)	10,000

What amount would John add back to his taxable income in calculating his net operating loss for the year?
a. $2,000
b. $3,000
c. $4,000
d. $10,000
e. Some other amount

12. Marsha is married and owns her own business. She uses the cash receipts and disbursements method for tax purposes. During the current year her income, expenses and other items were as follows:

Gross receipts	$40,000
Cost of goods sold	24,000
General expenses	18,000
Uncollectible accounts receivable	6,000

What is Marsha's bad debt expense deduction for tax purposes?
a. $-0-
b. $2,000
c. $4,000
d. $6,000
e. Some other amount.

13. Use the same facts as in question number 12. If Marsha uses the accrual method of accounting for tax purposes, her bad debt deduction would be:
a. $-0-
b. $2,000
c. $4,000
d. $6,000
e. Some other amount.

14. Larry Legal and Associates, a professional corporation, loaned $125,000 to Leonard Litigious, one of the employees. Leonard left for Brazil the next day (he left a note that said "hasta la vista, baby"). As a result of Leonard's action, the corporation will never collect on the loan. What can Larry Legal and Associates deduct?
a. $125,000 short-term capital loss
b. $125,000 long-term capital loss
c. $125,000 ordinary loss
d. $3,000 short-term capital loss
e. Some other amount

15. During 19x3, Tierra Corporation incurred research and experimental expenses of $37,000. In 19x4, the corporation had another $50,000 of such expenditures. The Corporation began realizing benefits from

the project on October 31, 19x4. If the corporation elects the expense method for research and experimental expenditures, what amount may be deducted in 19x4?
a. $-0-
b. $37,000
c. $50,000
d. $87,000
e. Some other amount

16. Teri had the following casualties during the current year:

Personal casualty loss (after the $100 limit)	$12,000
Personal casualty gain (long-term asset)	$5,000

If Teri's adjusted gross income for the year is $45,000, what is her casualty loss deduction?
a. $-0-
b. $2,500
c. $5,000
d. $7,000
e. Some other amount

17. In 19x5, Ted (who is in the business of lending money) loaned Nick $10,000 to go on a vacation. During 19x5 (before paying back any of the loan), Nick declared bankruptcy. Nick expects to be able settle his debts for $.45 on the dollar. However, during 19x6, Nick was only able to pay $.35 on the dollar. How much should Ted deduct on his 19x5 tax return?
a. $-0-
b. $4,500
c. $5,500
d. $3,500
e. Some other amount.

18. In 19x3, Penny purchased $10,000 worth of East-West Airline's common stock. East-West Airline has since declared bankruptcy and shut down operations. As a result of a bankruptcy judge's ruling the East-West Airline stock became worthless in 19x7. Penny's appropriate tax treatment for loss (before any annual limits) on the stock in 19x7 is:
a. $10,000 ordinary loss
b. $10,000 long-term loss
c. $10,000 short-term loss
d. $-0- loss deduction
e. Some other amount

19. Jed, who is single had the following items for the current year:

Salary of $90,000
Gain of $30,000 on the sale of Sec. 1244 stock acquired two ago
Loss of $75,000 on the sale of Sec. 1244 stock acquired four months ago
Worthless stock of $7,000 acquired on April 30 or the prior year and became worthless on March 10 of the current year

What is Jed's AGI for the current year?

a. $38,000
b. $50,000
c. $15,000
d. $55,000
e. Some other amount

20. Dale parks her car on a hill and fails to properly set the brake or curb the wheels. As a result of Dale's negligence, the car rolls down the hill, damages Bill's front porch, injures Bill (who was sitting on the porch), and damages Dale's car. Due to the accident Dales is forced to pay the following amounts:

$1,650 for medical expenses for Bill's injuries
$2,800 for repairs to her car
$1,000 for repairs to Bill's porch
$120 for a fine for traffic violation

Which of the payments, if any, qualify for casualty loss treatment to Dale (before any limitations)?
a. $-0-
b. $2,800
c. $3,800
d. $5,450
e. $5.570

21. Andrew, a single taxpayer, sustained a NOL of $10,000 in 2000. Andrew had no taxable income in 1997 and 1998. For 1999, Andrew filed a tax return with the following amounts:

Adjusted Gross Income		$16,000.
Itemized Deductions		
Charitable	$3,000	
Interest	5,000	
Taxes	1,500	
Total deductions		($9,500.)
Exemption		($2,750.)
Taxable Income		$3,750.
Tax (15%)		$563.

What is Andrew's 1999 tax after applying the NOL carryback from 2000?
a. $-0-
b. $263
c. $363
d. $563
e. Some other amount

22. Use the same facts as in question number 21. What is Andrew's NOL carryover available for future years?
a. $-0-
b. $3,500
c. $6,500
d. $6,150
e. Some other amount.

23. John is a farmer who has a $20,000 NOL caused by a flooding casualty to his farm. The flooding was declared a qualified disaster area by the President of the U.S. How many years can John's carryback his NOL?
   a. Two-years
   b. Three-years
   c. Five-years
   d. The is no carryback allowed.

Problems

1. Tom, a married individual, had the following income and deductions for 1999:

Income:			
	Gross income from business	$71,720	
	Interest on savings account	600	$72,320.
Deductions:			
	NOL carryover from 1997	$ 300	
	Business expenses	75,000	
	Net loss on rental property	1,000	
	1999 personal exemptions (2)	5,500	
	Itemized deductions (no casualty loss)	16,000	(97,800.)
Taxable income (loss)			($25,480.)

Calculate Tom's NOL for 1999.

2. During 1999 Tim had the following casualty losses occurring in separate events:

Asset	Adj. Basis	FMV Before	FMV After
A	$2,000	$3,000	-0-
B	$2,000	$1,800	-0-
C	$3,000	$2,000	-0-
D	$2,000	$3,000	$500

Assets A and B are personal assets while C and D were used in Tim's business at the time of the casualty. The assets were not covered by insurance. Determine the amount of the deductible casualty loss (disregarding the 10 percent of adjusted gross income limitation where applicable) for:

Asset A ____________________

Asset B ____________________

Asset C ____________________

Asset D ____________________

SOLUTIONS TO CHAPTER 7

True or False

1. True (p. 7-3)
2. True (p. 7-3)
3. False Nonbusiness bad debts are deductible only when totally worthless. (p. 7-4)
4. True (p. 7-6)
5. False These expenditures do not qualify. (p. 7-17)
6. True (p. 7-5)
7. False Losses on worthless securities are usually treated as capital losses. (p. 7-6)
8. True (p. 7-6)
9. True (p. 7-8)
10. True (p. 7-9)
11. False Business casualty loss deductions are not subject to the $100 floor. (p. 7-13)
12. False Rust is not sudden and unexpected. (p. 7-9)
13. True (p. 7-9)
14. False They may be deducted in the prior year. (p. 7-11)
15. False The deduction is equal to the *lesser* of the adjusted basis of the property or the decrease in FMV of the property. (p. 7-12)
16. False The carryforward period is 20 years. (p. 7-19)
17. False A deduction for personal and dependency exemptions is not allowed in arriving at the taxpayer's NOL. (p. 7-20)
18. True (p. 7-17)
19. False The maximum amount of loss on Sec. 1244 stock that may be treated as an ordinary loss is $100,000 on a joint return. (p. 7-8)
20. False Preferred stock is included under Sec. 1244. (p. 7-8)
21. False Net operating loss carryovers and carrybacks must be added back to taxable income in arriving at the current year net operating loss. (p. 7-21)
22. True (p. 7-24)

Fill-in-the-Blanks

1. specific charge-off (p. 7-3)
2. ordinary (p. 7-5)
3. discovery (p. 7-10)
4. expense (p. 7-17)
5. sixty (p. 7-18)
6. two, twenty (p. 7-19)
7. economic (p. 7-20)
8. taxable (p. 7-23)

Multiple Choice

1. B (p. 7-7)
2. D (p. 7-8)

3. D (p. 7-17)
4. C (p. 7-5)
5. C The reimbursement is income to the extent the casualty loss resulted in a tax benefit. (p. 7-11)
6. B $250 (stereo) + $400 (TV) - $100 (limit) = $550. (p. 7-12)
7. D (p. 7-8)
8. D There is a net casualty gain, therefore all gains and losses are capital. (p. 7-15)

9. D

Fair market value before casualty	$55,000	
Fair market value after casualty	-13,000	
Decrease in fair market value	$42,000	
Lesser of decrease in FMV or adjusted basis	$40,000	
Insurance recovery	-23,000	
Gross loss	$17,000	
Per casualty limitation	-100	
Adjusted gross income limitation	-7,000	
Casualty loss deduction	$ 9,900	(p. 7-12)

10. B $50,000 + 6,000 = $56,000. (p. 7-17)
11. A $2,000 = $10,000 - [$6,000 + ($5,000 - 3,000)]. (p. 7-21)
12. A Since Marsha is a cash basis taxpayer the accounts receivable were never included in income, thus there is no deduction for the bad debts. (p. 7-3)
13. D (p. 7-3)
14. C Corporations can only have business bad debts, therefore the $125,000 is deductible as an ordinary deduction. (p. 7-5)
15. C (p. 7-17)
16. B

Casualty loss over casualty gain	$7,000	
Less 10% of AGI	4,500	
Deduction	$2,500	(p. 7-15)

17. C $.55 x $10,000 = $5,500. (p. 7-4)
18. B (p. 7-6)

19. A

Salary		90,000	
Sec. 1244 ordinary loss		-50,000	
LTCG	$30,000		
LTCL ($75,000 -$50,000)	-25,000		
Worthless Security	-7,000		
		-2,000	
AGI		$38,000	(p. 7-25)

20. B The medical expenses do not qualify because they are not damage to Dale's property. The damage to the porch does not qualify because it is not Dale's porch. The traffic fine does not qualify because of Sec. 162(f) (public policy limitations). (p. 7-14)

21. A

Adjusted Gross Income		$16,000
Less: NOL		(10,000.)
Recomputed AGI		$6,000
Itemized Deductions		
Charitable	$3,000	
Interest	5,000	

		Taxes	1,500	
		Total deductions		($9,500.)
		Exemption		(2,700.)
		Taxable Income		$(6,200.)
		Tax		$-0- (p. 7-19)

22.	B	Adjusted Gross Income		$16,000
		Itemized Deductions		
		Charitable	$3,000	
		Interest	5,000	
		Taxes	1,500	
		Total deductions		($9,500.)
		Exemption (not allowed)		-0-
		Modified taxable income		$6,500
		NOL		-10,000.
		Modified taxable Income		6,500.
		NOL carry forward		$3,500. (p. 7-24)

23. B NOL casualties have a three-year carryback. (p. 7-20)

Problems

1.	Taxable income (loss) for 1999			($25,480.)
	Add:			
	NOL from 1997			$ 300.
	1999 personal exemptions			5,500.
	Itemized deductions	16,000		
	Less: Interest income	-600	15,400	21,200.
	Net operating loss for 1999			($4,280.) (p. 7-21)

2. Asset A $1,900 = Lesser of decrease in FMV ($3,000 - 0) or adjusted basis ($2,000); $2,000 - 100 = $1,900.

Asset B $1,700 = Lesser of decrease in FMV ($1,800) or adjusted basis ($2,000); $1,800 - 100 = $1,700.

Asset C $3,000 = Adjusted basis of $3,000. (Note, complete destruction and business property therefore no $100 limitation)

Asset D $2,000 = Lesser of decrease in FMV ($3,000 - 500) or adjusted basis ($2,000); (p. 7-12)

CHAPTER 8
DEPRECIATION, COST RECOVERY, AMORTIZATION, AND DEPLETION

CHAPTER HIGHLIGHTS

The tax law provides for the recovery of the cost of assets through depreciation, cost recovery, amortization, or depletion. This chapter looks at the methods by which capitalized costs may be recovered under the Code. In addition, the types of assets that qualify for some form of capital recovery are discussed.

I. ACCELERATED COST RECOVERY SYSTEM (ACRS)

A. General Considerations.

The accelerated cost recovery system applies to most property acquired after December 31, 1980. ACRS is designed to aid capital formation by providing a rapid write-off for capital goods. The recovery periods under ACRS are based on the classification of property into "classes." ACRS was revised by the Tax Reform Act of 1986, so that the classification of property depends on whether the property was placed in service before January 1, 1987, in which case the original ACRS rules apply, or after December 31, 1986, in which case the modified ACRS (MACRS) rules apply.

B. Personalty: Recovery Periods and Methods.

The cost of eligible personalty (and certain realty) is recovered based on recovery classes. The recovery class lives are a follows.

Post-1986 Acquisitions:

3-year: ADR midpoints of 4 years and less (except autos and light duty trucks), certain horses.

5-year: ADR midpoints of more than 4 years and less than 10 years, autos, light duty trucks, R&D equipment, etc.

7-year: Property that is not included in another class, includes office furniture, fixtures, and equipment.

10-year: ADR midpoints of 16 years or more but less than 20 years.

15-year: ADR midpoints of 20 years or more but less than 25 years.

20-year: ADR midpoints of 25 years or more.

The post-1986 ACRS rates are based on the 200 percent declining balance method (3, 5, 7, and 10-year classes) or 150 percent declining balance method (15- and 20-year classes), using the half-year convention in both the year of acquisition and the year of disposition, and disregarding salvage value. In certain cases, a mid-quarter convention may be required.

C. Realty: Recovery Periods and Methods.

Pre-1987 real estate under ACRS is written off over 15, 18, or 19 years depending on the date the property was placed in service. The pre-1987 rates are based on 175% declining balance. Depreciation for 15-year property and certain 18-year property uses a full month convention. Eighteen-year real property placed in service after June 22, 1984, and 19-year recovery property use a mid-month convention. (See text for the various ACRS tables).

Post-1986 real estate is written off over 15 years (land improvements), 27½ years for residential realty, or 31½ years (39 years after May 12, 1993) for nonresidential realty. Residential and nonresidential realty can only use the straight-line method. Property depreciated under the 27½-year, 31½-year, or 39-year class uses a mid-month convention.

D. Straight-line Election Under ACRS and MACRS. Instead of using the accelerated methods under ACRS, taxpayers may elect to use the straight-line method of depreciation. The pre-1987 straight-line recovery periods are as follows:

3-year property: 3, 5, or 12 years
5-year property: 5, 12, or 25 years
10-year property: 10, 25, or 35 years
15-year property: 15, 35, or 45 years
18-year property: 18, 35, or 45 years
19-year property: 19, 35, or 45 years

The election of the straight-line method is a class-by-class election for other than real property in the 15-, 18-, or 19-year classes. For real property, the straight-line election was available on a property-by-property basis. The half-year, monthly, or mid-month conventions continue to apply when the straight-line election is made.

Depreciation under the post-1986 straight-line election is based on the property's class life using a half-year or mid-quarter convention, whichever is applicable. The straight-line method is required for real property acquired after 1986.

See the text for various tables for calculating straight-line ACRS or MACRS.

E. Election to Expense. Section 179 permits an election to expense a limited amount of the cost of certain depreciable assets used in a trade or business up to a $18,500 annual limit in 1998. The amount expensed cannot exceed the taxable income derived from the taxpayer's trade or business. Furthermore, the amount expensed is reduced dollar-for-dollar when property placed in service exceeds $200,000 for the year.

F. Business and Personal Use of Autos and Other Listed Property. A taxpayer must show that listed property used for both business and personal use is used predominantly for business (greater than 50%) to use the statutory percentage methods under ACRS or MACRS. If the property is not used predominantly for business, the depreciable basis must be recovered using straight-line deprecation under the ADS. Recapture rules apply where the business usage of listed property depreciated under the statutory percentage method drops below the greater than 50 percent requirement.

Under the "luxury auto" rules, the deduction for depreciation expense on passenger automobiles is limited. The amount of these annual limits changes each year. See the textbook for the current years annual limits.

These limits are imposed before the percentage reduction for personal use of the automobile. Also, the annual limits apply to any election to expense under Sec. 179.

G. Alternative Depreciation System (ADS). For post-1986 property the ADS must be used in calculating depreciation expense for the following:

1) the alternative minimum tax calculation

2) property used outside the U.S.

3) property leased or otherwise used by a tax-exempt entity

4) property financed by tax-exempt bonds

5) certain imported property

6) determining earnings and profits

In most cases the ADS requires the use of the straight-line method, except with regard to the alternative minimum tax calculation of depreciation on personalty which uses the 150 percent declining balance method.

Taxpayers may elect to use the 150% declining balance method to compute the regular tax rather than the normal 200% MACRS method. Thus, there will be no difference between regular and alternative minimum tax. (Note: the taxpayers must use the ADS recovery periods if this election is made).

See text for the ADS calculation.

II. AMORTIZATION

Purchased intangible property, such as goodwill, used in a trade or business or for the production of income may be amortized over 15 years under Section 197.

III. DEPLETION

A. Payment for natural resources is recovered through depletion. However, intangible drilling and development costs can be handled in one of two ways. Such costs can either be (1) expensed in the year incurred, or (2) capitalized (added to the depletable basis) and written off through depletion. These costs include the cost of making property ready for drilling, erecting derricks, and drilling the well.

B. Depletion Methods. The owner of an interest in a wasting asset is entitled to a depletion deduction. The tax law allows for two types of depletion, cost and percentage.

Cost depletion is based on the adjusted basis of the asset. The basis is divided by the estimated recoverable units of the asset to arrive at a cost per unit. This cost is multiplied by the units sold to arrive at the deduction allowed. The cost per unit may be redetermined on a prospective basis, based on revised estimates of the recoverable units.

Percentage depletion is based on a percentage specified in the Code that is applied to the gross income from the property to arrive at the amount of depletion allowed. Such depletion may not exceed 50 percent of the taxable income from the property before the depletion allowance. Special limitations apply to the use of percentage depletion for certain oil and gas wells. The cost basis of the asset must be reduced by the percentage depletion claimed although the calculation is made without reference to the basis of the asset.

If intangible drilling costs are capitalized, the basis for cost depletion is increased. If such costs are expensed, the 50 percent limit for the percentage depletion deduction will be decreased.

IV. REPORTING PROCEDURES

A. Sole proprietors engaged in a trade or business should file a Schedule C with their Form 1040. Part I of Schedule C is used for reporting items of income. Part II is used for reporting deductions such as bad debts, depletion, and depreciation. If the business requires the use of inventories and the computation of cost of goods sold, Part II must also be completed.

B. If depreciation is claimed, it generally should be supported on a Form 4562.

KEY TERMS:

Depreciation

Amortization

Realty/Personalty

ACRS/MACRS

Sec. 179 Election

Listed Property

Depletion

TEST FOR SELF-EVALUATION

True or False

Indicate which of the following statements are true or false by circling the correct answer.

T F 1. If MACRS or depreciation is not claimed for a particular year, the basis for the asset remains unchanged.

T F 2. Computers and light-duty trucks are five-year class MACRS property.

T F 3. The depreciable basis of personal use property converted to business use is the lower of its adjusted basis or fair market value on the date of conversion.

T F 4. The alternative depreciation system must be used on all automobiles.

T F 5. Cost depletion is determined by dividing the fair market value of the asset by the estimated recoverable units expected.

T F 6. Under ACRS, the cost of an assets is recovered over a predetermined period that is generally shorter than the useful life of the asset or the period the asset is used to produce income.

T F 7. Assets such as land, stock, antiques are not eligible for cost recovery.

T F 8. Assets that do not decline in value on a predictable basis are not depreciable under ACRS.

T F 9. Cellular telephones, computers (not used in a regular business), and automobiles are listed property and subject to certain limits on MACRS.

T F 10. Depreciation, depletion, and amortization are different words to describe the process of deducting the cost of an asset.

T F 11. Under MACRS an automobile acquired in 1998 and used in a business is seven-year recovery property.

T F 12. The cost of residential rental real estate acquired after 1986 is written off over 27½ years under MACRS.

T F 13. For 1999 the maximum amount that can be expensed under Sec. 179 is $19,000.

T F 14. If more than 40 percent of the nonrealty assets acquired during a year are acquired in the last quarter of the tax year, then the taxpayer must use the mid-quarter MACRS tables to calculate the cost recovery deduction for all personal property placed in service during the year.

T F 15. The annual limits for automobile depreciation do not apply to the election to expense under Sec. 179.

T F 16. ACRS and other depreciation, amortization, and depletion are reported on Form 4562.

T F 17. The Sec. 179 expense election is available for real property or for property used in the production of income.

T F 18. A taxpayer who leases a passenger automobile must include an *inclusion amount* in gross income.

T F 19. Sec. 197 intangible property includes goodwill, going concern value, sports franchises, trademarks, and trade names.

T F 20. Generally, intangible property is amortized over a 15-year period, beginning in the month in which the property was acquired.

T F 21. Land can generally be depleted under the tax law.

Fill-in-the-Blanks

Complete the following statements with the appropriate word(s) or amount(s).

1. Post-1993 nonresidential real estate is written off over _________ years.

2. The taxpayer must have an _____________ interest in property in order to be entitled to a depletion deduction.

3. Percentage depletion may not exceed ____________ percent of the taxable income from the property before the allowance for depletion.

4. An automobile acquired in 1998 is __________ year property under MACRS.

5. For 1999, the maximum amount that can be expensed annually under Sec. 179 is $___________.

6. The two methods of depletion under the tax law are called __________ depletion and ___________ depletion.

7. For listed property to meet the business usage test, the percentage of use for business must exceed ______ percent.

8. _____________ depletion is computed without considering the cost.

Multiple Choice

Choose the best answer for each of the following questions.

1. On January 4 of the current year Byrne purchased a patent that qualifies as a Sec. 197 intangible. The cost of the patent was $204,000. In the current year Byrne may amortize how much of the patent's cost?
   a. $-0-

b. $204,000
c. $13,600
d. $10,000
e. Some other amount

2. On January 3, 1998, Heather purchased land for $150,000. She plans to build an apartment building on the land. The apartment will have an estimated useful life of 30 years. She does in fact build the apartment building in 1998 for $400,000. How much of the land cost can be depleted by Heather this year?
a. $-0-
b. $150,000
c. $5,000
d. $10,000
e. Some other amount

3. White Corporation acquired an asset (10-year property) on June 6, 1998, for $60,000. The asset is not an automobile, but it is listed property. White used the asset 40 percent of the time for business, 50 percent of the time for the production of income, and 10 percent for the personal use of the shareholder. A Sec. 179 election is not made, what is the cost recovery for 1998?
a. $2,700
b. $3,000
c. $5,400
d. $6,000
e. Some other amount

4. Black Corporation acquired an asset (10-year property) on July 20, 1998 for $60,000. The asset is not an automobile, but it is listed property. Black used the asset 60 percent of the time for business, 30 percent of the time for the production of income, and 10 percent for the personal use of the shareholder. A Sec. 179 election is not made, what is the cost recovery for 1998?
a. $2,700
b. $3,000
c. $5,400
d. $6,000
e. Some other amount

5. The Big Tex Oil Company purchases an oil lease for $1,000,000. After exploration, oil is discovered and it is estimated that 100,000 barrels of oil will be recovered from the lease. If during 1998 Big Tex produces 15,000 barrels of oil from the lease and sells 12,000 barrels, what is the amount of cost depletion allowed Big Tex?
a. -0-
b. $120,000
c. $150,000
d. $1,000,000
e. Some other amount

6. The Pit Sulfur Company has gross income of $200,000 from certain property (not oil and gas property) subject to depletion. The expenses related to that property are $140,000, and a statutory depletion rate of 22 percent is applicable. What is the amount of depletion using percentage depletion?
a. -0-

b. $44,000
c. $30,000
d. $13,200
e. Some other amount

7. On July 1, 1999, farmer John acquires a new tractor at a cost of $30,000. If John is married and files a joint return for 1999, what amount can John expense under Sec. 179 and what amount is subject to regular MACRS depreciation (assuming John has adequate taxable income from his business of farming)?
   a. $0, $30,000
   b. $19,000, $30,000
   c. $11,500, $19,000
   d. $19,000, $11,000
   e. Some other amounts

8. Sun Corporation acquires $200,000 worth of three-year property and $210,000 worth of five-year property in 1998. If the election to expense is not made, what is Sun's MACRS deduction using the half-year convention?
   a. $108,660
   b. $101,500
   c. $81,500
   d. $97,205

9. For 1999, what is the maximum amount of qualified expense property that can be placed in service during the year without causing a reduction in the Sec. 179 expense ceiling?
   a. $100,000
   b. $125,000
   c. $150,000
   d. $200,000
   e. Some other amount

10. Under MACRS, the cost recovery tables for real estate uses a:
   a. half-year convention
   b. mid-quarter convention
   c. mid-month convention
   d. semi-annual convention
   e. None of the above

11. On September 1, 1998, Mike *places in service* an automobile with a cost of $50,000. The car is used 90 percent for business and 10 percent for personal use. The 1998 luxury auto limits are:

	1998
First year	$3,160
Second year	5,000
Third year	2,950
Subsequent years	1,775

   What is Mike's 1999 MACRS deduction?
   a. $5,000

b. $4,500
c. $2,950
d. $2,655
e. Some other amount

12. Using the information in Question 11 above, and assuming the same business use percentage in 2000, what is Mike's MACRS deduction in 2000?
a. $3,160
b. $2,844
c. $5,000
d. $4,500
e. Some other amount

13. Maggie acquires an apartment building on June 3, 1999, for $600,000. What is Maggie's cost recovery deduction for calculating earnings and profits during 1999 under the alternative depreciation system (ADS)?
a. $8,124
b. $10,769
c. $7,993
d. $15,000
e. Some other amount

14. The percentage depletion rate on coal is:
a. 22%
b. 15%
c. 14%
d. 10%
e. 5%

15. Daniel purchases for $400,000 an apartment building in Canada. The apartment is purchased during March 1999. What is Daniel's depreciation deduction for the first year?
a. $7,916
b. $11,516
c. $10,052
d. $8,742
e. Some other amount

16. Tim purchases a cellular telephone for his business automobile. Cellular telephones are listed property. The phone is used 80% for business calls and 20% for personal calls. What method of cost recovery must Tim use on the phone?
a. Straight-line reduced by personal use percentage
b. Straight-line subject to recovery limits, reduced by personal use percentage
c. Statutory percentage reduced by personal use percentage
d. Statutory percentage subject to recovery limits, reduced by personal use percentage
e. None of the above

17. Harry purchased a seven-year business asset (not listed property) on July 30, 1999, at a cost of $100,000. Harry did not elect to expense under Sec. 179 nor did he elect straight-line cost recovery. Harry sold the asset on February 11, 2002. What is Harry's cost recovery for 2002?

a. $-0-
b. $12,490.00
c. $6,245.00
d. $3,122.50
e. Some other amount

18. Karen purchased an automobile on June 15, 1998, at a cost of $20,000. The 1998 Luxury Auto limits are as follows:

	1998
First year	$3,160
Second year	5,000
Third year	2,950
Subsequent years	1,775

Karen used the car 75% for business use and 25% for personal use in 1998. In 1999 Karen used the automobile 40% for business and 60% for personal use. What is Karen's excess depreciation to be recaptured in 1999?
a. $-0-
b. $870
c. $1,500
d. $2,370
e. Some other amount

19. On February 11, 19x1, Ann leases and places in service a passenger automobile worth $41,500. The lease is for five years. During 19x1 she uses the automobile 80% for business and 20% for personal use. Assuming the IRS table amount for 19x1 is $202, how much must Ann include in gross income for 19x1?
a. $-0-
b. $202.00
c. $161.60
d. $143.00
e. Some other amount

20. On June 1, 1999, Gwen purchased a dental practice from George for $267,000. The purchase price was allocated $225,000 to the tangible assets of the practice and $42,000 to goodwill. What is the amount of Gwen's deduction for amortization of goodwill for 1999?
a. $-0-
b. $1,633
c. $2,800
d. $42,000
e. Some other amount

Use the legend provided below to indicate for each asset (#21 to #27) which write off method would be used for tax purposes:

Legend
A = MACRS
B = Amortization

C = Depletion

_____ 21. Patent

_____ 22. The costs of drilling an oil well

_____ 23. Delivery truck

_____ 24. The cost of clearing land to start a coal mine

_____ 25. Trademark

_____ 26. Goodwill

_____ 27. Apartment Building

Problems

1. Each of the following assets was acquired in 1999. Determine the appropriate MACRS recovery class for each.

_____ a. A used delivery truck

_____ b. A used office building

_____ c. A new farm tractor

_____ d. A new duplex held for rental

_____ e. A used apartment building

_____ f. A new computer

2. On August 8, 1999, Steve acquired an apartment building (27½-year property) as an investment. The apartment cost $500,000 and has an estimated salvage value of $100,000. Using the table in the text, give the MACRS deduction for the first four years for this apartment.

Year 1 _______

Year 2 _______

Year 3 _______

Year 4 _______

SOLUTIONS TO CHAPTER 8

True or False

1.	False	The basis decreases by the amount of allowable MACRS depreciation. (p. 8-4)
2.	True	(p. 8-6)
3.	True	(p. 8-4)
4.	False	The regular MACRS may be used for autos meeting the more than 50 percent business use test. (p. 8-13)
5.	False	Adjusted basis is used, not fair market value. (p. 8-29)
6.	True	(p. 8-3)
7.	True	(p. 8-4)
8.	True	(p. 8-4)
9.	True	(p. 8-13)
10.	True	(p. 8-2)
11.	False	Automobiles are five-year property. (p. 8-6)
12.	True	(p. 8-9)
13.	True	(p. 8-11)
14.	True	(p. 8-7)
15.	False	The limit does apply to any amount expensed under Sec. 179. (p. 8-14)
16.	True	(p. 8-24)
17.	False	The election under Sec. 179 is not available. (p. 8-11)
18.	True	(p. 8-16)
19.	False	Sports franchise are not Sec. 197 property. (p. 8-20)
20.	True	(p. 8-19)
21.	False	Land cannot be depleted. (p. 8-20)

Fill-in-the-Blanks

1. 39 (p. 8-9)
2. economic (p. 8-20)
3. fifty (p. 8-22)
4. five (p. 8-6)
5. $19,000 [1999] (p. 8-11)
6. cost, percentage (p. 8-21)
7. fifty (p. 8-14)
8. Percentage (p. 8-22)

Multiple Choice

1.	C	$204,000 ÷ 15 = $13,600 (p. 8-19)
2.	A	Land cannot be depleted. (p. 8-20)
3.	A	$60,000 x .05 x .90 = $2,700. Straight-line must be used because the business usage test has not been met. (p. 8-15).
4.	C	$60,000 x .10 x .90 = $5,400. MACRS can be used because the business usage test has been met. (p. 8-14).
5.	B	($1,000,000/100,000 barrels) x 12,000 barrels = $120,000. (p. 8-21)

6.	C	($200,000 - 140,000) x 50% = $30,000 maximum. (p. 8-22)
7.	D	(p. 8-11) [1999]
8.	A	($200,000 x 33.33%) + ($210,000 x 20%) = $108,660. (p. 8-31)
9.	D	(p. 8-12) [1999]
10.	C	(p. 8-9)
11.	B	$5,000 (max) x 90% = $4,500 [1999] (p. 8-14)
12.	D	$2,950 (max) x 90% = $2,655 [1999] (p. 8-14)
13.	A	$600,000 x 1.354% = $8,124, Table 8-10. (p. 8-18)
14.	D	(p. 8-23)
15.	A	$400,000 x 1.979% = $7,916, Table 8-10. (p. 8-18)
16.	C	(p. 8-14)
17.	C	$100,000 x 12.49% x ½ = $6,245, Table 8-2. (p. 8-7)

18.	B	MACRS for 1998 $3,160 x 75% =	$2,370
		Straight-line for 1998 $20,000 x .10 x 75% =	-1,500
		Recapture amount [1999]	$ 870
		(p. 8-16)	

19.	D	$202 x (323 days/365 days) x 80% = $143.00 (p. 8-16)
20.	B	($42,000/15) x (7/12) = $1,633 (p. 8-19)
21.	B	(p. 8-19)
22.	C	(p. 8-21)
23.	A	(p. 8-6)
24.	C	(p. 8-21)
25.	B	(p. 8-19)
26.	B	(p. 8-19)
27.	A	(p. 8-9)

Problems

1.
- a. 5-year
- b. 39-year
- c. 7-year
- d. 27½-year
- e. 27½-year
- f. 5-year (see pp. 8-6 to 8-9)

2.
Year 1 $500,000 x 1.364% = $6,820
Year 2 $500,000 x 3.636% = $18,180
Year 3 $500,000 x 3.636% = $18,180
Year 4 $500,000 x 3.636% = $18,180 (Table 8-9)

CHAPTER 9
DEDUCTIONS:
EMPLOYEE EXPENSES

CHAPTER HIGHLIGHTS

This chapter identifies and categorizes employee expenses. In certain situations, employee expenses are treated as expenses incurred in a trade or business and thus are deductions *for* adjusted gross income (AGI). Most employee business expenses are deductible *from* adjusted gross income as itemized deductions. The factors that decide whether an individual is an employee or self-employed are also discussed.

I. EMPLOYEE VERSUS SELF-EMPLOYED

A. One major problem in taxation is to determine if an employer-employee relationship exists or if an individual is self-employed. An employer-employee relationship exists when the employer has the right to specify the results and the ways and means by which the results will be obtained.

B. A self-employed person is required to file a Schedule C and all allowable expenses incurred will be deductions for adjusted gross income. In addition, statutory employees are allowed to file a Schedule C and deduct these expenses for AGI.

II. EMPLOYEE EXPENSES IN GENERAL

Employee expenses fall into one of the following categories: Transportation, Travel, Moving, Education, Entertainment, and Miscellaneous.

III. TRANSPORTATION EXPENSES

A. Qualified Expenditures. A taxpayer is permitted a deduction from AGI subject to the 2% floor for unreimbursed, employment-related transportation expenses. An example of such expenses would include those incurred by an employee commuting to a second job from a first job. However, the cost of commuting from home to work and back is not deductible.

B. Computation of Automobile Expenses. In computing automobile expenses a taxpayer has two choices, actual cost or an automatic mileage method. In 1998, under the automatic mileage method a taxpayer can deduct 32.5 cents (31.0 cents after March 31, 1999) per mile for all business miles. Parking fees and tolls can be deducted in addition to the amount calculated under the automatic mileage method.

See the text for restrictions that apply to changing from one method to another, the use of a fully-depreciated vehicle, and the use of more than one vehicle for business purposes.

IV. TRAVEL EXPENSES

A. Definition of Travel Expenses. An employee may be allowed a deduction for unreimbursed travel expenses subject to the 2% of adjusted gross income limitation. Travel expenses include transportation costs and meals (reduce by a certain percentage) and lodging while away from home in the pursuit of a trade or business, along with reasonable laundry and incidental expenses. Entertainment expenses are not included as travel and are discussed elsewhere.

B. Away-from-Home Requirement. To meet the away from home test, an employee must be away from home overnight. An overnight stay is a period substantially longer than an ordinary day's work and requires rest, sleep, or relief from the work period. To be in travel status a taxpayer must be away from his tax home for a temporary period. Generally, if a taxpayer has a work assignment of less than one year it is regarded as temporary. If the work assignment is more than one year it is regarded as indefinite.

C. Restrictions on Travel Expenses. Expenses related to attending a convention, seminar, or similar meetings are disallowed unless the expenses are related to a trade or business of the taxpayer.

No deduction is allowed for travel that, by itself, is deemed to be educational by the taxpayer. This rule does not apply with respect to a deduction for travel necessary to engage in an activity that gives rise to a business deduction related to education.

Expenses incurred to attend conventions outside North America are disallowed unless the taxpayer can show that it is as reasonable for the convention to be held in a foreign location as in the North American area.

D. Combined Business and Pleasure Travel. If a trip combines both business and pleasure and is within the United States, transportation is deductible only if the trip is primarily for business. If the trip is primarily a vacation, expenses relating to business, other than transportation, are still deductible. Special rules apply for trips outside the United States.

V. MOVING EXPENSES

A. Moving expenses are deductible by employees for adjusted gross income. Reimbursements from the employer must be included in gross income. The two basic tests that must be met for moving expenses to be deductible are the distance test and the time requirement test.

B. Distance Test. The distance test requires that the taxpayer's new job location be at least 50 miles farther from the taxpayer's old residence than the old residence was from the former place of employment.

C. Time Requirements. A time requirement is also necessary for an employee to qualify for the moving expense deduction. An employee must be employed full-time at the new location for 39 weeks in the twelve-month period following the move and a self-employed individual must work in the new location for 78 weeks during the next two years.

D. When Deductible. Moving expenses are deductible in the year of payment. However, if the employee is to be reimbursed for the expenses in the following year, an election can be made to deduct the expenses in that year.

E. The following categories of moving expenses are deductible:

Cost of moving household and personal effects

Traveling from former to new place of residence

Note: Meals are not deductible and Mileage is at 10 cents per mile (for 1998).

VI. EDUCATION EXPENSES

A. General Requirements. An employee may deduct expenses (subject to the 2% limit) for education as ordinary and necessary business expenses provided such items were incurred either (1) to maintain or improve existing skills required in the present job, or (2) to meet the express requirements of the employer or the requirements imposed by law to retain the employment status. However, expenses are not deductible if they are required to meet the minimum educational standards for the taxpayer's job or if they qualify the taxpayer for a new trade or business.

B. Requirements Imposed by Law or by the Employer for Retention of Employment. Many states require that teachers take additional courses to retain their position. Such expenses would qualify as deductible since they are incurred in meeting requirements imposed by law or the employer for retention of employment.

C. Maintaining or Improving Existing Skills. The deductibility of educational expenses said to "maintain or improve existing skills" is a heavily litigated subject. The deduction is disallowed in cases where the deduction qualifies the taxpayer for a new trade or business. For example, the expenses of a business executive or accountant incurred in obtaining a law degree are specifically not deductible under this provision.

D. Classification of Specific Items. Education expenses for employees are deductible as itemized deductions on an individual's tax return.

E. Other Provisions Dealing With Education. Note, other aspects of educational expenses (e.g., scholarships and employer reimbursement) are discussed in other chapters in this textbook.

VII. ENTERTAINMENT EXPENSES

A. Dollar Limitations. Deductions for meals and entertainment (including facilities) are limited to 50% of the otherwise allowable amount. This rule applies to taxes and tips relating to meals and entertainment. Cover charges, parking, and room rental fees are also subject to the 50% rule. Certain employees are allowed a higher percentage of meal allowance. In 1999 and 2000, air transportation workers, interstate truck and bus drivers, train crews, dispatchers, and merchant marines are allowed 60% of the their qualified meals as a deduction.

B. Classification of Expenses. Entertainment expenses can be categorized as those "directly related to" business and those "associated with" business. "Directly related to" expenses are those related to an actual business meeting or discussion. "Associated with" expenses are those that promote the general goodwill of the business; however, the entertainment must serve a specific business purpose.

C. Restrictions upon Deductibility. Business meals are deductible if the following requirements are met:

the meal is directly related to or associated with the active conduct of a trade or business, and

the expense is not lavish or extravagant, and

the taxpayer (or an employee) is present at the meal.

The tax law denies any deduction for club dues except for service organizations (Lions Club, Rotary, etc.).

A deduction for the cost of a ticket for an entertainment activity is limited to the face value of the ticket. Deductions for skyboxes at sports arenas are generally disallowed except to the extent of the cost of a regular ticket.

Business gifts are limited to $25 per donee per year. Excluded from the $25 limit are gift wrapping, shipping, certain gifts costing $4 or less, and gifts used for advertising.

VIII. OTHER EMPLOYEE EXPENSES

A. Office in the Home. There was no deduction for an office in the home unless it is used exclusively and on a regular basis as the taxpayer's principal place of business or as a place of business that is used by patients, clients, or customers. If the office is used in connection with the taxpayer's business as an employee, the use of the office must also be for the convenience of the employer. The deductions for an office in the home cannot exceed gross income from the business activity reduced by all other deductible expenses attributable to the business but not allocable to the use of the home itself (unless the item would otherwise be deductible).

The U.S. Supreme Court has ruled (in *Soliman*) that the majority of the income earning activity must take place in the home office. However, for tax years after 1998, the tax law was amended to partially overturn the *Soliman* decision. Starting in 1999, a home qualifies as a principal place of business if both the following are true:

1) The office is used by the taxpayer to conduct administrative or management activities of a trade or business, and

2) there is no other fixed location of the trade or business where the taxpayer conducts these activities.

B. Miscellaneous Employee Expenses. Miscellaneous employee expenses such as special clothing, union dues, and professional expenses are deductible subject to the 2% of AGI limitation.

C. Contributions to IRAs. Individuals are allowed a deduction for adjusted gross income of up to $2,000 ($4,000 for spousal account) per year to an IRA. See Chapter 19 for the details on IRA contribution limits.

IX. CLASSIFICATION OF EMPLOYEE EXPENSES

A. Accountable Plans. Employee expenses are reimbursed under accountable plans or non-accountable plans. For a plan to be accountable two requirements must be met. The employee must: (1) Adequately account for (substantiate) the expenses and (2) Return any excess reimbursement or allowance.

Substantiation requires the employee provide the following items to the employer:

The amount of the expense

The time and place of travel or entertainment (or date of gift)

The business purpose of such expense

The business relationship of the person entertained (or receiving the gift)

The amount of an expenditure can be substantiated by a deemed substantiation (per diem) method. By using such a method the amount of the expense is proved. The maximum amount deemed substantiated is equal to the lesser of the per diem allowance or the Federal per diem rate, which varies by area and location. When the per diem method is used, the place, date, business purpose, and business relationship must still be substantiated in the normal manner.

B. Nonaccountable Plan. Under a nonaccountable plan an adequate accounting or reimbursement is not required. In such plans any reimbursement is reported in its entirety as wages on the employee's W-2. Any allowable expenses are treated in the same manner as unreimbursed expenses. Thus the employee is subject to the 50% limit on meals and entertainment, the 2% miscellaneous itemized deduction limit, etc.

C. Reporting Procedures. The reporting requirements for employee expenses depend upon whether the amount is reimbursed or unreimbursed and whether the amount is paid under an accountable plan or a nonaccountable plan.

X. LIMITATION (2%) ON ITEMIZED DEDUCTIONS

After classifying deductions as *for* or *from* AGI, it is necessary to group the itemized (deductions from AGI) deductions into two groups. The deductions in the first group are deductible in full for taxpayers who itemize while the second group of deductions are added and reduced by 2% of AGI.

A. Miscellaneous itemized deductions subject to the 2% of AGI limitation include:

All Sec. 212 expenses other than rent and royalty expenses

All unreimbursed employee expenses (after a 50% reduction, if applicable)

Professional dues and subscriptions

Union dues and work uniforms

Employment-related education expenses

Malpractice insurance premiums

Job hunting expenses

Office in the home and outside sales expenses

Legal, accounting, and tax return fees

Hobby expenses

Investment expenses

Custodial fees for income-producing property or IRAs

Collection fees for interest and dividends

Appraisal fees for establishing the amount of casualty losses or charitable deductions

B. Miscellaneous itemized deductions not subject to the 2% of AGI limitation are:
Work-related handicapped expenses

Gambling losses to the extent of gambling winnings

Certain terminated annuity payments

KEY TERMS:

Substantiation Requirements

Meals & Entertainment

Transportation & Travel

Moving Expenses

Educational Expenses

Office-in-the-Home

TEST FOR SELF-EVALUATION

True or False

Indicate which of the following statements are true or false by circling the correct answer.

T F 1. Expenses of self-employed taxpayers are deductible for adjusted gross income as trade or business expenses.

T F 2. An employer-employee relationship exists if the employer has the right to specify the result and the ways and means by which the result is to be attained.

T F 3. A self-employed individual is required to file Schedule C of Form 1040.

T F 4. Unreimbursed employee travel expenses are a deduction from adjusted gross income.

T F 5. All miscellaneous deductions are subject to the 2 percent of AGI limitation.

T F 6. To the extent employee expenses are reimbursed under an accountable plan, they are deductions for adjusted gross income.

T F 7. A taxpayer may switch to the automatic mileage method on an automobile if in prior years he had used MACRS or Sec. 179 expensing on that automobile.

T F 8. Travel and transportation expenses are defined in the same manner for tax purposes.

T F 9. Commuting expenses from home to one's place of employment are not deductible.

T F 10. An employee will be allowed a deduction for the cost of commuting from a primary job to a second job.

T F 11. Taxpayers must always use the automatic mileage method to determine an automobile expense deduction.

T F 12. If a taxpayer has two or more vehicles in use at the same time, he or she may use the automatic mileage method.

T F 13. A taxpayer cannot change to the automatic mileage method if the election to expense has been made or accelerated depreciation has previously been taken.

T F 14. Unreimbursed travel expenses are an itemized deduction (subject to the 2% floor).

T F 15. Union dues are deductible (subject to the 2% of adjusted gross income limitation) for tax purposes.

T F 16. In 1999, to be deductible, a home office must be used by a taxpayer to conduct administrative or management activities and there is no other fixed location of the trade or business where to taxpayers conducts these activities.

T F 17. All business gift deductions are limited to $25 per donee.

T F 18. Law school expenses are always deductible.

T F 19. The cost of a Bar or CPA exam review course is generally deductible.

T F 20. The business mileage deduction is 32.5 cents per mile for 1999.

T F 21. Expenses of moving household and personal belongings are not subject to a dollar limitation.

T F 22. In 1999, qualified business meals are only 50 percent deductible for nontransportation workers.

T F 23. For convention travel expenses to be deductible, the convention attended must be *directly related* to the taxpayer's trade or business.

T F 24. Travel as a form of education is not allowed as a deduction for individual taxpayers.

T F 25. If an employee receives reimbursement under a nonaccountable plan, then reimbursement is reported on the employee's W-2 and any allowable expenses are deductible in the same manner as unreimbursed expenses.

Fill-in-the-Blanks

Complete the following statements with the appropriate word(s) or amount(s).

1. In order to claim a deduction for travel expenses, a taxpayer must be away from home for a ______ period.

2. To qualify for a moving expense deduction, the taxpayer's new job location must be at least________ miles farther from the taxpayer's old residence than the old residence was from the former place of employment.

3. To satisfy the time requirement for the moving expense deduction, a self-employed individual must work in the new location for __________ weeks during the next two years and an employee must be employed for __________ weeks during the next 12 months.

4. If an education expense qualifies the taxpayer for a __________ trade or business the amount is not deductible.

5. If a convention is held outside __________, the deduction of the convention expenses may be limited.

6. Educational expenses incurred to maintain or improve _________ skills or to meet the requirements of an _________ are usually deductible.

7. Entertainment expense deductions are categorized as those __________ related to business and those ___________ with business.

8. The cost of special clothing specifically required as a condition of __________ and not adaptable to __________ wear is deductible.

Multiple Choice

Choose the best answer for each of the following questions.

1. Which of the following educational expenses would be deductible?
   a. Travel expenses for general knowledge.
   b. CPA review course expenses.
   c. Law school educational expenses.
   d. Expenses of a senior in college who has already accepted a job.
   e. None of the above are deductible

2. The substantiation requirements for business entertainment under Sec. 274 do not include:
   a. The amount
   b. Credit card receipts
   c. The business purpose
   d. The business relationship
   e. None of the above

3. An employee drove her automobile 6,000 miles on business during January through March of 1999. Using the automatic mileage method (32.5 cents per mile in the first quarter of 1999), her deduction for unreimbursed expenses (before any applicable 2% limit) is:
   a. $1,950 for AGI
   b. $1,950 from AGI
   c. $600 for AGI
   d. $600 from AGI
   e. Some other amount

4. Which of the following miscellaneous expenses is not subject to the 2 percent of adjusted gross income limitation?
   a. Unreimbursed employee expenses
   b. Outside sales expenses
   c. Union dues
   d. Investment expenses
   e. Gambling losses to extent of gambling winnings

5. Cathy is an outside sales person. She has set aside one room in her house as a home office where she does administrative work related to her job. Cathy no other office available to her. For the year, depreciation expense is $150 and other maintenance expenses are $250 on the home office. If Cathy's Schedule C net income (without the home office items) is $45,000, how much of these expenses are deductible by Cathy in 1999?
   a. -0-
   b. $150
   c. $250
   d. $400
   e. Some other amount

6. Toni is a self-employed consultant and while traveling spends $120 on meals and $200 on transportation and lodging. What is the amount of Toni's deduction for these expenditures in 1999?
   a. $260
   b. $320
   c. $256
   d. $280
   e. Some other amount

7. Terry, an employee of an accounting firm, spent $600 on dues to professional organizations and $250 for subscriptions to professional journals. Terry's AGI is $30,000. Assuming Terry itemizes deductions, how much (after the 2% limit) may she deduct?
   a. $-0-
   b. $850
   c. $600
   d. $250
   e. Some other amount

8. Which of the following would be an employer-employee relationship?
   a. A plumber who comes to your home to do work
   b. A CPA who prepares a tax return
   c. A physician who pays a nurse to help him in his office
   d. A gardener who takes care of individual lawns for a monthly fee
   e. None of the above

9. A self-employed CPA moves from California to Texas to establish a new practice. To qualify for a moving expense deduction, which of the following must be true?
   a. He must work for another CPA in Texas for one year
   b. He must have been in practice for three years in California
   c. He must obtain a license to practice from the state of Texas
   d. He must work full time in the new location for 78 weeks during the next two years
   e. None of the above

10. Fran is a CPA who has a small tax practice in her home in addition to working her regular job. The gross income from this practice is $5,500 for the year. Based on square footage, the portion of mortgage interest and real estate taxes allocable to the business amount to $3,000. The allocable portion of maintenance, utilities, and depreciation is $3,500. Assuming no other expenses related to the business were incurred, what amount of the maintenance, utilities, and depreciation is deductible by Fran?
    a. $-0-
    b. $3,500
    c. $2,500
    d. $500
    e. Some other amount

11. Mike, a staff accountant for a CPA firm, incurred the following expenses:

Travel	$200
Transportation	$500
Dues and Subscriptions	$300

Mike gave his employer an adequate accounting and received a reimbursement under an accountable plan of $1,000 to cover these expenses. What amount is deductible from adjusted gross income?
a. $-0-
b. $60
c. $300
d. $700
e. Some other amount

12. In 1999, Rachel, an employee of the Big CPA firm, spent $3,000 for business expenses (none of which are subject to the 50% limitation). She was reimbursed $4,000 for these expenses. *An adequate accounting was not made to her employer.* If Rachel's AGI was $50,000 for the year and her employer included $4,000 on her W-2, what amount of the employee business expenses may she deduct as an itemized deduction?
a. $-0-
b. $2,000
c. $3,000
d. $5,000
e. Some other amount

13. Uriah had travel expenses of $1,500 substantiated by credit card receipts. He has a diary that provides the business purpose and relationship for $800 of these expenses. How much will Uriah be allowed as a deduction, before considering any limitation based on adjusted gross income?
a. a maximum of $25 per day
b. $700
c. $800
d. $1,500
e. Some other amount

14. Under the deemed substantiation method of accounting for expenses, what is the maximum amount that taxpayers are allowed as a deduction without being required to substantiate the amount of the expense?
a. The federal per diem amount
b. $138 per day
c. All expenses up to $25 per day
d. The state per diem rate of the state in which they live
e. None of the above

15. Statutory employees report income and deductions on which of the following Forms or Schedules?
a. Form 2106
b. Schedule B
c. Schedule E
d. Form 2106 and Schedule A
e. None of above

16. Kate, a self-employed CPA, attended a two-day course on auditing. She incurred the following expenses:

Airfare	$ 500
Taxi	40
Meals	200

Lodging	300
Laundry	20
Total	$1,060

How much can Kate claim as a deduction *for* AGI in 1999?
a. $-0-
b. $1,060
c. $960
d. $1,040
e. Some other amount

17. Jason, a professor of history at a local university, attended an investment seminar. He incurred the following expenses:

Airfare	$300
Meals	100
Lodging	200
Total	$600

What is Jason's miscellaneous itemized deduction (before any 2% limit) in 1999?
a. $-0-
b. $540
c. $580
d. $600
e. Some other amount

18. In 1999, Ted incurred the following unreimbursed expenses at his country club in connection with his employment as a salesman:

Annual dues to country club	$3,000
Business meals (directly related)	2,000
Personal meals	1,000
Days of business use (directly related)	60
Days of personal use	40

What is Ted's entertainment deduction *before* any 2% limitation?
a. $2,000
b. $1,000
c. $4,000
d. $3,040
e. Some other amount

19. Todd purchased his automobile in 1998 for $15,000. It was used 80% for business purposes. Todd drove the car for 10,000 business miles in 1998 (the 1998 depreciation rate is $.12). What is Todd's basis in the business portion of the automobile at the beginning of 1999?
a. $15,000
b. $12,000
c. $10,800
d. $9,200

e. Some other amount

20. The foreign convention expense limitation rules would apply to a convention held in which of the following?
a. Mexico
b. Hawaii
c. Alaska
d. Guam
e. Venezuela

21. Peter, a civil engineer working for Amber Company, incurs a total of $5,200 in business expenses, consisting of the following:

Transportation (no commuting)	$1,500
Meals and lodging away from home	2,000
Dues and subscriptions	750
Entertainment	950
Total	$5,200

Peter received reimbursement of $3,400 from his employer under an accountable plan. His itemized deductions before any limitations for 1999 would be:
a. $-0-
b. $1,500
c. $1,800
d. $5,200
e. Some other amount

22. Reed, a traveling sales representative (a statutory employee) of Pink Company, incurs the following job related business expenses:

Transportation (no commuting)	$4,000
Meals and lodging away from home	5,000
Dues and subscriptions	1,000
Entertainment	2,000
Total	$12,000

Reed received no reimbursement from his employer. What amount may Reed deduct *for* adjusted gross income in 1999 before any 50% limitation for meals and entertainment?
a. $-0-
b. $4,000
c. $8,000
d. $12,000
e. Some other amount

23. Lori Legal is a self-employed lawyer. She has to fly to Hawaii on business to see a client. Lori decides to incorporate a vacation into her trip to the islands. Round trip airfare is $600. Of the 10 days out of town, Lori consulted with her client for three days. How much of the airfare can Lori deduct on her schedule C as a business expense?
a. $-0-

b. $180
c. $540
d. $600
e. Some other amount

24. During 19x1, Duke changed jobs and moved from Dallas to Phoenix. Duke had the following expenses in connection with the move:

Cost of moving household goods	$4,000
Meals	300
Lodging	500

Duke drove his car the 1,150 miles from Dallas to Phoenix (assume the 19x1 moving mileage rate is $.10). What is his moving expense deduction for 19x1?
a. $4,000
b. $4,300
c. $4,500
d. $4,615
e. $4,800

25. Chad is an employee of Haddock Corporation, a commercial real estate broker. He takes a client to dinner and incurs the following expenses (all of which can be substantiated):

Taxi	$25
Drinks before dinner	40
Meal cost	135
Tips	35
Total	$235

If Chad is reimbursed by Haddock for $235 (under an adequate accounting plan), how much of the reimbursement is income to Chad in 1999?
a. $-0-
b. $117.50
c. $130.00
d. $205.00
e. $235.00

26. Same as number 25. What is Haddock's tax deduction?
a. $-0-
b. $117.50
c. $130.00
d. $205.00
e. $235.00

27. Tom is a self-employed interstate truck driver and while traveling spends $120 on meals and $200 on transportation and lodging. What is the amount of Tom's deduction for these expenditures in 1999?
a. $260
b. $266
c. $320

d. $160
e. Some other amount

Use the legend provided below to indicate for items listed (#28 to #34) how it would be deducted for an individual taxpayer.

Legend
A = Deduction for AGI
B = Deduction from AGI, subject to the 2% limit
C = Deduction from AGI, not subject to the 2% limit

____ 28. Union dues of an employee

____ 29. Qualified Moving expenses

____ 30. Home office expenses of an employee

____ 31. Gambling losses (to extent of gambling winnings)

____ 32. Education expenses of a self-employed CPA

____ 33. Work related expenses for handicapped individuals

Problems

1. In 1999, Dorothy moved from San Francisco to San Diego to obtain a better job. She paid $4,000 to have her personal and household goods moved. During the move, Dorothy incurred $125 in transportation expense, lodging expense of $150, and meal expense of $50. In selling her residence, Dorothy incurred $6,500 in selling expenses. Dorothy received no reimbursement for her moving expenses. Calculate Dorothy's moving expense deduction using the following worksheet.

Moving household goods	$__________
Transportation	__________
Lodging	__________
Meals	__________
House sale expenses	__________
Moving expense deduction	$__________

2. Ray, a college professor, incurred the following business-related expenses for which he was not reimbursed.

Mileage (100% after March 1999)	16,500 miles
Travel (includes meals of $200)	$750
Air transportation	$600

Calculate Ray's employee business expense deduction for 1999 (before any 2% limitation).

Mileage	$ ___________
Travel	$ ___________
Transportation	$ ___________
Total	$ ___________

3. Chee, a college professor, accepted a position with the IRS in Washington, D.C. The assignment was designated as temporary and was for a 12-month period. Chee left his wife and children in Houston and rented an apartment in Washington during his employment. Chee's AGI for the year is $50,000. He incurred the following expenses, none of which were reimbursed by the IRS.

Airfare to and from Washington, D.C.	$2,000
Rent on Washington apartment	$10,000
Meals, in Washington	$5,000

What amount is deductible by Chee? Is the deduction for AGI or from AGI? $___________

SOLUTIONS TO CHAPTER 9

True or False

1. True (p. 9-3)
2. True (p. 9-3)
3. True (p. 9-3)
4. True (p. 9-7)
5. False Only certain deductions are subject to the 2% limitation. (p. 9-25)
6. True (p. 9-22)
7. False Taxpayers may not switch to the automatic mileage method. (p. 9-6)
8. False They are different categories of deductions. (pp. 9-4, 7)
9. True (p. 9-4)
10. True (p. 9-5)
11. False They may use actual operating costs. (p. 9-6)
12. False Employees with two vehicles must use actual operating costs. (p. 9-6)
13. True (p. 9-6)
14. True (p. 9-7)
15. True (p. 9-25)
16. True (p. 9-19)
17. False Gift wrapping, mailing, etc. may exceed the $25 limit. (p. 9-19)
18. False The taxpayer is being qualified for a new trade or business; therefore, the education expenses are not deductible. (p. 9-14)
19. False The taxpayer has not met the minimum standards for the job. (p. 9-13)
20. True (p. 9-6)
21. True (p. 9-12)
22. True (p. 9-16)
23. True (p. 9-8)
24. True (p. 9-9)
25. True (p. 9-24)

Fill-in-the-Blanks

1. temporary (p. 9-7)
2. 50 (p. 9-11)
3. 78, 39 (p. 9-12)
4. new (p. 9-13)
5. North America (p. 9-10)
6. existing, employer (p. 9-13)
7. directly, associated (p. 9-17)
8. employment, regular (p. 9-21)

Multiple Choice

1. E (p. 9-13)
2. B (p. 9-22)
3. B 20,000 miles x $.32½ = $1,950 from AGI. [1999] (p. 9-6)

4.	E	(p. 9-25)
5.	D	(p. 9-19)
6.	A	(50% of $120) + $200 = $260. (p 9-7, 15)
7.	D	$600 + 250 - (2% of $30,000) = $250. (p. 9-25)
8.	C	(p. 9-3)
9.	D	(p. 9-12)
10.	C	$5,500 - 3,000 = $2,500. (p. 9-20)
11.	A	All of the expenses are reimbursed. (p. 9-22)
12.	B	$3,000 - (2% of $50,000) = $2,000. (p. 9-24)
13.	C	(p. 9-22)
14.	A	(p. 9-23)
15.	E	Statutory employees report on Schedule C. (p. 9-3)
16.	C	$500 + 40 + (50% x $200) + 300 + 20 = $960. (p. 9-13)
17.	A	Investment seminar expenses are not deductible. (p. 9-13)
18.	B	$2,000 x 50% = $1,000, only the business meals are deductible at 50%. (p. 9-15)
19.	C	($15,000 x 80%) - ($.12 x 10,000 miles) = $10,800. [1999] (p. 9-6)
20.	E	(p. 9-10)
21.	C	$5,200 - $3,400 = $1,800 (p. 9-23)
22.	D	All statutory employee expenses are deductible for AGI. (p. 9-4)
23.	A	Nothing can be deducted because the trip was not primarily for business. Only three of 10 days was spent engaged in business. (p. 9-10)
24.	D	$4,000 + $500 +($.10 x 1,150 miles) = $4,615. (p. 9-12)
25.	A	(p. 9-22)
26.	C	$25 + 50%($40 + $135 + $35) = $130. (p. 9-25)
27	B	(55% of $120) + $200 = $266. (p 9-7, 16)
28.	B	(p. 9-25)
29.	A	(p. 9-12)
30.	B	(p. 9-25)
31.	C	(p. 9-25)
32.	A	(p. 9-3)
33.	C	(p. 9-22)

Problems

1.

Moving household goods	$4,000
Transportation	125
Lodging	150
Meals	-0-
Qualified house sale expenses	-0-
Moving expense deduction	$4,275

(p. 9-12)

2.

Mileage 16,500 x $.31 [1999]	$5,115	
Travel (50% of $200) + $550	650	
Transportation	600	
Total	$6,365	(p. 9-4, 6, 16)

3. The expenses are deductible from AGI, subject to the 2% limit. Chee's total deduction would be as follows:

Airfare	$ 2,000
Rent	10,000
Meals 50%($5,000)	2,500
Total	$14,500
2% of $50,000	-1,000
Deduction	$13,500

(p. 9-7)

CHAPTER 10
DEDUCTIONS AND LOSSES:
CERTAIN ITEMIZED DEDUCTIONS

CHAPTER HIGHLIGHTS

Personal expenses are generally disallowed as deductions. However, Congress has identified certain personal expenses which are allowed as itemized deductions. This chapter summarizes the provisions which allow deductions for medical expenses, state and local taxes, certain interest expense, and charitable contributions. The limitations which apply to these deductions are also discussed.

I. MEDICAL EXPENSES

A. General Requirements. Taxpayers are allowed a deduction for medical expenses (net of any reimbursement) for the care of the taxpayer, spouse, and dependents. Medical expenses are deductible only to the extent that they exceed seven and one half percent of adjusted gross income.

B. Medical Expenses Defined. The term medical care means expenditures incurred for the "diagnosis, cure, mitigation, treatment, or prevention of disease," or for "affecting any structure or function of the body."

Expenses to improve the taxpayer's general health such as programs to stop smoking or to lose weight are not deductible. Expenses for unnecessary cosmetic surgery are not deductible.

If a patient is placed in a nursing home for personal or family reasons, expenses are deductible only to the extent of actual medical or nursing attention received. If the patient is placed in the home primarily for medical reasons, the expenses are fully deductible.

The expenses of keeping a dependent at a special school for the mentally or physically handicapped may be deductible as medical expenses.

C. Capital Expenditures for Medical Purposes. Capital expenditures for medical care are deductible to the extent that the cost exceeds the increase in value of the related property. However, the cost of capital expenditures that enable a handicapped individual to live independently and productively are fully deductible subject to the seven and one half percent of adjusted gross income limitation.

D. Medical Expenses Incurred for Spouse and Dependents. Medical expenses for dependents are deductible if they are legitimate medical expenses. The gross income test and joint return test need not be met for a dependent to qualify for the medical deduction.

E. Transportation and Lodging Expenses for Medical Treatment. Expenditures for transportation to and from the point of treatment are deductible as medical expenses. If a taxpayer uses a personal automobile, a mileage allowance of 10 cents per mile in 1999 may be claimed as a medical expense or the taxpayer may use actual out-of-pocket costs. Qualified lodging that is part of medical care is deductible up to $50 per night per person.

F. Amounts Paid for Medical Insurance Premiums. Medical insurance premiums are included in medical expenses subject to the seven and one-half percent limitation. A self-employed person who is not covered under a medical plan may deduct as a business expense (*for* AGI) up to 60 percent in 1999 of medical insurance premiums paid for coverage for his or her family. Any excess premiums can be claimed as a medical expense.

G. Year of Deduction. Medical expenses are deductible in the year paid by the taxpayer.

H. Reimbursements. If a taxpayer receives an insurance reimbursement for medical expenses deducted in a previous year, the reimbursement must be included as income in the year of receipt. The reimbursement is income only if the expense provided a tax benefit in the previous year.

If the taxpayer used the standard deduction amount in the year the medical expenses were paid instead of itemizing deductions, any reimbursements received need not be included in gross income.

I. Medical Savings Accounts. For tax years after 1997, taxpayers can set medical savings accounts (MSAs). These accounts are intended to be used with high-deductible health insurance. Contributions to these accounts are deductible and amounts used to pay for medical care not covered by high-deductible insurance are not subject to tax. However, distributions are taxable and subject to a 15% penalty if made before age 65, death, or disability. MSAs are available for a 4-year pilot project.

II. TAXES

A. Deductibility as a Tax. Taxpayers are allowed a deduction for the payment of certain state and local taxes to reduce the effect of multiple taxation. The law defines a tax as an enforced contribution extracted under legislative authority. Under Sec. 164, the following taxes are deductible:

1) State, local, and foreign real property taxes

2) State and local personal property taxes

3) State and local income taxes

4) The environmental tax

Federal income taxes, employee FICA taxes, estate, inheritance taxes, gift taxes, general sales taxes, and excise taxes cannot be deducted under this section.

B. Property Taxes, Assessments, and Apportionment of Taxes.

For personal property taxes to be deductible, they must be ad valorem (assessed in relation to the value of the property).

Generally, assessments for local benefits are not deductible and are added to the adjusted basis of the property.

Real estate taxes are apportioned between the buyer and seller on the basis of the number of days the property was held by each. This apportionment is required without regard to whether the tax is paid by the buyer or seller.

C. State & Local Income Taxes.

State and local taxes are deductible in the year paid by a cash basis taxpayer. Withholding and actual payments are deductible under this rule and state and local tax refunds are included in gross income, providing there was a tax benefit in the prior year.

State and local income taxes imposed on an individual are itemized deductions even if the source of the taxable income is from a trade or business or the production of income.

III. INTEREST

A. Allowed and Disallowed Items. Under the tax law, individual taxpayers are allowed a deduction (within certain limits) for the following kinds of interest:

1) Trade or business interest

2) Investment interest

3) Interest on passive activities

4) Qualified residence interest

5) Qualified education loan interest

Personal (consumer) interest is not deductible.

Investment interest is deductible only to the extent of net investment income. Disallowed investment interest may be carried over and deducted in future years.

Qualified residence interest includes acquisition indebtedness up to a maximum of $1,000,000 ($500,000, if married filing separately) on a taxpayer's first and second residences, and interest on home equity borrowing of up to $100,000 ($50,000, if married filing separately).

B. Restrictions on Deductibility and Timing Considerations. Deductions are allowed if the debt represents a bona fide obligation for which the taxpayer is liable. A taxpayer may not deduct interest paid on behalf of another. For interest to be deductible both the debtor and creditor must intend the loan to be repaid.

Interest must be paid to secure a deduction unless the taxpayer used the accrual method of accounting. Prepaid interest must be allocated to the tax years to which the interest payments relate.

C. Classification of Interest Expense. Interest expense can be either a deduction for or a deduction from adjusted gross income, depending on whether the loan is for business (other than that as an employee), investment, or personal purposes. Deductions for interest charges on personal indebtedness are reported as itemized deductions on Schedule A of Form 1040 (subject to limitations).

IV. CHARITABLE CONTRIBUTIONS

A. The Code permits the deduction of contributions made to qualified charitable organizations. The deduction is justified as a social consideration in the tax law.

B. Criteria for a Gift. To qualify as a charitable contribution, the gift must be made to a qualified organization. The major elements needed for a gift to be deductible are a donative intent, the absence of consideration, and acceptance by the donee.

If a contribution to a college or university carries the right to purchase athletic tickets, then 80% of the amount of the contribution is deductible.

Contributions of services are not allowed as a deduction. Out-of-pocket expenses incurred in the performance of donated services are allowed if there is no significant element of personal pleasure, recreation, or vacation in the donated services.

C. Qualified charitable organizations are:

1) States or possessions of the United States or any subdivision thereof

2) Organizations situated in the United States operated exclusively for religious, charitable, scientific, literary, or educational purposes or for the prevention of cruelty to children or animals

3) Veterans' organizations

4) Fraternal organizations operating under the lodge system

5) Certain cemeteries

D. Time of Deduction. Charitable contributions are deductible in the year paid for both cash and accrual basis taxpayers. However, an accrual basis corporation can pledge a contribution at the end of the year and deduct it if the amount is paid within two and one-half months after the close of the tax year.

E. Record keeping and Valuation Requirements. No deduction is allowed for contributions of $250 or more unless the taxpayer obtains *written substantiation* of the contribution from the charitable organization. The substantiation must specify the amount of cash and a description (but not value) of any property other than cash contributed.

F. Limitations on Charitable Contribution Deductions.

There are limitations placed on the amount of charitable contributions. For individuals, the general AGI limitations are:

1) 50 percent for contributions to certain public charities, all private operating foundations, and certain private nonoperating foundations.

2) 30 percent for contributions of cash and ordinary income property to private nonoperating foundations and contributions of appreciated capital gain property to 50 percent organizations. If the value of the capital gain property is reduced by any appreciation on the property, then the 50 percent limit applies.

3) 20 percent for contributions of long-term capital gain property to certain private nonoperating foundations. See text for calculation of limits.

If ordinary income property is contributed, the deduction is equal to the fair market value of the property less the amount of ordinary income which would have been reported if the property were sold.

Generally, contributions may be carried over for five years. Contributions made during the carryover years are deducted before carryover amounts are applied.

V. MISCELLANEOUS DEDUCTIONS

A. Taxpayers are allowed certain miscellaneous deductions if they exceed 2 percent of AGI. Examples of such deductions are: professional dues, uniforms, tax return preparation fees, job hunting expenses, safe-deposit box fees, investment expenses, appraisals for casualty losses, donated property, etc., hobby loss expenses, and unreimbursed employee expenses

Miscellaneous deductions not subject to the 2 percent limitation include: gambling losses, certain handicapped work expenses, federal estate tax or income in respect of a decedent, and certain unrecovered annuity investments

VI. OVERALL LIMITATION ON CERTAIN ITEMIZED DEDUCTIONS

Itemized deductions for high income taxpayers are subject to limits when AGI exceeds certain amounts. In 1999, the applicable itemized deductions are reduced by the lesser of 3 percent of the excess of adjusted gross income over $126,600 (single taxpayers and married taxpayers filing jointly), ***or*** 80% of the itemized deductions affected by the limit (see below). This limitation applies after all other limits (e.g., the 7.5% medical limitation) on itemized deductions have been applied.

The limitation applies to the following itemized deductions:

Taxes
Home mortgage interest
Charitable contributions
Unreimbursed employee expenses subject to 2% of AGI floor
All other expenses subject to the 2% of AGI floor

The following deductions are **not** subject to the itemized deductions limitation:

Medical expenses
Investment interest
Nonbusiness casualty and theft losses
Gambling losses

KEY TERMS:

Medical Expenses

Types of Interest

Taxes

Charitable Contributions

Miscellaneous Itemized Deductions

TEST FOR SELF-EVALUATION

True or False

Indicate which of the following statements are true or false by circling the correct answer.

T F 1. For medical expenses to be deductible, they must be for the taxpayer, spouse or dependents.

T F 2. The term "medical care expenditure" would include expenses that are not related to a particular ailment.

T F 3. Nursing home expenditures are always deductible as medical expenses.

T F 4. Under certain circumstances, capital expenditures can be deducted as medical expenses.

T F 5. The cost of special schools for the mentally or physically handicapped may be deductible as a medical expense.

T F 6. For other than self-employed taxpayers, 100 percent of medical insurance premiums are subject to the seven and one half percent of adjusted gross income floor.

T F 7. The term "medicine and drugs" does not include toothpaste, shaving lotion, deodorants, and hand lotions.

T F 8. The expense of unnecessary cosmetic surgery is not deductible as a medical expense.

T F 9. All medicine and drugs are deductible.

T F 10. If a taxpayer is reimbursed for medical expenses that were paid in a previous year, he or she must always include that amount in income.

T F 11. All amounts paid to a government are deductible under Sec. 164 as a tax.

T F 12. The IRS defines a tax as "an enforced contribution exacted under legislative authority in the exercise of taxing power, and imposed and collected for raising revenue to be used for public or governmental purposes."

T F 13. State and local income taxes are deductible for Federal tax purposes.

T F 14. For personal property taxes to be deductible, they must be ad valorem, that is, assessed in relation to the value of the property.

T F 15. Real property taxes include taxes assessed for local benefits such as new streets and sidewalks.

T F 16. Real property taxes are apportioned between the buyer and seller on the basis of the number of days each held the property.

T F 17. State income taxes are always deducted on the accrual method.

T F 18. For 1999, personal interest is not deductible by taxpayers.

T F 19. Cash contributions to needy individuals are deductible charitable contributions.

T F 20. Property donated to a charity is generally valued at fair market value at the time of the gift.

T F 21. Any charitable contribution is deductible for tax purposes.

T F 22. Interest on a principal residence mortgage is not deductible.

T F 23. For 1999, the investment interest expense deduction is limited to net investment income.

T F 24. The interest deduction is always a deduction for adjusted gross income.

T F 25. The estate and gift taxes are deductible for income tax purposes.

T F 26. Points paid by the seller on the sale of a personal residence are treated as a reduction in the sales price and are deductible to the purchaser of the house.

T F 27. In 1999, Robert drives 625 miles to obtain medical care for himself and his family. His deduction (before any limits) for medical millage is $62.50.

Fill-in-the-Blanks

Complete the following statements with the appropriate word(s) or amount(s).

1. Interest has been defined by the Supreme Court as __________ for the use or forbearance of money.

2. For an interest payment to be deductible by the taxpayer, the debt must be the taxpayer's ______________.

3. The tax law requires that prepaid interest except for "points" on a personal residence be __________ and allocated to the subsequent periods to which the interest payments relate.

4. Excess annual contributions to public charities subject to the 50 percent limitation are carried forward for __________ years.

5. Fees paid to mortgage loan companies for finding, placing, or processing a mortgage loan are commonly called __________.

6. To be deductible, a charitable contribution must be to a __________ organization.

7. Property donated to a charity is generally valued at fair __________ value.

8. The maximum limitation on charitable contributions for individuals is __________ percent of adjusted gross income.

Multiple Choice

Choose the best answer for each of the following questions.

1. Steve borrows $150,000 at 10% interest on January 3, 1999. The proceeds are used to purchase $100,000 worth of raw land and $50,000 worth of stock in Exxon. During 1999 the stock pays dividends of $2,500. Steve has deductible expenses on this investment property of $500 (after considering the 2% of adjusted gross income limitation). Assuming Steve pays interest of $15,000 (10% of $150,000) in 1999, how much is deductible?
   a. $2,000
   b. $12,500
   c. $2,500
   d. $15,000
   e. Some other amount

2. During 1999 Mary had adjusted gross income of $30,000 and she paid the following medical expenses:

Medical insurance	$560
Dental charges	600
Physicians' charges	1,000
Prescription drugs	100
Hospital costs	400

   Assuming Mary itemizes deductions, what is Mary's medical expense deduction?
   a. $-0-
   b. $2,660
   c. $410
   d. $1,160
   e. Some other amount

3. During the current year, Tim paid $66 for California license plates for his automobile. California plates are sold at a fee of $24 plus $2 per hundred dollar valuation of the automobile. Assuming Tim itemizes his deductions, how much, if any, may Tim claim as a deduction for taxes?
   a. $-0-
   b. $26
   c. $42
   d. $66
   e. Some other amount

For Questions 4 through 8, indicate the amount of the charitable contribution deduction Ted would be allowed in each of the independent situations.

4. In 1999 Ted donated an art object to Goodwill Industries, a qualified charity. The art object cost Ted $2,000 five months ago and has a fair market value of $3,000 on the date of donation.
   a. $-0-
   b. $2,000
   c. $2,500

d. $3,000
e. Some other amount

5. Assume the same situation as in Question 4, except the art object possesses a fair market value of $1,800 (not $3,000) on the date of donation.
a. $-0-
b. $1,800
c. $2,000
d. $1,600
e. Some other amount

6. Ted donated shares of Texaco stock to his church in satisfaction of last year's church pledge. Ted purchased the stock as an investment two years ago. The stock cost Ted $2,300 and possessed a fair market value of $2,700 on the date of donation.
a. $-0-
b. $2,300
c. $2,700
d. $2,500
e. Some other amount

7. Ted donated $650 of his time as a painter and paint with a cost basis to him of $200, to help fix up his church. How much can he deduct?
a. $-0-
b. $850
c. $650
d. $200
e. Some other amount

8. Ted works for the American Red Cross for free during each month of the current year. He would normally charge $400 per month for the type of work performed. What is Ted's charitable deduction?
a. $-0-
b. $400
c. $4,800
d. Some other amount

9. In 1999, what is the maximum amount of property contributions that a taxpayer may make to qualified organizations without being required to have *written substantiation*?
a. $-0-
b. $250
c. $249
d. $500
e. Some other amount

10. Pat is a cash basis taxpayer who had $1,000 of state income tax withheld from her salary in 1999. In addition, during 1999 she received a refund of 1998 state income taxes of $250. During 1999, Pat also made estimated state income tax payments of $600. For 1999, Pat's state income tax deduction is:
a. $-0-
b. $1,350
c. $1,000

d. $1,600
e. Some other amount

11. Gene owns his own home which he bought several years ago. His original mortgage, which was used to buy the house, is $150,000. In the current year he obtains a home equity loan on the house of $90,000. The interest on the original mortgage is $15,000 and on the new loan is $10,000. The fair market value of the house is $325,000. How much of this interest is deductible as "qualified residence interest?"
a. $-0-
b. $10,000
c. $15,000
d. $25,000
e. Some other amount

12. Which of the following items will not qualify as a medical expense deduction?
a. Eyeglasses
b. Insulin
c. A trip to Arizona for the general improvement of the taxpayer's health
d. Transportation to and from a doctor's office
e. None of the above

13. The prepaid interest rules of Sec. 461(g) apply to all prepaid interest payments except which of the following?
a. "Points" on the purchase of a rental house
b. Construction loans
c. Bank auto loans
d. "Points" paid by a buyer of a personal residence
e. None of the above

14. Big Booster gives $1,000 to his alma mater's athletic department. The contribution entitles him to four football tickets for $50 each. How much is Big's charitable contribution deduction?
a. $-0-
b. $1,000
c. $800
d. $640
e. Some other amount

Questions 15 to 17 use the following information.

Eric, who is single and has no dependents, had adjusted gross income of $80,000 in 1999, comprised of the following:

Salary	$74,000
Net investment income	6,000

During 1999, uninsured art objects owned by Eric, with a basis of $50,000 and a fair market value of $70,000, sustained casualty fire damage reducing the fair market value to $60,000. Also, during 1999, Eric made the following payments:

Interest on margin account to stockbroker	$18,000
Real estate taxes on a condominium (owned by Eric's mother, in which Eric resides)	3,000
State and city gasoline taxes	180
Medical insurance premiums	300
Unreimbursed dental expenses	4,500
Contribution to political committee of elected public official	500

Eric elected to itemize his deductions for 1999.

15. How much can Eric claim as taxes in itemized deductions on his 1999 return?
a. $0
b. $180
c. $3,000
d. $3,180
e. Some other amount

16. How much can Eric claim in his itemized deductions for medical and dental expenses on his 1999 return?
a. $2,400
b. $800
c. $300
d. $-0-
e. Some other amount

17. How much can Eric claim in his itemized deductions for the casualty loss on his 1999 return?
a. $-0-
b. $1,900
c. $2,000
d. $9,900
e. Some other amount

18. Carol, a resident of San Diego, travels with her dependent sick mother to see a specialist in San Francisco for medical treatment. The cost of the trip includes $400 ($200 each) for airfare and $450 for lodging in San Francisco for three nights. Disregarding the percentage limitation, what is Carol's medical deduction for this trip?
a. $-0-
b. $400
c. $850
d. $700
e. Some other amount

19. Xavier would otherwise qualify as Zack's dependent except for the joint return test. During 1999, Zack paid the following medical expenses:

Operation for Xavier	$2,000
Prescription drugs for Zack	1,200
Zack's dentists bills	3,000
Xavier's membership in health spa	2,500
Total	$8,700

Disregarding the percentage limitation, what is the total of Zack's deductible medical expenses?
a. $8,700
b. $6,200
c. $5,000
d. $4,200
e. Some other amount

20. During 1999 Saul, a self-employed individual taxpayer, paid the following amounts:

State income tax	$2,000
Federal income tax	$4,000
Real estate tax on land in Ireland	$1,000
State sales tax	$500
CPA license fee	$150

What amount can Saul deduct as an itemized deduction for taxes on Schedule A of Form 1040?
a. $3,500
b. $3,000
c. $2,000
d. $1,000
e. Some other amount

21. During 1999, Cecil is a resident of a state that imposes a state income tax. During the year, Cecil had the following transactions in regards to his state income taxes:

Taxes withheld	$6,000
Last year's state income tax refund	1,000
Estimated payments	2,000
Deficiency paid related to two years ago	3,000

If Cecil itemizes his deductions, how much may be claimed as a deduction for taxes on Schedule A?
a. $5,000
b. $8,000
c. $10,000
d. $11,000
e. Some other amount

22. During 1999, Scott sells his home to Ben for $200,000. After the sale, Ben pays the real estate taxes of $3,600 for the calendar year. For income tax purposes the deduction is apportioned $2,100 to Scott and $1,500 to Ben. Assuming the real estate taxes are not prorated in escrow, what is Ben's basis in the residence?
a. $200,000
b. $201,500
c. $202,100
d. $198,500
e. Some other amount

23. Tina purchased a new residence in January 1999, for $150,000 and paid points of $4,500 to obtain mortgage financing. The mortgage is for 30 years. Her regular interest on the mortgage for the year was $6,500. What is the maximum amount Tina can deduct for interest on her home in 1999?
   a. $4,500
   b. $6,500
   c. $6,650
   d. $11,000
   e. Some other amount

24. In 1999, Dale had the following income and deductions:

Salary	$110,000
Dividends income	35,450
State income taxes	15,000
Qualified residence interest	13,000
Charitable contributions	14,000

   Assuming Dale is single, what is the net amount of itemized deductions that she may claim on her federal income tax return?
   a. $825
   b. $27,500
   c. $41,435
   d. $42,000
   e. Some other amount

25. In 1999, Karen had the following income and deductions:

Salary	$250,000
Dividend income	35,450
Medical expenses (after the 7½% floor)	15,000
Qualified residence interest	5,000
Investment interest	14,000

   Assuming Karen is single, what is the net amount of itemized deductions that she may claim on her federal income tax return?
   a. $-0-
   b. $30,000
   c. $29,477
   d. $34,000
   e. Some other amount

26. In 1999, Casper had the following income and deductions:

Salary	$115,000
Dividends income	5,450
State income taxes	12,000
Qualified residence interest	13,000
Charitable contributions	14,000

Assuming Casper is married and files a joint return, what is the net amount of itemized deductions that he may claim on his federal income tax return?

a. $39,000
b. $27,000
c. $37,725
d. $1,275
e. Some other amount

27. During 1999, Doreen is a resident of California. During the year, Doreen had the following transactions in regards to her state income taxes:

State taxes withheld (California)	$4,000
Amount paid with last year's California tax return	3,000
Estimated payments (California)	2,000
Nonresident income taxes paid to the state of Arizona	3,000

If Doreen itemizes her deductions, how much may be claimed as a deduction for taxes on Schedule A?

a. $7,000
b. $9,000
b. $4,000
d. $12,000

28. In 1999, Rick establishes a qualified Medical Savings Account (MSA). His medical insurance has a deductible of $2,000. During the year Rick contributes $2,200 to his MSA. What is Rick's MSA deductions for 1999?

a. $-0-
b. $1,300
c. $2,000
d. $2,200
e. Some other amount

29. On qualified education loans, interest is deductible for the first _____ months during which payments are required.

a. 36
b. 48
c. 60
d. 72
e. None of the above

30. For 1999, the maximum interest deduction on a qualified education loan is?

a. $1,000
b. $1,500
c. $2,000
d. $2,500
e. None of the above

Problem

1. Ted and Joyce, both employees of Orange Corporation, had the following items of income and expense for 1999:

Adjusted gross income	$31,500
Medical insurance	500
Doctor bills	1,000
Prescription drugs	200
Hospital bills	1,000
Medical insurance reimbursement	1,200
State income tax	950
Real estate taxes	775
Qualified residence interest	7,150
Personal interest	625
Contribution to church (by check)	450
Tax return preparation fee	225
Professional dues	600
Contribution of used goods to Goodwill	150
Contribution carryover from 1998	625

They file a joint income tax return. Calculate Ted and Joyce's itemized deductions using the worksheet below.

Medical expenses	________	
Insurance reimbursement	________	
Total	________	
Less 7½% of AGI	________	
Medical Deduction		________
Taxes		________
Interest		________
Contributions		________
Miscellaneous (less 2% of AGI)		________
Total Deductions		________

SOLUTIONS TO CHAPTER 10

True or False

1. True (p. 10-2)
2. True (p. 10-3)
3. False The expenditure must be primarily for medical reasons. (p. 10-5)
4. True (p. 10-5)
5. True (p. 10-5)
6. True (p. 10-8)
7. True (p. 10-4)
8. True (p. 10-4)
9. False Only prescription drugs are deductible. (p. 10-4)
10. False The reimbursement is included in income only to the extent of the tax benefit derived in the prior year. (p. 10-9)
11. False Fees, unless incurred in a trade or business or as an investment expense, are not deductible. (p. 10-11)
12. True (p. 10-10)
13. True (p. 10-13)
14. True (p. 10-11)
15. False Assessments usually increase the value of the property and are added to the taxpayer's basis of the property. (p. 10-12)
16. True (p. 10-12)
17. False Individuals deduct state income taxes on the cash method. (p. 10-13)
18. True (p. 10-13)
19. False Contributions must be made to qualifying organizations. (p. 10-19)
20. True (p. 10-22)
21. False There are limits based on 50%, 30% and 20% of AGI. (p. 10-23)
22. False Qualified interest on residence mortgages is deductible. (p. 10-16)
23. True (p. 10-14)
24. False Interest for personal use is a deduction from AGI. (p. 10-18)
25. False Estate and gift taxes are not deductible. (p. 10-11)
26. True (p. 10-17)
27. True 625 miles x $.10 per mile = $62.50. [1999] (p. 10-7)

Fill-in-the-Blanks

1. compensation (p. 10-14)
2. obligation (p. 10-18)
3. accrued (p. 10-18)
4. five (p. 10-26)
5. "points" (p. 10-16)
6. qualified (p. 10-19)
7. market (p. 10-22)
8. 50 (p. 10-23)

Multiple Choice

1. A The deduction is limited to net investment income. (p. 10-14)

2. C

Drugs	$100	
Insurance	560	
Dental	600	
Physicians	1,000	
Hospitals	400	
Total	$2,660	
Less 7½% (AGI)	-2,250	
Medical deduction	$410	(p. 10-3)

3. C $66 - 24 = $42. (p. 10-10)
4. B $3,000 - ($3,000 - 2,000) = $2,000 since the property contributed is ordinary income property. (p. 10-23)
5. B $1,800 - zero = $1,800. (p. 10-23)
6. C Fair market value is used provided the stock is not contributed to a private nonoperating foundation. (p. 10-24)
7. D The donation of service is not deductible. (p. 10-20)
8. A The donation of free services is not deductible. (p. 10-20)
9. C (p. 10-22)
10. D $1,000 + 600 = $1,600 (p. 10-13)
11. D All of the debt is considered qualified residence interest. (p. 10-15)
12. C (p. 10-4)
13. D (p. 10-16)
14. D ($1,000 - 200) x 80% = $640 (p. 10-20)
15. A A taxpayer must own real estate to deduct any taxes on it. (p. 10-11)
16. D $4,500 + 300 - 7½% ($80,000) = $-0-. (p. 10-2)
17. B $10,000 - 100 - 10% ($80,000) = $1,900. (see a previous chapter)
18. D $400 (airfare) + (3 nights x $50 (per person) x 2 persons) = $700. (p. 10-7)
19. B $2,000 + 1,200 + 3,000 = $6,200. (p. 10-6)
20. B $2,000 + 1,000 = $3,000. (p. 10-11)
21. D $6,000 + 2,000 + 3,000 = $11,000. (p. 10-13)
22. C $200,000 + 2,100 = $202,100. (p. 10-12)
23. D $4,500 (points) + $6,500 (regular interest) = $11,000. (p. 10-16)
24. C $42,000 - 3%($145,450 - $126,600) = $41,435 [1999] (p. 10-30)

25. B Deductions not subject to 3% cutback:

Medical		$15,000
Investment interest		14,000
Deductions subject to 3% cutback:		
Qualified residence interest		5,000
Less the smaller of:		
3%($285,450 - $126,600), or	4,766	
80%(5,000)	4,000	-4,000
Allowable deductions		$30,000

(p. 10-30) [1999]

26. A AGI does not exceed the phase-out limit of $126,600, therefore there is no limit. [1999] (p. 10-30).
27. D $4,000 + $3,000 + $2,000 + $3,000 = $12,000. (p. 10-31).
28 B 65% of $2,000 = $1,300 (p. 10-10)
29 C (p. 10-14)
30. B (p. 10-14)

Problem

1.

Medical expenses		
($500 + 1,000 + 1,000 + 200)	$2,700	
Insurance reimbursement	-1,200	
Total	$1,500	
Less 7½% of AGI	-2,363	
Medical Deduction		0
Taxes ($950 + 775)		1,725
Interest		7,150
Contributions ($450 + 150 + 625)		1,225
Miscellaneous [$225 + 600 - (2% of AGI)]		195
Total Deductions		$10,295

CHAPTER 11
PASSIVE ACTIVITY LOSSES

CHAPTER HIGHLIGHTS

The treatment of at-risk amounts and passive losses are areas of concern for many taxpayers. The purpose of these rules is to limit the use of tax shelters to reduce a taxpayer's tax liability. The rules for application of the at-risk rules and the passive loss limitation are very complex, but must be understood in order to have a working knowledge of the U.S. income tax system.

I. THE TAX SHELTER PROBLEM

For many years tax shelters represented a popular way for taxpayers to avoid taxes. The ability of taxpayers to avoid or reduce tax through the use of tax shelters has been limited by the at-risk rules and the passive loss rules. These two provisions have made the tax shelter investments of the past nearly obsolete. If they make investments in many activities, especially real estate, taxpayers must have a working knowledge of these provisions because of their impact on tax liability.

II. AT-RISK LIMITS

A. The tax laws provide an at-risk limitation on losses from business and income-producing activities. A loss deduction is limited to the amount the taxpayer has at risk. The amount at risk is generally the sum of the following:

1) The adjusted basis of property and amount of cash contributed to the activity,

2) Any amount borrowed for use in the activity for which the taxpayer has personal liability, and

3) The taxpayer's share of the net earnings, decreased by the taxpayer's share of losses and withdrawals from the activity.

A taxpayer is not considered at risk with respect to borrowed amounts if either one of the following is true:

1) The taxpayer is not personally liable for repayment of the debt (nonrecourse loans).

2) The lender has an interest (other than as a creditor) in the activity (except to the extent provided by the Regulations).

Recapture of previously allowed losses occurs to the extent the at-risk amount is reduced below zero. This occurs when the amount at risk is reduced by distributions to the taxpayer, changes in the status of debt from recourse to nonrecourse, or by any arrangement that affects the taxpayer's risk of loss.

III. PASSIVE LOSS LIMITS

A. Classification and Impact of Passive Income and Losses.

The passive loss rules require income and losses to be classified into three categories. These categories are:

1) Active (wages, salaries, commissions, a trade or business in which the taxpayer is a material participant, etc.).

2) Portfolio (dividends, annuities, etc.).

3) Passive (rental income(with certain exceptions) or a trade or business in which the taxpayer is not a material participant).

Carryover of Suspended Losses. If a passive loss is disallowed because of insufficient passive income to offset it, it becomes suspended. The at-risk limitations are applied first, as well as other provisions which influence the determination of taxable income, before a taxpayer's suspended loss under the passive loss provisions can be determined. A taxpayer's basis in the investment is reduced by deductions even if the deductions are not allowed in the current year because of the passive loss rules. Suspended losses are carried over indefinitely and are applied against future years' passive income. If the passive activity is disposed of, the suspended losses can be offset against active and portfolio income. Suspended losses for each passive activity must be determined separately on a pro rata basis.

Passive Credits. Credits arising from passive activities can only be used against regular tax attributable to passive income. Any excess passive credits are carried over indefinitely into future years. If a taxpayer has a passive loss for a tax year, then no passive credits can be used. If the taxpayer's tax is calculated using the alternative minimum tax (see Chapter 12), then no passive credits can be used. The passive credit is lost if there is no regular tax generated when the activity is disposed of.

B. Taxpayers Subject to the Passive Loss Rules.

The passive loss rules apply to individuals, estates, trusts, closely-held C corporations, and personal service corporations. The reason that the passive loss rules apply to personal service corporations is to prevent taxpayers from sheltering personal service income by acquiring passive activities at the corporate level. A personal service corporation is a corporation which meets the following conditions:

1) The principal activity is the performance of personal services, and

2) Services are substantially performed by owner-employees.

There is one important exception to the above rules for corporations. A "closely held" C corporation can deduct passive losses against active income but not portfolio income.

C. Passive Activities Defined.

A passive activity is defined under Sec. 469 as:

1) Any trade or business in which the taxpayer does not "materially participate."

2) Any rental activity (regardless of the taxpayer's level of participation), subject to certain exceptions..

Identification of an Activity. Identifying what constitutes an activity is the first step in applying the passive loss rules. Taxpayers with several businesses need to determine whether a segment of a business is a separate entity or part of a single activity. The Regulations state a taxpayer can treat one or more businesses as a single activity if those activities form an *appropriate economic unit* for measuring gain or loss. Taxpayers should carefully consider all tax factors in deciding how to group their activities. Once a taxpayer's activities have been grouped, they cannot be regrouped unless there is a material change in facts and circumstances. There are special rules for grouping rental activities (see the textbook).

Material Participation. If a taxpayer materially participates in a nonrental activity, any loss from that activity will be treated as an active loss that can offset other active income. The Code provides that material participation requires the taxpayer to be involved in the operation of the activity on a regular, continuous, and substantial basis. The Regulations provide the specific tests as follows:

1) The individual participates in the activity for more than 500 hours during the year.

2) The individual's participation in the activity for the year constitutes substantially all the participation in the activity of all individuals (including nonowner employees) for the year.

3) The individual participates in the activity for more than 100 hours during the year, and the individual's participation in the activity for the year is not less than the participation of any other individual (including nonowner employees) for the year.

4) The activity is a significant participation activity for the taxable year, and the individual's aggregate participation in all significant participation activities during the year exceeds 500 hours. A significant participation activity is one in which the individual's participation exceeds 100 hours during the year.

5) The individual materially participated in the activity for any five taxable years (whether or not consecutive) during the ten taxable years that immediately precede the taxable year.

6) The activity is a personal service activity and the individual materially participated in the activity for any three preceding taxable years (whether or not consecutive).

7) Based on the facts and circumstances, the individual participates in the activity on a regular, continuous, and substantial basis during the year.

Rental Activities Defined. According to the tax law, a rental activity, subject to certain exceptions, is to be treated as a passive activity. A rental activity is defined as any activity where payments are principally for the use of tangible property.

There are six exceptions to the automatic treatment of an activity as a rental activity for purposes of the passive loss definition. These exceptions allow the activity to be excluded from automatic classification as a passive activity, but the activity is subject to the material participation test in order to avoid classification as a passive activity under the general rule. The six exceptions are as follows:

The average period of customer use for such property is seven days or less.

The average period of customer use for such property is 30 days or less, and significant personal services are provided by the owner of the property.

Extraordinary personal services are provided by the owner of the property without regard to the average period of customer use.

The rental of such property is treated as incidental to a nonrental activity of the taxpayer.

The taxpayer customarily makes the property available during defined business hours for nonexclusive use by various customers.

The property is provided for use in an activity conducted by a partnership, S corporation, or joint venture in which the taxpayer owns an interest.

D. Interaction of the At-risk and Passive Activity Limits.

A loss that is not allowed for a year because the taxpayer is not at risk with respect to the loss is suspended under the at-risk provision and it is not suspended under the passive loss rules. Also the taxpayer's basis is reduced by depreciation, even though the deduction is not currently useable because of the passive loss rules.

E. Special Passive Activity rules for Real Estate Activities.

For tax years after 1993, losses from real estate rental activities are not treated as passive losses for certain real estate owners. To qualify as a nonpassive activity treatment, a real estate professional must satisfy both of the following requirements:

1) More than half of the personal services that taxpayer performs in trades or businesses are performed in real property trades or businesses in which the taxpayer materially participates, and

2) The taxpayer performs more than 750 hours in these real estate property trades or businesses as a material participant.

Real Estate Rental Activities. There is a limited exception for rental real estate activity losses. Under this special provision, up to $25,000 of losses on rental real estate activities of an individual may be deducted against active and portfolio income. This annual $25,000 deduction is reduced by 50 percent of the taxpayer's AGI in excess of $100,000. Thus, the entire deduction is phased out when AGI reaches $150,000. If a married taxpayer files separately, then the $25,000 deduction is normally reduced to zero. Adjusted gross income is calculated without regard to the IRA deduction, social security benefits, and net losses from passive activities. To qualify for the $25,000 deduction, the taxpayer must actively participate in the rental activity and own 10% or more of all interests in the activity. The $25,000 allowance is considered only after all qualifying rental real estate losses and gains are netted against other passive income. Losses in excess of the $25,000 allowance are passive losses.

F. Dispositions of Passive Interests.

When a taxpayer disposes of his or her entire interest in a passive activity, any disallowed suspended losses are deductible. In general, if the current and suspended losses of passive activities exceed the gain realized or if the sale results in a realized loss, the sum of the following is treated as a loss which is not from a passive activity:

1) Any loss from the activity for the tax year (including suspended losses of the activity disposed of), plus

2) Any loss realized on the disposition in excess of net income or gain for the tax year from all passive activities (without regard to the activity disposed of).

A transfer of a taxpayer's interest in a passive activity by reason of the taxpayer's death results in the suspended losses being allowed (to the decedent) to the extent they exceed the amount (if any) of the stepped-up basis allowed. If a passive activity becomes an activity, suspended losses are allowed to the extent of income from the new active business.

KEY TERMS

At-Risk Limitations

Passive Activity Rules

Active Income

Portfolio Income

Passive Income

Material Participation

Active Participation

TEST FOR SELF-EVALUATION

True or False

Indicate which of the following statements are true or false by circling the correct answer.

T F 1. In general, the passive loss rules apply to real estate rental activities.

T F 2. All debt on property qualifies as an amount at risk.

T F 3. In general, the deduction of passive losses against active and portfolio income is not allowed.

T F 4. The $25,000 exception for rental real estate losses applies only to corporations and partnerships.

T F 5. In general, the special $25,000 allowance for rental real estate losses is reduced by 50% of a taxpayer's modified AGI over $100,000.

T F 6. An investment as a limited partner is generally a passive activity for purposes of the tax law.

T F 7. Credits from passive activities can be used to offset a taxpayer's regular tax liability arising from passive income or a taxpayer's alternative minimum tax liability arising from passive income.

T F 8. Passive credits are carried back three years and then forward for ten years, and if not used in that time period they are lost forever.

T F 9. The amount at-risk is decreased each year by the taxpayer's share of income and by the taxpayer's share of losses and withdrawals from the activity.

T F 10. Recapture of previously allowed losses occurs to the extent the at-risk amount is reduced below zero.

T F 11. Generally, a taxpayer's amount at-risk is separately determined with respect to separate activities.

T F 12. Passive loss rules apply to individuals, estates, trusts, closely held C corporations, and personal service corporations.

T F 13. Individual taxpayers are allowed to offset passive losses against portfolio income but not against active income.

T F 14. In general, personal service corporations are subject to the passive loss rules.

T F 15. If a taxpayer participates in an activity for more than 300 hours during the year, then he is considered to have materially participated in that activity.

T F 16. If a taxpayer's participation in an activity for the taxable year constitutes substantially all the participation in the activity of all individuals for the year, then the taxpayer materially participates in the activity.

T F 17. If a taxpayer materially participated in an activity for any five of the ten preceding tax years, then the taxpayer materially participates in the activity for the current year.

T F 18. If the average period of customer use of rental property is seven days or less, then the activity is considered a nonrental activity subject to the material participation standards.

T F 19. The owner of a public golf course that sells weekly and monthly passes would automatically be subject to the passive loss rules.

T F 20. When a passive activity is sold in a taxable transaction, the suspended loss can be used to offset any realized gain.

T F 21. In general, a taxpayer can treat one or more trade or business activities or rental activities as a single activity if those activities form an appropriate economic unit for measuring gain or loss.

T F 22. Jennifer owns a woman's clothing store in Los Angeles and a laundromat in San Diego. For passive activity purposes, each activity *must* be treated as a separate activity.

Fill-in-the-Blanks

Complete the following statements with the appropriate word(s) or amount(s).

1. Tax credits attributable to passive activities can be carried forward __________ or until the activity is disposed of in a taxable transaction.

2. A death transfer of a taxpayer's interest in an activity results in the suspended losses being allowed to the extent they exceed the ____________ in basis allowed.

3. In a disposition of a taxpayer's interest in a passive activity by gift, the suspended losses are added to the ___________ of the property.

4. Any passive activity losses disallowed for a taxable year may be carried ________.

5. To qualify for the $25,000 rental real estate loss deduction under the passive loss limitation rules, the taxpayer must __________ participate in the activity.

6. The passive activity provisions require classification of income into three categories. These are _________ income, ________ income, and _______ income.

7. Under the passive loss rules, interest and dividends are classified as _________ income.

8. Generally for individual taxpayers, passive losses can only offset ________ income.

9. If a taxpayer participates on a regular, continuous, and substantial basis in an activity, then he or she ________________ participates in the activity.

Multiple Choice

Choose the best answer for each of the following questions.

1. Colm invests $20,000 in a limited partnership which financed the rest of its operations by the use of nonrecourse loans. If Colm's share of the loss this year is $25,000, how much may he deduct on his tax return in the current year without regard to the limitations on the deduction of losses from passive activities?
   a. $-0-
   b. $5,000
   c. $20,000
   d. $25,000
   e. Some other amount

2. Art's AGI this year is $120,000 without deducting IRA contributions or passive losses. What is the maximum amount that Art can deduct if he has real estate losses of $18,000 from a rental house (Art actively participates in the activity)?
   a. $-0-
   b. $15,000
   c. $18,000
   d. $10,000
   e. Some other amount

3. Leonie's adjusted basis in a passive activity was $20,000 at the beginning of the year. Her loss from the activity during the year was $4,000 and she had no other passive activity income for the year. Her passive activity credits for the year were $1,000. At the end of the year her adjusted basis in the passive activity would be:
   a. $20,000
   b. $19,000
   c. $16,000
   d. $15,000
   e. Some other amount

4. In 1998, Dale invests $25,000 in a limited partnership. Dale's share of the partnership's 1998 loss was $5,000. For 1999, Dale's share of the partnership's income is $10,000. What is Dale's amount at-risk at the end of 1999?
   a. $-0-
   b. $25,000
   c. $30,000
   d. $15,000
   e. Some other amount

5. The passive loss rules are applied at the owner level for which of the following entities?
   a. S corporations
   b. Partnerships

c. C corporations
d. a. and b.
e. a. and c.

6. For 1999, Gray Inc., a closely-held C corporation (not a personal service corporation), has $600,000 of passive losses from rental activities, $500,000 of active business income, and $200,000 of portfolio income. How much of the passive loss may offset other income?
a. $-0-
b. $200,000
c. $300,000
d. $500,000
e. Some other amount

7. Same as number 6, except Gray is an individual. How much of the passive loss may offset other income?
a. $ -0-
b. $200,000
c. $300,000
d. $500,000
e. $600,000

8. Which of the following items is not portfolio income?
a. Interest on a savings account
b. Dividends on stock of a U.S. Corporation
c. Interest on U.S. Savings Bonds
d. Dividends on stock of a Foreign Corporation
e. All of the above are portfolio income

9. If an activity is a personal service activity, how many prior years must an individual participate in the activity to be considered a material participant in the activity after withdrawal from the activity?
a. One
b. Two
c. Three
d. Five
e. Seven

10. Rachel owns an apartment building and a gift shop in the same location. She materially participates in the gift shop business and is an active participant in the apartment rental business. The apartment building shows a $15,000 loss for the current year while the gift shop has a $25,000 profit. Assuming Rachel has no other income, she should report net income (loss) from these two ventures of?
a. ($15,000)
b. $25,000
c. $10,000
d. $40,000
e. Some other amount

11. Lola owns a business that is a passive activity. The business had a loss for 1999 determined as follows:

Operating income	$70,000
Dividends (on investments)	15,000
Total income	$85,000
Operating expenses	-$80,000
Investment interest	-8,000
Loss on sale of stock	-3,000
Net loss	-$6,000

What is Lola's passive loss from this business in 1999?
a. $-0-
b. ($6,000)
c. ($10,000)
d. ($3,000)
e. Some other amount

12. Jody sold an apartment building with an adjusted basis of $200,000 for $250,000. In addition, Jody has current and suspended losses associated with that specific apartment building of $60,000. How much of the $60,000 loss can Jody use to offset ordinary and portfolio income?
a. $-0-
b. $10,000
c. $50,000
d. $60,000
e. Some other amount

13. Fran, a physician, earned $300,000 from her medical practice in 1999. She received $55,000 in dividends and interest during the year. In addition, she incurred a loss of $60,000 from an investment in a passive activity. What is Fran's income for 1999 after considering the loss from the passive investment?
a. $300,000
b. $305,000
c. $355,000
d. $295,000
e. Some other amount

14. Which of the following would be a passive rental activity?
a. Ted rents "go-carts" to customers.
b. Ted owns a motel and rents rooms by the day to guests.
c. Ted rents tuxedos to customers for parties, etc.
d. Ted works 1,000 hours as a lawyer and spends 800 hours is renting apartments he owns.
e. None of the above

15. Clancy spends 20 hours a week, for 50 weeks a year operating a clothing store. He also owns a restaurant in another state which is managed by a full-time employee. Which of the activities (if any) are a passive activity?
a. The clothing store
b. The restaurant
c. Both are passive activities
d. Neither is a passive activity
e. None of the above

16. Carla dies owning a passive activity with an adjusted basis of $50,000. Its fair market value at that date was $85,000. There are suspended losses relating to the property of $10,000. What is the passive loss deduction allowed on Carla's final tax return?
   a. $-0-
   b. $5,000
   c. $10,000
   d. $15,000
   e. Some other amount

17. In 1999, Clay invests $50,000 in the West Tex Oil Partnership. The $50,000 was obtained by the use of nonrecourse loans. West Tex has a loss of $70,000 applicable to Clay's interest during the year. What is Clay's amount at-risk at the beginning of the next year?
   a. $-0-
   b. $20,000
   c. $50,000
   d. $70,000
   e. Some other amount

18. Iris made investments in three passive activities during the year. The income and loss from operations were as follows:

Activity 1	($60,000)
Activity 2	(40,000)
Activity 3	50,000
Net passive loss	($50,000)

   What is the amount of suspended loss allocated to Activity 2?
   a. $-0-
   b. $50,000
   c. $40,000
   d. $20,000
   e. Some other amount.

19. Ralph owns the following businesses and participates in each of them as follows:

Activity	Hours of Participation
A	150
B	100
C	300
D	225

   In which of these activities is Ralph a material participant?
   a. None of them
   b. Activities C and D
   c. Activities A, C, and D
   d. Activity C only
   e. All of them

20. Ralph owns the following businesses and participates in each of them as follows:

Activity	Hours of Participation
A	150
B	125
C	300
D	225

In which of these activities is Ralph a material participant?
a. None of them
b. Activities C and D
c. Activities A, C, and D
d. Activity C only
e. All of them

21. In 1999, Dawn performed personal service activities as follows: 800 hours as a tax planner, 500 hours in real estate development and leasing, and 500 hours in real estate rental activities. Her income from tax planning is $48,000 and she has a loss of $22,000 from the real estate development and leasing and a loss of $20,000 from the real estate rental activities. How much of the $42,000 loss may she deduct against her tax planning income.
a. $-0-
b. $20,000
c. $22,000
d. $42,000
e. Some other amount

22. Leon acquired an interest in a bakery four years ago. The loss from the activity is $60,000 in the current year. He has AGI of $150,000 before considering the loss from the bakery. Leon does not materially participate in the operation of the bakery. What is his AGI considering this investment?
a. $150,000
b. $120,000
c. $90,000
d. Some other amount

23. Trout Corporation earned $500,000 from operations in 1999. Trout also received $36,000 in interest income on various portfolio investments. During the year, Trout paid $175,000 to acquire a 40% interest in a passive activity that produced a total loss of $100,000. If Trout is a personal service corporation, what is its taxable income?
a. $536,000
b. $496,000
c. $436,000
d. $460,000
e. Some other amount

24. Same as number 23 except that Trout Corporation is a closely-held nonpersonal service corporation.
a. $536,000
b. $496,000
c. $436,000
d. $460,000

e. Some other amount

25. Bob's adjusted basis in a passive activity is $20,000 at the beginning of 1999. His losses from the activity in 1999 are $8,000. What is Bob's deduction for 1999?
   a. $-0-
   b. $8,000
   c. $12,000
   d. $20,000
   e. Some other amount

26. Same as number 25. What is Bob's adjusted basis and amount at-risk at the end of 1999?
   a. $-0-
   b. $8,000
   c. $12,000
   d. $16,000
   e. Some other amount

27. Same as number 25. What is Bob's suspended passive loss that is carried into the year 2000?
   a. $-0-
   b. $8,000
   c. $12,000
   d. $16,000
   e. Some other amount

Use the legend provided below to indicate for each situation (#28 to #33) if that taxpayer materially participates in the activity:

Legend
A = Materially participates
B = Does not materially participate

____ 28. Able works 600 hours this year in the activity. What is his status?

____ 29. Betty works 210 hours this year in the activity and she is the only person working in the activity. What is her status?

____ 30. Charles works 140 hours this year in the activity and he hires one part-time employee who works 300 hours this year. What is his status?

____ 31. Debbie is a CPA. She spent four years in full-time practice many years ago. This year she works in an activity in which she prepares a small number of tax returns. What is Debbie's status for 1999 with respect to the tax return preparation?

____ 32. Eddie, who owns 50% of a gas station, was a material participant from 1994 to 1998. He retired at the end of 1998. What is Eddie's status in 1999 if he still is involved in the gas station?

____ 33. Fay participates in three activities A, B, and C. She spends 300 hours in activity A, 250 hours in activity B, and 85 hours in activity C. What is Fay's status with respect to activity B?

SOLUTIONS TO CHAPTER 11

True or False

1. True (p. 11-18)
2. False The debt cannot be nonrecourse debt. (p. 11-5)
3. True (p. 11-3)
4. False It applies to individuals. (p. 11-22)
5. True (p. 11-22)
6. True (p. 11-18)
7. False Passive credits can only be used against regular tax attributable to passive income. (p. 11-9)
8. False Passive activity credits carry forward for an indefinite period until the activity is disposed of. (p. 11-9)
9. False The taxpayer's share of income increases the amount at-risk. (p. 11-4)
10. True (p. 11-5)
11. True (p. 11-3)
12. True (p. 11-10)
13. False Passive losses cannot offset portfolio income or active income. (p. 11-3)
14. True (p. 11-10)
15. False The test is more than 500 hours per year. (p. 11-15)
16. True (p. 11-15)
17. True (p. 11-16)
18. True (p. 11-19)
19. False Exception 5 to general rental rule. (p. 11-20)
20. True (p. 11-24)
21. True (p. 11-12)
22. False The activities may be grouped into a single entity. (p. 11-12)

Fill-in-the-Blanks

1. indefinitely (p. 11-9)
2. step-up (p. 11-24)
3. basis (p. 11-25)
4. forward (p. 11-26)
5. actively (p. 11-22)
6. active, portfolio, passive (p. 11-3)
7. portfolio (p. 11-6)
8. passive (p. 11-3)
9. materially (p. 11-14)

Multiple Choice

1. C Limited to his amount at risk in the activity. (p. 11-4)
2. B $25,000 - (50% of AGI ($120,000) over $100,000) = $15,000 maximum. (p. 11-22)
3. C (p. 11-20)
4. C $25,000 - 5,000 + 10,000 = $30,000. (p. 11-4)
5. D (p. 11-10)

6.	D	Under an exception, closely-held corporations can offset passive losses against active income. (p. 11-10)
7.	A	Individuals cannot offset passive losses against portfolio income or active income. (p. 11-3)
8.	E	(p. 11-6)
9.	C	(p. 11-17)
10.	C	\$25,000 - 15,000 = \$10,000. (p. 11-22)
11.	C	\$70,000 - 80,000 = (\$10,000). (p. 11-4)
12.	B	\$50,000 - 60,000 = (\$10,000). (p. 11-24)
13.	C	\$300,000 + 55,000 = \$355,000. (p. 11-3)
14.	D	Ted did not spend more than 50% of his time in the rental activity. (p. 11-21)
15.	B	There is no material participation in the restaurant. (p. 11-14)
16.	A	The suspended loss is deductible only to the extent it exceeds the step-up in basis. (p. 11-24)
17.	A	There would be a \$20,000 unused loss for 1999. (p. 11-4)
18.	D	\$50,000 x (\$40,000/\$100,000) = \$20,000 (p. 11-8)
19.	C	Material participation is achieved through test #4. (p. 11-16)
20.	E	Material participation is achieved through test #4. (p. 11-16)
21.	D	The rental activity is not passive since Dawn spends more than 50% of her time devoted to real estate activities and her material participation in those activities exceeds 750 hours. (p. 11-21)
22.	A	The passive loss is not allowed (p. 11-14).
23.	A	\$500,000 + \$36,000 = \$536,000. (p. 11-10).
24.	B.	\$500,000 - (40% of \$100,000) + \$36,000 = \$496,000. (p. 11-10).
25.	A	The passive loss limit applies and therefore nothing is deductible. (p. 11-6)
26.	C	\$20,000 - \$8,000 = \$12,000. (p. 11-6)
27.	B	The \$8,000 disallowed by the passive loss rules is carried into the next year. (p. 11-6)
28.	A	(p. 11-15)
29.	A	(p. 11-15)
30.	B	(p. 11-15)
31.	A	(p. 11-17)
32.	B	(p. 11-16)
33.	A	(p. 11-16)

CHAPTER 12
ALTERNATIVE MINIMUM TAX

CHAPTER HIGHLIGHTS

This chapter deals with those situations where there is an alternative computation of tax liability for individuals and corporations, the alternative minimum tax. The purpose of the alternative minimum tax is to ensure taxpayers with economic income pay some tax. In general, the alternative minimum tax is a special tax on "loopholes" that keeps taxpayers from using several tax preferences in combination to avoid most of their tax liability.

I. THE INDIVIDUAL ALTERNATIVE MINIMUM TAX

A. The AMT Formula. The alternative minimum tax (AMT) must be paid if it produces a greater tax liability than an individual taxpayer would otherwise pay. This "extra" tax prevents certain taxpayers from completely avoiding the Federal income tax through the use of special favorable tax provisions.

The calculation of the AMT requires the determination of alternative minimum taxable income (AMTI). In its simple form, AMTI is calculated as:

Taxable income
Plus: Positive AMT adjustments
Minus: Negative AMT adjustments
Equals: Taxable income after AMT adjustments
Plus: Tax preferences
Equals: Alternative minimum taxable income

The AMT adjustments are timing differences because of separate regular tax and AMT treatments of various items (such as depreciation). Because the adjustment can be both positive and negative they are added or subtracted from taxable income as the case may be.

B. AMT Formula: Other Components. The complete formula for computing the alternative minimum tax is shown below.

The Individual AMT Formula

Regular taxable income:
+/-: Adjustments
Plus: Tax Preferences
Equals Alternative minimum taxable income
Minus: Exemption
Equals: Alternative minimum tax base
Times: 26% or 28% alternative minimum tax rate
Equals: Tentative minimum tax before foreign tax credit
Minus: Alternative minimum tax foreign tax credit
Equals: Tentative minimum tax
Minus: Regular tax liability
Equals: Alternative minimum tax (if positive)

The noncorporate AMT tax rate for individuals is 26% of AMT base up to $175,000 and 28% over any AMT base over $175,000. For taxable capital gains after May 6, 1997, net (long-term) capital gains included in the AMT base are taxed at the favorable alternative tax rates for capital gains (20 percent or 10 percent) instead of the AMT statutory rates.

The alternative minimum tax exemption is equal to $45,000 for married taxpayers filing joint returns, $33,750 for single taxpayers and head of household, and $22,500 for married taxpayers filing separate returns. The 25 percent phase-out of the exemption begins when alternative minimum taxable income exceeds the following:

$112,500 for single taxpayers

$150,000 for married taxpayers filing jointly

$75,000 for married taxpayers filing separately

C. AMT Adjustments. The AMT *adjustments* include:

1) Circulation expenditures

2) Certain depreciation on post-1986, pre-1999 real property

3) Certain depreciation on post-1986 personal property

4) Certain excess amortization on post-1986, pre-1999 pollution control facilities

5) Expenditures Requiring 10-year write-off for AMT

6) Use of the completed contract method of an accounting

7) Incentive stock options

8) Adjusted gains or losses on asset dispositions

9) Alternative tax NOL deduction

10) Certain itemized deductions

Casualty losses

Gambling losses

Charitable contributions

Medical expenses over 10% of AGI

Estate tax on income in respect of a decedent

Qualified interest

11) The standard deduction (if a taxpayer did not itemize)

12) The personal and dependency exemptions

D. AMT Preferences. The AMT tax *preferences* are always an addition to taxable income. Tax preferences include the following:

1) Percentage depletion

2) Intangible drilling costs

3) Interest on certain private activity bonds

4) Certain excess depreciation on pre-1987 property

5) Certain post-1986, pre-1999 amortization on pollution control facilities

6) Forty-two percent exclusion for certain small business stock

E AMT Credit. To provide equity for taxpayers when timing differences reverse, the regular tax liability may be reduced by a tax credit for prior years' minimum tax liability attributable to timing differences. The credit is not available in connection with AMT exclusions, which represent permanent differences rather than timing differences. Examples of AMT exclusions are the standard deduction, exemptions, excess percentage depletion, etc. The credit may be carried over indefinitely.

II. THE CORPORATE ALTERNATIVE MINIMUM TAX

A. Small Corporations. For tax years after 1997, the AMT does not apply to "qualified small corporations." A Corporation with average annual gross receipts of less than $5 million for the prior three-year period is a qualified small corporation. A corporation can continue to qualify for this exemption if its average gross receipts for the preceding three-year period do not exceed $7.5 million.

B. The corporate alternative minimum tax is similar to the individual AMT. The tax preferences that apply to the calculation of the alternative minimum tax for individual taxpayers also apply to corporations. However, corporations have certain adjustments which differ from those that apply to individuals. The AMT rate for corporations is 20% instead of the individual rate of 26% or 28%.

The corporate AMT tax formula is:

Taxable income:
Plus: Income tax NOLs
+/-: AMT adjustments
Plus: Tax preferences
Equals: AMTI before ATNOL
Minus: ATNOL (limited to 90%)
Equals: Alternative minimum taxable income (AMTI)
Minus: Exemption
Equals: Alternative minimum tax base
Times: 20% alternative minimum tax rate
Equals: AMT before AMT foreign tax credit
Minus: AMT foreign tax credit (may be limited to 90%)
Equals: Tentative AMT
Minus: Regular tax before credits less the regular foreign tax credit
Equals: Alternative minimum tax

C. AMT Adjustments. Corporate AMT adjustments include the following:

1) Certain depreciation on post-1986, pre-1999 real and personal property

2) Certain excess mining exploration costs

3) Certain long-term contract timing differences

4) Differences in gains and losses for asset dispositions

5) Post-1986, pre-1999 amortization on pollution control facilities

6) Alternative tax net operating loss

7) Adjusted current earnings (ACE) adjustment

The adjusted current earnings (ACE) adjustment is equal to 75% of the difference between adjusted current earnings and unadjusted AMTI.

D. Tax Preferences. The tax preferences that apply to individuals also apply to corporations.

E. The exemption amount for corporations is $40,000, reduced by 25% of the amount by which AMTI exceeds $150,000.

KEY TERMS:

AMT Adjustments

AMT Preferences

AMT Credit

AMT Exemption

AMT Tax Rate

TEST FOR SELF-EVALUATION

True or False

Indicate which of the following statements are true or false by circling the correct answer.

T F 1. The alternative minimum tax is beneficial to most high-income individual taxpayers.

T F 2. For 1999, the maximum rate for the individual alternative minimum tax is 28 percent.

T F 3. The AMT exemption for single taxpayers is $33,750 before any phase out.

T F 4. The AMT exemption is reduced 25 cents on the dollar for AMTI above specified amounts.

T F 5. Casualty losses are allowed in calculating alternative minimum taxable income for individuals.

T F 6. Tentative AMT less the regular tax liability is the AMT due.

T F 7. The standard deduction is allowed in computing alternative minimum taxable income (AMTI) for individual taxpayers.

T F 8. The alternative tax net operating loss cannot offset more than 90% of alternative minimum taxable income.

T F 9. The difference between modified ACRS depreciation and the ADS (alternative depreciation system) is an adjustment for AMT purposes, arising as a result of a timing difference.

T F 10. Intangible drilling costs in excess of 50% of net income from oil, gas, and geothermal properties is an AMT tax preference.

T F 11. For AMT purposes, the cost of certified pollution control facilities placed in service after 1986 and before 1999 must be depreciated using the ADS over the appropriate class life.

T F 12. Qualified housing interest is deductible in calculating the alternative minimum tax.

T F 13. The corporate AMT tax rate is 25%.

T F 14. The ACE adjustment may be either positive or negative.

T F 15. For 1999, losses from passive activities are not deductible in computing either the regular income tax or the AMT.

T F 16. For long-term contracts, the AMT computation requires that taxpayers use the percentage-of-completion method.

T F 17. For the individual AMT calculation, medical expenses are deductible to the extent they exceed 7.5 percent of AGI.

T F 18. In arriving at alternative minimum taxable income, alternative minimum tax adjustments may either increase or decrease taxable income.

T F 19. An individual's regular tax liability may be reduced by a credit for prior years' minimum tax liability attributable to timing differences.

T F 20. The corporate AMT exemption is $40,000 reduced by 25% of the excess of AMTI over $100,000.

T F 21. A passive loss computed for regular income tax purposes may differ from the passive loss computed for AMT purposes.

T F 22. High income taxpayers must reduce AMTI by the amount of any itemized deductions disallowed because of the 3% floor.

T F 23. The IRS requires that certain items (e.g., percentage depletion) that are limited for income tax purposes be refigured using a different limitation for AMT purposes.

T F 24. For property placed in service after 1998, the AMT adjustment for *real property* cost recovery is eliminated because the AMT recovery period is the same as for MACRS.

T F 25. For *personal property* placed in service in 1999, if a taxpayer elects to use the 150 percent declining-balance method for regular income tax depreciation, there are no AMT adjustments.

Fill-in-the-Blanks

Complete the following statements with the appropriate word(s) or amount(s).

1. The corporate AMT foreign tax credit may be limited to _______ percent of AMT liability before the AMT foreign tax credit.

2. The __________ __________ _________ adjustment is a special alternative minimum tax adjustment for corporate taxpayers which attempts to indirectly impose conformity between tax accounting and financial accounting methods.

3. Form _________ is the individual AMT form.

4. The individual AMT credit may be carried forward _________.

5. The alternative minimum tax exemption amount for married taxpayers filing jointly is $_________ for 1999.

6. ______ is the sum of a taxpayer's regular taxable income, plus or minus adjustments, and tax preferences.

7. Corporations are subject to an AMT adjustment equal to __________ percent of the excess of ACE over AMTI (before the ACE adjustment).

Multiple Choice

Choose the best answer for each of the following questions.

1. For 1999, Carolyn's taxable income is $300,000. She has tax preferences of $75,000 and positive adjustments of $40,000. If she is a single taxpayer, what is Carolyn's alternative minimum taxable income?
   a. $300,000
   b. $375,000
   c. $415,000
   d. $340,000
   e. Some other amount

2. Refer to question number 1, what is Carolyn's tentative minimum tax?
   a. $99,600
   b. $112,700
   c. $116,200
   d. $107,900
   e. Some other amount

3. Which of the following is not allowed as a deduction in computing the alternative minimum tax?
   a. Gambling losses (to the extent of winnings)
   b. State income taxes
   c. Charitable contributions
   d. Casualty losses

4. Carol is single and has AMTI of $140,000. What is Carol's exemption amount for the AMT?
   a. $45,000
   b. $22,500
   c. $26,875
   d. $33,750
   e. Some other amount

5. Refer to question #4. Carol is married and files a joint tax return. What is her AMT exemption?
   a. $26,875
   b. $22,500
   c. $33,750
   d. $45,000
   e. Some other amount

6. On nonresidential real property placed in service after 1986 and before January1, 1999, the AMT depreciation (ADS) is based on a life of how many years?
   a. 27.5 years
   b. 31.5 years
   c. 35 years
   d. 40 years

e. None of the above

7. In 1999, Tom incurs mine exploration costs of $200,000 which are deducted for regular income tax purposes. What is Tom's adjustment in computing AMTI for 1999?
   a. $-0-
   b. $200,000 positive
   c. $180,000 positive
   d. $160,000 negative
   e. Some other amount

8. Refer to question number 7, what is Tom's adjustment for 2000, assuming no additional mine exploration costs were incurred in 2000?
   a. $-0-
   b. $20,000 negative
   c. $40,000 negative
   d. $200,000 positive
   e. Some other amount

9. For 1999 Amber Corporation (not an AMT "small corporation") has adjusted current earnings of $400,000 and the corporation has unadjusted alternative minimum taxable income of $100,000. What is Amber Corporation's ACE (adjusted current earning) adjustment for the AMT?
   a. $-0-
   b. $300,000 positive
   c. $225,000 positive
   d. $150,000 positive
   e. Some other amount

10. In 1999, Ted incurred a net operating loss of $200,000. Ted had no AMT adjustments, but deducted tax preferences of $30,000. What is Ted's ATNOL carryover into 2000?
    a. $30,000
    b. $170,000
    c. $200,000
    d. $230,000
    e. Some other amount

11. Don, whose AGI is $70,000, incurred medical expenses of $10,000 during the year. What is Don's adjustment, if any, for the individual AMT?
    a. $-0-
    b. $1,750 negative
    c. $1,750 positive
    d. $7,000 negative
    e. Some other amount

12. In the current year, Fern has modified ACRS depreciation of $30,420 on a nonresidential building placed in service last year (prior to January 1, 1999). Her AMT depreciation under ADS is $23,960. Fern's adjustment for computing AMTI is?
    a. $6,460 positive
    b. $6,460 negative
    c. $23,960 positive
    d. $30,420 negative

e. Some other adjustment

13. Bob owns a rental duplex. His basis for regular tax purposes is $93,000 while the basis for AMT purposes is $95,000. Bob sells the duplex for $105,000 for an income tax gain of $12,000 and an AMT gain of $10,000. What is Bob's AMT adjustment from the sale?
a. $-0-
b. $2,000 positive
c. $2,000 negative
d. $10,000 positive
e. $10,000 negative

14. The corporate alternative minimum tax ACE adjustment applies to which of the following?
a. S corporations
b. C corporations
c. Regulated investment companies
d. Real estate investment trusts
e. The ACE adjustment applies to all of the above

15. For regular income tax purposes, Andy had net investment income of $30,000 before deducting investment interest. He incurred investment interest of $45,000 during the year. Also, Andy had interest income on private activity bonds of $12,000. What is Andy's investment interest deduction for AMT purposes?
a. $-0-
b. $12,000
c. $30,000
d. $42,000
e. Some other amount

16. The AMT credit is available for which of the following differences between regular taxable income and AMTI?
a. Circulation expenditures
b. Standard deduction
c. Personal exemptions
d. Excess percentage depletion
e. None of the above

17. D owns mineral property that qualifies for a 15 percent depletion rate. At the beginning of 1999 the basis of the property is $5,000. Gross income from the property during the year was $120,000. What is D's tax preference generated by the property?
a. $-0-
b. $5,000
c. $13,000
d. $18,000
e. Some other amount

18. Beige Corporation (not a "small Corporation"), a calendar year taxpayer, has alternative minimum taxable income (before the ACE adjustment) of $500,000 for 1999. If Beige's adjusted current earnings (ACE) are $1,200,000. What is the amount of Beige Corporation's ACE adjustment?
a. $-0-
b. $525,000 positive

c. $375,000 positive
d. $900,000 negative
e. Some other amount

19. Using the information in question 18, what is Beige Corporation's tentative minimum tax for 1999?
a. $-0-
b. $205,000
c. $215,250
d. $240,000
e. Some other amount

20. In 1999, Black Corporation (a calendar year taxpayer) had the following transactions:

Taxable income	$500,000
Interest on private activity bonds (issued in 1989)	60,000
Excess percentage depletion	150,000

Assuming Black Inc. is not a small corporation, what is Black's AMTI for 1999?
a. $710,000
b. $560,000
c. $500,000
d. $650,000
e. Some other amount

21. Sarajane has total nonrefundable credits of $20,000, regular tax liability of $66,000, and tentative AMT of $50,000. How much of the nonrefundable credits can Sarajane claim in the current year?
a. $-0-
b. $16,000
c. $20,000
d. $4,000
e. Some other amount

22. Norm has the following items in 1999:

Adjusted Gross Income	$45,000
Medical expenses	$10,000
Other Itemized Deductions	$8,000
Taxable income	$27,000

Assuming that Norm is subject to the AMT this year, the adjustment required from the above is:
a. $-0-
b. $1,125
c. $2,125
d. $4,125
e. Some other amount

23. Paul had $22,000 in interest income from corporate bonds, $14,000 interest income from private activity bonds, and $7,000 from preferred stock. What is the amount of investment income Paul must report for AMT purposes?
a. --0-

b. $7,000
c. $21,000
d. $43,000
e. Some other amount

24. Refer to question #23. Paul incurred investment interest expense of $12,000 related to the corporate bonds and $9,000 related to the private activity bonds. He also incurred $6,000 interest on a home equity loan and used the proceeds to purchase the preferred stock. What amount of investment interest can Paul use in calculating his regular tax and his AMT tax?
a. $12,000; $12,000
b. $12,000; $27,000
c. $18,000; $21,000
d. $27,000; $27,000
e. Some other amounts

25. Refer to questions #23 and #24. What is Paul's AMT adjustment for investment interest?
a. $-0-
b. $6,000
c. $9,000
d. $15,000
e. Some other amount

26. Billy Bob had intangible drilling costs (IDC) of $90,000 for the current year. His net oil and gas income for the same period was $70,000. What is Billy Bob's tax preference for IDC?
a. $-0-
b. $9,000
c. $35,500
d. $45,500
e. $81,000

27. Roger, a single taxpayer, has taxable income of $110,000 for 1999. He had positive AMT adjustments of $55,000, negative AMT adjustments of $10,000, and tax preferences of $59,500. What is Roger's AMTI?
a. $-0-
b. $155,000
c. $165,000
d. $169,500
e. $214,500

28. In 1999, Bill has an AMT base of $400,000 including a net (long-term) capital gain of $30,000. The AMT tax rate applied to the net (long-term) capital gain is?
a. 15%
b. 20%
c. 22%
d. 26%
e. 28%

29. Black Corporation has average annual sales for $3,500,000 for the three-year period prior to the current tax year. It has an AMT base of for 1999 of $120,000. What is Black's tentative AMT for 1999?
a. $-0-

b. $24,000
c. $31,200
d. $33,600
e. Some other amount

Problem

1. Tim and Mary Kelley are married taxpayers who file a joint tax return. For the current tax year, the Kelley's have AGI of $70,000 (including $30,000 of investment income). They have excess percentage depletion of $60,000 and interest income on private activity bonds of $20,000. The amount of their investment interest expense for the year is $25,000, and they made charitable contributions of $5,000. If the Kelley's regular taxable income for the current year is $29,000, determine the following amounts.

a. What is the amount of their regular income tax? ______________

b. What is the amount of their tentative minimum tax? ______________

c. What is Kelley's total tax liability? ______________

SOLUTIONS TO CHAPTER 12

True or False

1. False The AMT ensures that high-income taxpayers pay some amount of tax. (p. 12-2)
2. True (p. 12-8)
3. True (p. 12-8)
4. True (p. 12-8)
5. True (p. 12-17)
6. True (p. 12-6)
7. False The standard deduction is not allowed. (p. 12-20)
8. True (p. 12-16)
9. True (p. 12-11)
10. False Intangible drilling costs in excess of 65% of net income from such properties is an AMT tax preference. (p. 12-21)
11. True (p. 12-28)
12. True (p. 12-18)
13. False The rate is 20%. (p. 12-26)
14. True (p. 12-29)
15. True (p. 12-15)
16. True (p. 12-13)
17. False The percent of AGI is 10%. (p. 12-18)
18. True (p. 12-4)
19. True (p. 12-24)
20. False The adjustment to the exemption is for AMTI over $150,000. (p. 12-26)
21. True (p. 12-14)
22. True (p. 12-17)
23. True (p. 12-21)
24. True (p.12-10)
25. True (p. 12-12)

Fill-in-the-Blanks

1. 90 (p. 12-28)
2. adjusted current earnings (p. 12-29)
3. 6251 (p. 12-25)
4. indefinitely (p. 12-24)
5. $45,000 (p. 12-8)
6. AMTI (p. 12-7)
7. 75 (p. 12-29)

Multiple Choice

1. C $300,000 + 75,000 + 40,000 = $415,000. (p. 12-6)
2. B (26% x $175,000) + (28% x [$415,000 - $175,000]) = $112,700. (p. 12-6)
3. B (p. 12-17)
4. C $33,750 - 25% ($140,000 - 112,500) = $26,875. (p. 12-8)
5. D (p. 12-8)

6.	D	(p. 12-10)
7.	C	$200,000 - ($200,000/10 years) = $180,000. (p. 12-12)
8.	B	$0 - ($200,000/10 years) = ($20,000). (p. 12-12)
9.	C	($400,000 - 100,000) x 75% = $225,000. (p. 12-29)
10.	B	$200,000 - 30,000 = $170,000. (p. 12-16)
11.	C	[$10,000 - 7.5%($70,000)] - [$10,000 - 10%($70,000)] = $1,750. (p. 12-18)
12.	A	$30,420 - 23,960 = $6,460 positive. (p. 12-10)
13.	C	$12,000 income tax gain - $10,000 AMT gain = $2,000 AMT negative adjustment. (p. 12-14)
14.	B	See footnote 43. (p. 12-29)
15.	D	$30,000 + 12,000 = $42,000. (p. 12-19)
16.	A	(p. 12-26)
17.	C	(15% x $120,000) - $5,000 = $13,000. (p. 12-21)
18.	B	75% x ($1,200,000 - 500,000) = $525,000. (p. 12-26)
19.	B	($500,000 + 525,000) x 20% = $205,000. (p. 12-27)
20.	A	AMTI: $500,000 + 60,000 + 150,000 = $710,000. (p. 12-21)
21.	B	$66,000 - $50,000 = $16,000 (p. 12-9)

22. B

$10,000 - ($45,000 x 7.5%) =	$6,625	
$10,000 - ($45,000 x 10%) =	$5,500	
	$1,125	(p. 12-18)

23. D $22,000 + $14,000 + 7,000 = $43,000 (p. 12-19)

24. B

	Regular	AMT	
Corporate	$12,000	$12,000	
Private Activity	-0-	$9,000	
Preferred St.	-0-	$6,000	
Total	$12,000	$27,000	(p. 12-20)

25.	D	$27,000 - $12,000 = $15,000 (p. 12-20)
26.	C	$90,000 - ($90,000/10 years) - 65%($70,000) = $35,500. (p. 12-21)
27.	E	$110,000 + $55,000 - $10,000 + $59,500 + $214,500. (p. 12-6)
28.	B	(p. 12-9)
29.	A	Black qualifies for the small corporation exemption from the AMT. (p. 12-26)

Problem

1. a. $4,350 = 15% x $29,000
   b. $19,500 = 26% x ($70,000 + 60,000 + 20,000 - 25,000 - 5,000 - 45,000 (exemption))
   c. $19,500 = $4,350 regular tax + $15,150 alternative minimum tax (p. 12-23)

CHAPTER 13
TAX CREDITS AND
PAYMENT PROCEDURES

CHAPTER HIGHLIGHTS

This chapter discusses the tax credits available to taxpayers. The credits are primarily designed to get taxpayers to undertake certain activities that are deemed to be economically or socially desirable. Payment procedures used by taxpayers to pay income and employment taxes to the federal government are also discussed.

I. OVERVIEW AND PRIORITY OF CREDITS

A. Refundable Versus Nonrefundable Credits. Certain credits are refundable while others are nonrefundable. Refundable credits are refunded to the taxpayer even if the amount of the credit exceeds the taxpayer's tax liability.

The major refundable and nonrefundable credits are as follows:

Refundable Credits:
Taxes withheld on wages
Earned income credit

Nonrefundable Credits:
Child and dependent care credit
Credit for the elderly and disabled
Foreign tax credit
Adoption expenses credit
General business credits: Tax rehabilitation credit, Business energy credit, Work opportunity credit, Research activities credit, Low-income housing credit, Welfare to Work Credit

B. General Business Credit. Special rules apply to the general business credit. For any tax year, the general business credit is limited to the taxpayer's *net income tax* reduced by the greater of:

The *tentative minimum tax*, or

25% of the *net regular tax liability* over $25,000.

C. Treatment of Unused General Business Credits. For tax years beginning before 1998 any unused credit must be carried back three years and forward 15 years. For tax years after 1997 there is a one year carryback and 20 year carryforward period. The unused credit carryovers are treated in a FIFO manner.

II. SPECIFIC BUSINESS-RELATED TAX CREDIT PROVISIONS

A. Tax Credit for Rehabilitation Expenditures. Taxpayers are allowed a credit for rehabilitating industrial and commercial buildings and certified historic structures. Currently, the credit is 10 percent for nonresidential buildings, other than certified historic structures, originally placed in service before 1936 and 20 percent for residential and nonresidential certified historic structures. To qualify for the credit, the expenditure must exceed the greater of the adjusted basis of the property before the rehabilitation or $5,000.

The rehabilitation credit must be recaptured if the property is disposed of prematurely or if it ceases to be qualifying property.

B. Business Energy Credits. Most business energy credits have expired. However, two of the credits remain to encourage the conservation of natural resources and to develop alternate (to oil & gas) energy sources. These are the credits for solar energy property (10%) and geothermal property (10%).

C. Work Opportunity Credit. Taxpayers may take a credit for wages paid to certain targeted employees hired before June 30, 1999. The credit is equal to 40 percent of the first $6,000 of wages per employee for the first year of employment. Eligible employees include certain disadvantaged individuals (e.g., high-risk youths, ex-felons, food stamp recipients, veterans, summer youth employees). The wage expense deduction is reduced by the amount of the credit claimed. The credit is allowed for qualified summer youth employees. The maximum wages eligible for this credit are $3,000 per employee at a tax credit rate of 40 percent.

D. Welfare-to-Work-Credit. A welfare-to work credit is available to employers hiring individuals who have been long-term recipients of welfare. The credit is 35 percent of the first $10,000 of qualifies wages paid to an employee in the first year of employment, plus 50 percent of the first $10,000 of qualified wages in the second year of employment. Employers cannot claim both the work opportunity credit and the welfare-to-work credit for wages paid to the same qualified employee. This credit does not apply to employees hired after June 30, 1999.

E. Research Activities Credits.

Incremental Research Credit. To encourage research and experimentation, taxpayers are allowed a 20 percent credit for qualifying incremental expenditures. The credit only applies to qualified expenditures that exceed a base amount, determined by multiplying the average annual gross receipts of the taxpayer for the four preceding tax years by the taxpayer's "fixed base" percentage. The base amount may not be less than 50 percent of the qualified research expenses in the credit year. This credit is available through June 30, 1999.

The following expenditures do not qualify for the research credit:

1) Research conducted after the beginning of commercial production.

2) Surveys such as marketing research, testing, and routine data collection.

3) Research conducted outside the United States.

4) Research in the social sciences, arts, or humanities.

Qualified research expenditures can be expensed for tax purposes one of two ways:

1) The taxpayer can use the full credit and reduce the expense deduction by the amount of the credit, or

2) The taxpayer can use the full expense deduction and reduce the credit by 50% of the credit times the maximum corporate tax rate.

Basic Research Credit. Corporations (other than S Corporations) are allowed an additional 20 percent credit for basic research expenditure amounts paid to a qualified research organization, in excess of a base amount.

F. Low-Income Housing Credit. Owners of qualified low-income housing projects are allowed a credit based on the qualified basis of the property.

G. Disabled Access Credit. This credit is available for eligible access expenditures paid or incurred by an eligible small business after November 5, 1990. The credit is 50% of the eligible expenditures that exceed $250 but do not exceed $10,250. An eligible small business must satisfy one of the following:

1) Have gross receipts for the previous year of $1,000,000 or less, or

2) Have no more than 30 full-time employees during the previous year.

The depreciable basis of the access property is reduced by the amount of the credit.

III. OTHER TAX CREDITS

A. Earned Income Credit. The earned income credit is designed to help certain low-income taxpayers. In 1999, the earned income credit is determined by multiplying a maximum amount of earned income (based on the number of children the taxpayer has by the appropriate earned income credit percentage (see Table 13-2 in text). The credit is subject to phase out as the taxpayer's adjusted gross income or earned income reaches a certain level (see Table 13-2 in text) and once the taxpayer's earned income or adjusted gross income exceeds a certain amount, no credit is available. It is not necessary for taxpayers to compute the earned income credit because the IRS publishes Earned Income Credit Tables as part of the instruction package for Form 1040 and 1040A.

The earned income credit is a form of negative income tax because a taxpayer can receive a credit (refund) even if no tax is due.

B. Tax Credit for Elderly or Disabled Taxpayers. To qualify for the credit for the elderly, the taxpayer must be 65 years old, or if under 65 must be retired with a permanent and total disability and have income from a public or private employer because of the disability. For taxpayers age 65 or older, the maximum credit is equal to 15 percent of $5,000 (single taxpayers or one spouse over 65), $7,500 (married with both spouses over 65), or $3,750 (married filing separately). The base amount is reduced by excluded social security and railroad retirement benefit payments, and one-half of adjusted gross income over certain amounts ($7,500 for single taxpayers, head of household and surviving spouses; $10,000 for married filing jointly; and $5,000 for married filing separately).

C. Foreign Tax Credit. Individual and corporate taxpayers may claim a tax credit for foreign income tax paid on income earned and subject to tax in another country or U.S. possession. Unused foreign tax credits may be carried back two years and forward five years.

An overall limitation on the foreign tax credit is based on the following formula.

$$\frac{\text{Foreign taxable income}}{\text{Total taxable income}} \times \text{U.S. tax liability before the FTC}$$

D. Child Tax Credit. Individual taxpayers are allowed a tax credit based on their number of children under age 17. For 1999 and later years it is $500. The credit is phased out for married filing joint taxpayers with AGI over $110,000 and over $75,000 for single taxpayers. The total credit is reduced by $50 for each $1,000 (or part thereof) of AGI over the threshold amount.

E. Credit for Child and Dependent Care Expenses.

Taxpayers are allowed a credit for employment-related child and dependent care expenses. The credit is 30 percent of unreimbursed expenses reduced by 1 percent for every $2,000 (or fraction thereof) of AGI over $10,000, but not below 20 percent. The maximum qualifying expenses in any single year are $2,400 for one qualifying individual and $4,800 for two or more individuals. The eligible expenses are further limited to the taxpayer's earned income. For married taxpayers, the limitation applies to the spouse with the least amount of earned income. A taxpayer qualifies for the credit if he or she maintains a household for either of the following:

1) A dependent under age 13

2) A dependent or spouse who is physically or mentally incapacitated

Special rules allow taxpayers with spouses who are students to qualify for the credit. A spouse who is a full-time student is deemed to have earned income of $200 per month for one qualifying individual or $400 per month if there are two or more qualifying individuals in the household.

Taxpayers are not allowed to use amounts reimbursed to the taxpayer by an employer for dependent care and excluded from gross income. See Chapter 5 for this exclusion.

The taxpayer must provide the name, address, and taxpayer identification number of the provider of the child or dependent care.

F. Education Tax Credits. There are two new credits available to help with educational expenses, the *HOPE Scholarship Credit* and the *Lifetime Learning Credit.* These nonrefundable credits are available for qualifying tuition and related expenses incurred by students pursuing undergraduate or graduate degrees or vocational training. Room, board, and book costs do not qualify.

The HOPE Credit is a maximum credit of $1,500 per year (100% of the first $1,000 of tuition expenses plus 50% of the next $1,000 of tuition) for the first two years of post-secondary education.

The Lifetime Learning Credit is a maximum of 20 percent of tuition expenses (up to $5,000 per year). The Lifetime Learning Credit is intended for individuals who are beyond the first two years of post-secondary education. Beginning in 2003, the Lifetime Credit will be available on the first $10,000 of qualifying costs each year.

The education credits are available for qualified tuition and related expenses incurred by a taxpayer, a taxpayer's spouse, or a taxpayer's dependent.

Both education credits are phased out when a taxpayer's AGI exceeds certain amount. See textbook.

IV. PAYMENT PROCEDURES

A. Procedures Applicable to Employers.

Employers are required to withhold Federal income tax and the employees' share of FICA tax from employees' paychecks. The IRS publishes a list of which employees and wages require Federal income and employment tax withholding. The payment procedure involves the following three steps.

1) Ascertain which employees and wages are covered by employment taxes and withholdings.

2) Arrive at the amount to be paid/withheld.

Report and pay the proper amount to the IRS on a timely basis.

B. FICA Taxes. The FICA tax is comprised of two components: the Social Security tax and the Medicare tax. The Social security tax is 6.2% of wages to a maximum wage amount of $72,600 for 1999. The Medicare tax is 1.45% of wages with no limit. These amounts are paid by both the employee and by the employer (in other words the IRS collects each amount twice).

C. Amounts of Income Tax Withholding. The procedure for withholding involves the following steps.

1) Have the employee complete Form W-4.

2) Determine the employee's payroll period.

3) Compute the tax to be withheld using the wage-bracket table or the percentage method.

In using the wage-bracket method an employer simply looks up the tax to be withheld in a table provided by the IRS. The tables are available for various pay periods (weekly, biweekly, monthly, etc.) and for single and married taxpayers.

The percentage method of calculating withholding requires the following procedures:

Step 1 Multiply the amount of one allowance (see text for appropriate amounts) by the employee's total allowances.

Step 2 Reduce the employee's wages by the amount in step one.

Step 3 Use the results in step two to compute the withholding using the proper percentage-method table (see text).

Reporting and payment procedures require that the employer file the following forms with the IRS:

1) Form SS-4 provides the employer with an identification number that must be used on all forms filed with the IRS and the Social Security Administration.

2) Form W-2 is a summary of each employee's wages and the amount of federal income tax and FICA tax withheld. The Form W-2 must be furnished to the employee by January 31 of the following year.

3) Form W-3 is a summary of withholdings for all employees and is filed with the Social Security Administration along with a copy of each Form W-2.

4) Form 940 or 940EZ is used for the employer's annual accounting for FUTA.

5) Form 941 must be filed quarterly summarizing employment taxes for the quarter. Any undeposited amounts must be deposited or accompany this form.

Withholding on Pensions. Income tax withholding for pension payments is mandatory under the tax law unless the taxpayer elects to have no tax withheld.

Backup Withholding. Certain taxpayers may be subject to "backup withholding" on interest and dividend payments. The backup withholding is designed to make sure that taxpayers report all their investment income. For example backup withholding applies if a taxpayer does not give his or her identification number to a bank so that any income can be reported on Form 1099.

D. Procedures Applicable to Self-Employed Persons.

Taxpayers who have income other than wages or who are self-employed may be required to make estimated tax payments (Form 1040ES). One-fourth of the required annual payment is due on April 15, June 15, and September 15 of the current year and January 15 of the following year. The required annual payment is the lesser of the following amounts:

1) 90% of the current year's tax.

2) 100% of last year's tax (the return must cover the full 12 months of the preceding tax year). The 100% is increased to 105% if AGI on the proceeding tax year's return exceeds $150,000 ($75,000 if married filing separately).

No payment is required if the estimated tax is under $1,000. An underpayment occurs when any installment is less than 25 percent of the required annual payment.

The Self-Employment (SE) Tax. Self-employed taxpayers are required to pay a self-employment tax, which is to provide for Social Security benefits. Individuals with net earnings from self-employment of $400 or more are subject to this tax. The SE tax consists of two separate parts, the Social Security tax and the Medicare tax. Each part has a rate and a ceiling amount. For 1999 these amounts are:

	Rate	**Ceiling**
Social Security tax	12.4%	$72,600
Medicare tax	2.9%	No limit
Total	15.3%	

Taxpayers are allowed an income tax deduction for one-half of the self-employment tax paid and a deduction at one-half the self-employment tax rate for purposes of determining the self-employment tax. The 1999 SE worksheet is as follows:

1. Net earnings from self-employment _______

2. Multiply line 1 by 92.35% _______

3. If line 2 is $72,600 or less, multiply the amount on line 2 by 15.3% _______

4. If the amount on line 2 is more than $72,600 multiply the excess of line 2 over $72,600 by 2.9% and add $11,107.80 _______

Self-employed taxpayers are allowed a deduction for AGI for one-half the amount of self-employment tax paid. For example (using the above formula), if a taxpayer's 1999 self-employment income is $55,000, his SE tax is $7,771.25. Of that amount, one-half, $3,885.63 is deductible.

The Social Security ceiling amounts are reduced by any wages the taxpayer has that are subject to the regular Social Security tax (FICA). Schedule SE is used to calculate the self-employment tax.

KEY TERMS:

Refundable Credits

Nonrefundable Credits

Earned Income Credit

Child Care Credit

Rehabilitation Credit

Research Credits

TEST FOR SELF-EVALUATION

True or False

Indicate which of the following statements are true or false by circling the correct answer.

T F 1. In 1999, a taxpayer has three qualifying children and earned income of $9,500. This taxpayer's earned income credit is $3,800.

T F 2. The basic research credit is 25 percent for basic research payments over a base amount.

T F 3. The rate for the low-income housing credit is set monthly by the IRS.

T F 4. The rehabilitation credit is intended to discourage business from moving out of the inner city and to preserve historic structures.

T F 5. For 1999, the earned income credit for a taxpayer with one child is the appropriate percentage of the first $6,800 of earned income, reduced by the appropriate percentage of adjusted gross income (or, if greater, earned income) over $12,460.

T F 6. The earned income credit is a form of negative income tax and can be refunded even if no tax is due.

T F 7. For 1999, to be eligible for the earned income credit, an individual must maintain a household that is the principal abode of a qualifying child.

T F 8. The tax credit for the elderly is 20 percent of the Sec. 22 amount, reduced by excluded social security, railroad retirement benefits, and certain pension amounts.

T F 9. The maximum dependent care credit for three qualifying children is $800.

T F 10 Amounts spent for the care of a taxpayer's spouse may qualify for the dependent care credit.

T F 11. A transfer of property to a qualified basic research organization does not qualify for the 20 percent basic research credit.

T F 12. The maximum amount of general business credit than can be taken in one year is equal to the taxpayer's net income tax reduced by the greater of the tentative minimum tax or 25% of net regular tax over $25,000.

T F 13. If an employee has no regular payroll period, then he or she is considered to be paid on a daily basis.

T F 14. The wage-bracket method of withholding calculation requires more computation than the percentage method.

T F 15. Employers can always wait until the end of their taxable year before filing the required form for payroll withholding, and they do not have to deposit the withholding until the end of the year.

T F 16. The penalty for underpayment of estimated tax may be avoided by single individuals with AGI under $150,000 if they timely file quarterly payments (including amounts withheld) that are equal to or exceed the prior year's tax liability.

T F 17. Individuals with net earnings from self-employment of $200 or more are subject to the self-employment tax.

T F 18. The backup withholding rate is 31 percent.

T F 19. In 1999, self-employment tax is 60 percent deductible for income tax purposes.

T F 20. S corporations and personal service corporations (PSCs) are allowed the basic research credit.

T F 21. In 1999, a taxpayer's only income is self-employment income of $90,000. The amount of her Medicare tax is $2,410.34.

T F 22. In 1999, a married taxpayer has a monthly salary of $1,875 and he claims two exemptions on his W-4 form. His monthly withholding using the percentage method is $133.05.

T F 23. In 1999, Earl has $20,000 of income from Country A, which imposes a 30% tax. His U.S. taxable income is $57,250 and he files single with one exemption. Assume his U.S. income tax is $19,000. Earl's maximum foreign tax credit (FTC) is $4,750.

T F 24. Unused foreign tax credit is carried back 3 years and forward 5 years.

T F. 25. In order to qualify for the adoption expenses credit, a child must be under 18 years old or physically or mentally incapable of self-care.

Fill-in-the-Blanks

Complete the following statements with the appropriate word(s) or amount(s).

1. The purpose of the foreign tax credit is to mitigate __________ taxation.

2. The foreign tax credit calculation is based on a(n) __________ limitation.

3. The maximum employment-related child and dependent care expenses that may be considered in calculating the child and dependent care credit is __________ for one qualifying individual and __________ for two or more qualifying individuals.

4. A full-time student is deemed to have earned income of __________ per month for one qualifying individual for purposes of the child care credit.

5. For 1999, individuals with net earnings from self-employment of $400 or more, are subject to a Social Security tax rate of 12.4% of self-employment income up to __________ and a Medicare tax rate on self-employment income of 2.9% of self-employment income up to __________.

6. Form __________ is the Employer's Quarterly Federal Tax Return.

7. The child and dependent care credit ranges from ______ to ______ percent.

8. The tax credit for rehabilitation expenditures on certified historical structures is ____ percent.

9. Unused general business credits carry back _______ years and forward _______ years for years after December 31, 1997.

10. The earned income credit is an example of a _________ credit and the foreign tax credit is an example of a ___________ credit.

11. A dependent under the age of ______ qualifies for the child and dependent care credit.

Multiple Choice

Choose the best answer for each of the following questions.

1. Ted and his wife, Wilma, pay $3,000 to keep their son, Ted Jr., in a day care center. Ted Jr. is five years old. Ted's earnings are $12,000 and Wilma's earnings are $15,000. What amount of child care credit can Ted and Wilma claim on a joint return assuming no other income or losses for the year?
   a. $-0-
   b. $480
   c. $504
   d. $900
   e. None of the above

2. Given the same situation as in Question 1, except Wilma's earnings are only $1,500, what is the child care credit Ted and Wilma can claim on a joint return?
   a. $-0-
   b. $315
   c. $504
   d. $420
   e. None of the above

3. Tim is 68 years old and single. He has adjusted gross income of $5,000 and does not receive any social security benefits. What is Tim's tax credit for the elderly?
   a. $-0-
   b. $375
   c. $750
   d. None of the above

4. Given the same situation as in Question 3, except Tim's adjusted gross income is $13,000, what is Tim's elderly tax credit?
   a. $-0-
   b. $750.00
   c. $337.50
   d. None of the above

5. Teri maintains a household for her child, who is 13 years old. Teri's adjusted gross income is $10,000, all from salary. How much is Teri's 1999 earned income credit?
   a. $-0-
   b. $2,312
   c. $3,400
   d. $4,000
   e. Some other amount

6. For 1999, Gray Corporation has $110,000 worth of excess qualified incremental research expenditures. What is Gray's incremental research credit?
   a. -0-
   b. $20,000
   c. $55,000
   d. $22,000
   e. None of the above

7. Bill and Betty have one child, Bobby, who is six years old. Bill's earnings are $15,000 and Betty's are $14,000. Other income includes interest on a savings account at San Diego Federal Savings and Loan of $450. They paid $2,600 to the Tiny Tot Day Care Center to keep Bobby so they could both work. What is their child care credit?
   a. $-0-
   b. $480
   c. $520
   d. $2,600
   e. Some other amount

8. The basic research credit rate is:
   a. 10%
   b. 15%
   c. 20%
   d. 22%
   e. Some other amount

9. Sheila spends $60,000 to rehabilitate a commercial building originally placed in service in 1910. The building is not a certified historic structure. What is Sheila's rehabilitation credit on the building?
   a. $-0-
   b. $6,000
   c. $9,000
   d. $12,000
   e. Some other amount

10. Same as the above question, what is Sheila's rehabilitation credit if the building is a certified historic structure?
    a. $-0-
    b. $6,000
    c. $9,000
    d. $12,000
    e. Some other amount

11. Toni has net earnings from self-employment of $30,000. What is Toni's self-employment tax for 1999?
    a. $4,590.00
    b. $4,238.86
    c. $2,295.00
    d. $1,860.00
    e. Some other amount

12. Tilly has net earnings from self-employment of $90,000. What is Tilly's self-employment tax for 1999?
    a. $11,412.74
    b. $12,716,60
    c. $11,107.80
    d. $13,770.00
    e. Some other amount

13. Tina has net earnings from self-employment of $200,000. What is Tina's self-employment tax for 1999?
    a. $11,107.80
    b. $28,259.10
    c. $14,358.70
    d. $30,600.00
    e. Some other amount

14. Which of the following taxpayers would not be subject to the penalty for the underpayment of estimated tax?
    a. The taxpayer did not have the cash to make the payments
    b. The taxpayer's estimated payments this year exceed his tax liability for the prior year
    c. The taxpayer's CPA forgets to fill out the appropriate forms and send them to the taxpayer
    d. The estimated payments this year are equal to 70% of the current tax liability
    e. None of the above

15. Which of the following forms is the Employer's Annual Federal Unemployment Tax Return?
    a. Form SS-4
    b. W-2
    c. 940 or 940EZ
    d. 941
    e. None of the above

16. Joyce is married and earns a monthly salary of $2,950 in January 1999. If she claims two exemptions, how much must be withheld from her salary using the *wage-bracket tables* found in the text?
    a. $320
    b. $286
    c. $257
    d. $292
    e. Some other amount

17. Adrian is married and earns a salary of $2,950 per month in March 1999. If he claims two exemptions, calculate Adrian's withholding using the *percentage method.*
    a. $263.34
    b. $361.80
    c. $295.05
    d. $375.00

e. Some other amount

18. If backup withholding applies, the payor must withhold at what rate?
 a. 20%
 b. 25%
 c. 28%
 d. 31%

19. In 1999, White, an eligible small business, made $12,000 of capital improvements that qualify for the disabled access credit. What is the amount of White's credit?
 a. $-0-
 b. $5,000
 c. $6,000
 d. $5,875
 e. Some other amount

20. During March 1999, Yellow Corporation incurred the following research expenditures:

In-house	$100,000
Paid to Tech University for research	$60,000

What is the total of Yellow's qualified research expenditures for 1999?
 a. $-0-
 b. $60,000
 c. $139,000
 d. $160,000
 e. Some other amount

21. During 1999, Jan earned $45,000 in wages subject to FICA. Jan also had net earnings of $30,000 from an outside consulting business. Jan sold IBM stock for a gain of $4,000 during the year. What is the amount of Jan's net earnings from self-employment for purposes of determining the Social Security portion of the self-employment tax?
 a. $-0-
 b. $27,600
 c. $30,000
 d. $72,600
 e. Some other amount

22. Which of the following is a refundable credit:
 a. Withholding
 b. Child care credit
 c. Foreign tax credit
 d. Rehabilitation credit
 e. All of the above are refundable

23. Orange Corporation's general business credit for 1999 is $75,000. The net income tax for the year is $125,000 and the tentative AMT is $15,000. Assuming Orange has no other tax credits for the year, the general business credit allowed is:
 a. $15,000
 b. $75,000

c. $100,000
d. $110,000
e. Some other amount

24. Green Corporation's general business credit for 1999 is $75,000. The net income tax for the year is $125,000 and the tentative AMT is $70,000. Assuming Green has no other tax credits for the year, the general business credit allowed is:
a. $70,000
b. $55,000
c. $75,000
d. $110,000
e. Some other amount

25. In 1999, Ray and Michelle pay $2,000 in adoption fees and $5,500 in legal fees to adopt a new baby. How much is their adoption expenses credit?
a. $-0-
b. $2,000
c. $5,000
d. $5,500
e. Some other amount

26. Same as number 25. If Ray and Michelle's AGI is $100,000 for 1999, what is the amount of their adoption expense credit?
a. $-0-
b. $5,000
c. $5,500
d. $1,875
e. Some other amount

27. In May 1999 Green Corporation hired two individuals who are certified as long-term family assistance recipients. Each employee is paid $11,000 in 1999. What is Green's welfare-to-work credit for 1999?
a. $-0-
b. $3,500
c. $7,000
d. $7,700
e. Some other Amount

28. Same as #27. Both employees continue to work in 1999 and are paid $12,000 each. What is Green's welfare-to-work credit for 1999?
a. $-0-
b. $5,000
c. $7,000
d. $10,000
e. Some other Amount

29. Bob and Jane have two children, ages 10 and 12. Their AGI for 1999 is $115,300. What is Bob and Jane's child tax credit?
a. $800
b. $700
c. $300

d. $1,000
e. Some other amount

30. Lew and Martha are married and have AGI of $70,000. The have two children, Bill and Betty. In Fall 1999, Bill started his freshman year of college and Betty was enrolled for her junior year. Bill's qualified tuition expenses were $1,700 and Betty's were $3,000 for the fall semester. Bill and Betty are dependents of Lew and Martha and both are full-time students. What is Lew and Martha's HOPE Credit for 1999?
a. $-0-
b. $1,350
c. $1,500
d. $340
e. Some other amount

31. Same as #30. What is Lew and Martha's Lifetime Learning Credit for 1999?
a. $-0-
c. $1,500
c. $600
d. $1,350
e. Some other amount

32. John is single and has one child who is qualified for the HOPE Credit. In the Fall 1999, John pays $2,400 in tuition for his son to attend college. John's AGI for 1999 is $52,000. What is his Hope Credit for 1999?
a. $-0-
b. $600
c. $900
d. $1,500
e. Some other amount

Problems

1. For 1999, Annette has net earnings from self-employment of $52,000. Use the following worksheet to calculate her SE tax.

1.	Net earnings from self-employment	_______
2.	Multiply line 1 by 92.35%	_______
3.	If line 2 is $68,400 or less, multiply the amount on line 2 by 15.3%	_______
4.	If the amount on line 2 is more than $68,400 multiply the excess over $68,400 by 2.9% and add $10,465.20	_______

2. For 1999, Bridget has net earnings from self-employment of $87,000. Use the following worksheet to calculate her SE tax.

1.	Net earnings from self-employment	_______
2.	Multiply line 1 by 92.35%	_______
3.	If line 2 is $68,400 or less, multiply the amount on line 2 by 15.3%	_______
4.	If the amount on line 2 is more than $68,400 multiply the excess over $68,400 by 2.9% and add $10,465.20	_______

SOLUTIONS TO CHAPTER 13

True or False

1. True $9,500 x 40% = $3,800. (p. 13-15)
2. False The credit is 20%. (p. 13-12)
3. True See footnote #15 (p. 13-13)
4. True (p. 13-7)
5. True (p. 13-15)
6. True (p. 13-15)
7. False Taxpayers 25 to 64 years old do not have to have a qualifying child. (p. 13-16)
8. False The credit is 15 percent. (p. 13-16)
9. False The maximum credit is 30% x $4,800 = $1,440. (p. 13-22)
10. True (p. 13-21)
11. True (p. 13-12)
12. True (p. 13-6)
13. True (p. 13-32)
14. False The wage-bracket method is where the amount is simply looked up using the appropriate table. (p. 13-32)
15. False Employers must deposit employment taxes at least quarterly. (p. 13-35)
16. True (p. 13-36)
17. False Individuals with net earnings from self-employment of $400 or more are subject to the self-employment tax. (p. 13-37)
18. True (p. 13-35)
19. False It is 50% deductible. (p. 13-37)
20. False They are not allowed the credit. (p. 13-12)
21. True $90,000 x 92.35% = $83,114 x 2.9% = $2,410.34. [1999] (p. 13-37)
22. False 15% x [$1,875 - 2($225) - $538] = $133.05. [1999] (p. 13-36)
23. True $20,000 x 30% = $6,000 available FTC.
    $20,000/($57,250 + $2,750 (1999 exemption) + $20,000) x $19,000 = $4,750 Maximum FTC [1999] (p.13- 19)
24. False It is 2 year back and 5 years forward. (p. 13-19)
25. True (p. 13-19)

Fill-in-the-Blanks

1. double (p. 13-18)
2. overall (p. 13-19)
3. $2,400, $4,800 (p. 13-22)
4. $200 (p. 13-22)
5. $72,600, no limit [1999] (p. 13-39)
6. 941 (p. 13-35)
7. 20, 30 (p. 13-22)
8. 20% (p. 13-8)
9. 1, 20 (p. 13-6)
10. refundable, nonrefundable (p. 13-5)
11. 13 (p. 13-21)

Multiple Choice

1.	C	Credit from text: 21% of $2,400 (maximum) = $504. (p. 13-22)
2.	D	28% of $1,500 = $420. (p. 13-22)
3.	C	15% of $5,000 = $750. (p. 13-16)
4.	C	15% of ($5,000 - (($13,000 - 7,500)/2)) = $337.50. (p. 13-17)
5.	B	34% of $6,808 = $2,312. (p. 13-15) [1999]
6.	D	(20% x $110,000) = $22,000. (p. 13-11)
7.	B	$2,400 x 20% = $480. (p. 13-22)
8.	C	(p. 13-12)
9.	B	$60,000 x 10% = $6,000. (p. 13-8)
10.	D	$60,000 x 20% = $12,000. (p. 13-8)
11.	B	$30,000 x 92.35% = $27,705 x 15.3% = $4,238.86 (p. 13-38)
12.	A	$90,000 x 92.35% = $83,115; [($83,115 - $72,600) x 2.9%] + $11,107.80 = $11,412.74. [1999] (p. 13-38)
13.	C	$200,000 x 92.35% = $184,700; [($184,700 - $72,600) x 2.9%] + $11,107.80 = $14,358.70. [1999] (p. 13-38)
14.	B	(p. 13-36)
15.	C	(p. 13-35)
16.	D	See table in text. [1999] (p. 13-33)
17.	C	15% x ($2,950.00 - (2 x $225.00) - $538) = $295.05 [1999] (p. 13-32)
18.	D	(p. 13-35)
19.	B	50% x ($10,250 maximum - $250) = $5,000. (p. 13-14)
20.	C	$100,000 + (65% x $60,000) = $139,000. (p. 13-11)
21.	B	$72,600 - 45,000 = $27,600. [1999] (p. 13-37)
22.	A	(p. 13-5)

23. B

Net income tax	$125,000
Less: the greater of	
$15,000 (tentative AMT), or	
25% x ($125,000 - $25,000)	-25,000
Maximum business credit allowed	100,000
Allowable business credit	$75,000

(p. 13-6)

24. B

Net income tax	$125,000
Less: the greater of	
$70,000 (tentative AMT), or	
25% x ($125,000 - $25,000)	-70,000
Maximum business credit allowed	55,000
Allowable business credit	$55,000

(p. 13-6)

25.	C	$5,000 is the maximum credit. (p. 13-20)
26.	D	$5,000 - [($5,000*($25,000/$40,000))] = $1,875 (p. 13-19)
27.	C	$7,000 = 35% x 10,000 x 2 employees (p. 13-10) [1999]
28.	D	$10,000 = 50% x $10,000 x 2 employees (p. 13-10) [1999]
29.	B	$700 = ($500 x 2) - $300 ($50 for each $1,000 over $110,000) (p. 13-20) [1999]
30.	B	$1,350 = (100% x $1,000) + (50% x $700) Note, Betty is not eligible for the Hope Credit because she is past two years of college. (p. 13-24)

31. C $600 = 20% x $3,000 (p. 13-24)

32. A $-0-, which is a $1,500 credit [(100% x $1,000) + (50% x $1,000)] less a phase out of $1,500 ($52,000 - $40,000)/$10,000 x $1,500]. (p. 13- 24)

Problems

1.	1.	Net earnings from self-employment	$52,000	
	2.	Multiply line 1 by 92.35%	48,022	
	3.	If line 2 is $72,600 or less, multiply the amount on line 2 by 15.3%	$7,347	[1999]
	4.	If the amount on line 2 is more than $72,600 multiply the excess over $72,600 by 2.9% and add $11,107.80	______	
2.	1.	Net earnings from self-employment	87,000	
	2.	Multiply line 1 by 92.35%	80,345	
	3.	If line 2 is $72,600 or less, multiply the amount on line 2 by 15.3%	______	
	4.	If the amount on line 2 is more than $72,600 multiply the excess over $72,600 by 2.9% and add $11,107.80	$11,332.41	[1999]

CHAPTER 14
PROPERTY TRANSACTIONS:
DETERMINATION OF GAIN
OR LOSS AND BASIS CONSIDERATIONS

CHAPTER HIGHLIGHTS

When a taxpayer disposes of property, the following four questions must be answered: (1) Is there a *realized* gain or loss?; (2) If so, is the gain or loss *recognized?; (3)* If the gain or loss is recognized, is it *ordinary or capital?;* and (4) What is the *basis* of any replacement property? This chapter (and the next chapter) deals with the determination of realized and recognized gain or loss and the determination of the basis of replacement property. Chapters 16 and 17 address the classification of gain or loss as either ordinary or capital.

I. DETERMINATION OF GAIN OR LOSS

A. Realized Gain or Loss.

The realized gain or loss is the difference between the amount realized and the adjusted basis of the property.

The term "sale or other disposition" is defined broadly in the tax law. The term includes nearly all dispositions of property such as trade-ins, casualties, condemnations, and bond retirements.

The "amount realized" from the sale or other disposition of property is the sum of money received plus the fair market value of other property received, reduced by the costs of transferring the property. The amount realized includes any liability (including nonrecourse debt) on the property assumed by the buyer.

The "adjusted basis" of the property disposed of is its original cost basis adjusted to the date of disposition. The adjustments consist of adding capital additions and subtracting capital recoveries. Capital additions include the cost of capital improvements and betterments made to the property and amortization of bond discounts. The major capital recoveries are depreciation, certain corporate distributions, and amortization of bond premiums.

The basis in property must be reduced by the amount of any deductible casualty or theft loss. The basis is also reduced by any insurance proceeds received. In addition, if the insurance proceeds result in the recognition of gain, the basis must be increased by the recognized gain.

B. Recognized Gain or Loss. Recognized gain is the amount of the realized gain that is included in the taxpayer's gross income. A recognized loss is deductible for tax purposes. As a rule, the entire gain or loss realized will be recognized unless specific relief is found in the Code.

C. Nonrecognition of Gain or Loss.

In certain cases, realized gain or loss is not recognized for tax purposes. Several such exceptions include nontaxable exchanges, losses on the sale, exchange, or condemnation of personal use assets, gains on the sale of a personal residences, and certain transactions between related parties.

Losses realized on the sale, exchange, or condemnation of personal use property are not recognized for tax purposes, whereas gains realized on such property are generally fully taxable.

D. Recovery of Capital Doctrine.

The recovery of capital doctrine states that a taxpayer is entitled to recover the cost or other basis of property acquired and is not taxed on that amount. The cost of depreciable property is recovered through annual depreciation deductions and the basis is reduced by the amount of the depreciation taken.

The relationship between the recovery of capital doctrine and the concepts of realized and recognized gain or loss can be summarized as follows:

1) A realized gain (or loss) that is never recognized results in the permanent recovery of more (or less) than the taxpayer's cost or other basis for tax purposes.

2) When recognition of a realized gain (or loss) is postponed, a temporary recovery of more (or less) than the taxpayer's cost or other basis results for tax purposes.

II. BASIS CONSIDERATIONS

A. Determination of Cost Basis.

The basis of property is generally its cost, where cost is the amount paid for the property in cash or other property. The basis of property acquired in a "bargain purchase" is its fair market value.
The Regulations require that taxpayers must adequately identify stock that is sold. If the stock cannot be identified, the IRS will assume FIFO for determining the basis of the shares sold.

When a taxpayer acquires multiple assets in a lump-sum purchase, it is necessary to allocate the total cost among the individual assets. This allocation is based on the relative fair market value of the individual assets acquired. Special allocation rules apply when the purchase involves a business with goodwill as one of the assets purchased.

Shares of common or preferred stock received as nontaxable stock dividends must be allocated as part of the basis of the common stock owned. This allocation is done based on relative fair market value.

If a taxpayer receives nontaxable rights to purchase additional stock and the fair market value of the rights is less than 15 percent of the fair market value of the stock with respect to which they were distributed, the basis in the rights is zero unless the taxpayer elects to allocate part of the cost of the stock to the rights. If the value of the rights is 15 percent or more of the fair market value of the stock, then the rights must be allocated as part of the stock's basis using relative fair market values. The holding period of nontaxable rights received includes the holding period of the stock on which the rights were distributed. However, if the rights are exercised, the holding period of the new stock begins the day the rights are exercised.

B. Gift Basis.

When property owned by a taxpayer is received by gift, there is no-cost basis, so a basis must be assigned to the asset. For gifts, the basis for dispositions that result in a gain is the donor's adjusted basis. However, if the property is disposed of at a loss, the basis to the donee is the lower of the donor's adjusted basis or fair market value on the date of the gift. If property is disposed of at an amount that falls between the basis for gain and the basis for loss, no gain or loss is realized. Gift property is called "dual basis" property.

An adjustment to the basis of property acquired by gift may be required for gift tax paid. For gifts before 1977, the full amount of the gift tax is added to the donor's basis up to the fair market value of the property. The following formula is used to calculate the donee's gain basis for gifts after 1976:

Post-1976 Gift Tax Adjustment

Donee's gain basis = donor's adjusted basis +
{unrealized appreciation ÷ fair market value} x gift tax paid

The holding period of property acquired by gift begins on the date the property was acquired by the donor if the gain basis rule applies. Otherwise, if the loss basis rule (FMV) for gifts applies, the holding period starts on the date of the gift.

C. Property Acquired from a Decedent.

The basis of property acquired from a decedent is generally its fair market value at the date of death or the alternate valuation date. The alternate valuation date is six months after the date of death and may be elected only if the value of the gross estate and estate tax liability will be reduced.

The holding period for property acquired from a decedent is always long-term.

The basis of community property at the time of death of one spouse becomes the fair market value of the entire amount of the property, not just the decedent's share.

D. Disallowed Losses.

Under Sec. 267, realized losses from sales or exchanges of property, directly or indirectly, between certain related parties are not recognized. If property is acquired in such a transaction, the basis is the property's cost to the transferee. However, if a subsequent sale or other disposition of the property results in a realized gain, the amount of the gain is reduced by the loss that was previously disallowed. If the original sale involves a personal use asset, any gain realized in a subsequent sale is not reduced by the previously disallowed loss.

The most common related party transactions are those between family members, and those between an individual and a corporation in which the individual owns directly or indirectly more than 50 percent of the stock.

If a taxpayer acquires stock or securities in a "wash sale" under Sec. 1091, any loss on the sale of the stock replaced by the substantially identical stock or securities will be disallowed. The basis in the replacement stock or securities will be the cost plus any disallowed loss. A wash sale occurs when a taxpayer sells or exchanges stock or securities and within 30 days before or after such sale or exchange acquires substantially identical stock or securities. If the taxpayer acquires less than the number of shares sold in a wash sale, any loss must be prorated based on the number of shares acquired relative to the number of shares sold.

A recognized loss on "tax straddles," such as buy and sell orders in the same commodity, is limited to the amount by which the realized loss exceeds any unrealized gain on the offsetting position. Losses that are not recognized are treated as having occurred in the following taxable year.

E. Conversion of Property from Personal to Business or Income-Producing Use.

The basis for loss and depreciation for property converted from personal to business or income-producing use is the lower of the property's adjusted basis or fair market value on the date of conversion. The basis for gain is the adjusted basis on the date of conversion.

Depreciation is calculated for tax purposes using the basis for loss. The basis for gain, however, must also be adjusted for depreciation to determine the gain or loss on disposition.

F. Additional Complexities in Determining Realized Gain or Loss.

Amount realized. Calculating the amount realized on a transaction can be complex. There are numerous positive and negative adjustments that have to be made in arriving at the amount realized. The following are examples of such adjustments:

1) Mortgage(s) assumed by purchaser,

2) Seller's property taxes paid by the purchaser,

3) Broker's commissions, and

4) Points paid by seller.

Adjusted basis. Determining the adjusted basis of property can also be complex. There are many items that cause adjustments to the original basis of property (especially real estate). The following are examples of such adjustments:

1) Depreciation,

2) Recording costs,

3) Title fees,

4) Survey costs,

5) Attorney's fees,

6) Appraisal fees, and

7) Capital improvements.

KEY TERMS

Amount Realized

Adjusted Basis

Gain or Loss Realized

Gain of Loss Recognized

Gift Basis

Disallowed Losses

TEST FOR SELF-EVALUATION

True or False

Indicate which of the following statements are true or false by circling the correct answer.

T F 1. A realized gain and a recognized gain are the same thing.

T F 2. Trade-ins are not dispositions and would not cause a gain or loss to be recognized.

T F 3. The amount realized from a sale or disposition of property includes property received at fair market value.

T F 4. The amount realized from a sale or disposition of property does not include any liability assumed by the buyer.

T F 5. The term, "fair market value," is defined by the courts as the price at which property will change hands between a willing seller and a willing buyer when neither is compelled to sell nor buy.

T F 6. The amount realized is reduced by the costs to transfer the property.

T F 7. The adjusted basis of property is the original basis plus capital recoveries, less capital additions.

T F 8. Depreciation is an example of capital recovery.

T F 9. The tax law assumes all gains that are realized will be recognized unless otherwise stated.

T F 10. A realized loss from the sale or disposition of a personal use asset is not recognized for tax purposes.

T F 11. Under the cost recovery doctrine, a taxpayer may recover the cost of property acquired and will be taxed on that amount.

T F 12. The cost of depreciable property is recovered through annual depreciation deductions.

T F 13. The original basis of property is generally its cost, which is paid for by cash or other property.

T F 14. The basis of property acquired in a bargain purchase is its cost.

T F 15. If stock lots cannot be identified, the Regulations make a LIFO presumption.

T F 16. A lump sum cost is allocated based on relative fair market values of the individual assets acquired.

T F 17. For gifts, the basis to the donee for income tax purposes is the lesser of fair market value at the date of the gift or the donor's adjusted basis, if the gift is later sold for a loss.

T F 18. If stock rights are exercised, the holding period of the newly acquired stock begins with the date the rights are exercised.

T F 19. The basis of property converted to business use is always fair market value on the date of conversion.

T F 20. The wash sale provision applies to both gains and losses.

T F 21. A loss on the sale of stock to which the wash sale provisions apply, will be disallowed if substantially identical stock or securities are acquired within thirty days before or after the date of the sale or exchange.

T F 22. Both the decedent's share and the surviving spouse's share of community property have a basis equal to the fair market value on the date of death.

Fill-in-the-Blanks

Complete the following statements with the appropriate word(s).

1. The basis for loss is the lesser of the donor's adjusted basis or fair ________ value on the date of the gift.

2. For gifts made before 1977, any gift tax paid is __________ to the donor's basis up to the fair market value of the property.

3. For gifts made after 1976, the basis of the gifted property must be increased by the amount of gift taxes paid that are due to the net unrealized _________ of the gifted property.

4. The basis of property acquired from a decedent is its fair market value at the date of__________ or the alternate valuation date.

5. In a wash sale, the realized loss that is not recognized is __________ to the basis of the replacement stock.

6. If property is converted from personal to business or income-producing use, the basis for loss and depreciation is the lesser of the property's adjusted ___________ or fair market value on the date of conversion, while the basis for gain is the adjusted basis on the date of____________.

Multiple Choice

Choose the best answer for each of the following questions.

1. In 1988, Don acquired Texaco stock at a cost of $300,000. This stock was worth $275,000 on the date of Don's death, March 1, 1999. Nine months before Don's death the stock was worth $400,000. The

alternate valuation date is not used. If the securities are sold by Don's heirs, the basis for determining gain or loss is:
a. -0-
b. $275,000
c. $300,000
d. $400,000
e. Some other amount

2. Under the Internal Revenue Code, the holding period for property acquired from a decedent is always:
a. Long-term
b. Short-term
c. Determined by the date acquired by the decedent
d. Determined by the date of death
e. Some other amount

3. On January 2, 1999, Todd converts his house into rental property. The basis of the house is $100,000 and its fair market value on the date of conversion is $88,000. Todd's basis for depreciation is:
a. -0-
b. $88,000
c. $100,000
d. $12,000
e. Some other amount

4. Assume the same situation as in Question 3. Todd's basis for gain in the event the property is later sold would be:
a. $88,000 less any depreciation
b. $100,000 less any depreciation
c. $88,000 with no depreciation allowed
d. Some other amount

5. Assume the same situation as in Question 3. Todd's basis for loss in the event the property is later sold would be:
a. $88,000 less any depreciation
b. $60,000 less any depreciation
c. $60,000
d. Some other amount

6. On July 1, 1999, Ted sells 100 shares of Green, Inc. stock (basis of $4,000) for $3,500. On July 18, 1999, he purchases 50 shares for $1,800. Ted's recognized loss on the sale is:
a. -0-
b. $500
c. $250
d. Some other amount

7. Assume the same situation as in Question 6. Ted's basis in the 50 shares purchased on July 18, 1999, would be:
a. -0-
b. $1,800
c. $2,300

d. $2,050
e. Some other amount

8. John Deaux of Lake Charles, Louisiana, sold common stock acquired two years ago to his brother, Don, at the current market price of $6,000. John's basis in the stock is $8,000. He should report:
a. Neither a gain nor a loss
b. A long-term capital loss of $2,000
c. An ordinary loss of $2,000
d. A short-term capital loss of $2,000
e. A Sec. 1231 gain of $2,000

9. Assume the same situation as in Question 8. The stock market recovered rapidly and later Don Deaux sold the stock to an unrelated third party for $9,000. His recognized gain would be:
a. -0-
b. $3,000
c. $1,000
d. $2,000
e. Some other amount

10. During 1999, Tim received a gift of property with a fair market value of $8,000. The property had an adjusted basis to the donor of $8,500. There was no gift tax paid on the transfer. If Tim sold the property for $8,700, the gain or (loss) would be:
a. $200
b. $700
c. $500
d. Some other amount

11. Assume the same situation as in Question 10, except the property is sold for $7,500. What is the gain or (loss)?
a. $500 gain
b. $500 loss
c. $1,000 loss
d. Some other amount

12. Assume the same situation as in Question 10, except that the property is sold for $8,200. What is the gain or (loss)?
a. No gain or loss
b. $300 loss
c. $200 gain
d. Some other amount

13. Tony sells his house with a basis of $40,000 for $50,000 in cash. The buyer assumes Tony's mortgage of $60,000. The amount of gain realized on this transaction is:
a. -0-
b. $10,000
c. $20,000
d. $70,000
e. Some other amount

14. Tina buys an automobile from her employer for $8,000. The fair market value of the car is $12,000 and its basis to the employer is $14,000. Tina's basis in the automobile is:
    a. $4,000
    b. $8,000
    c. $12,000
    d. $14,000
    e. Some other amount

15. Andrew sells real estate to Lupe for $100,000 cash and Lupe assumed Andrew's mortgage of $225,000. Andrew paid brokers' commissions of $19,000 and points of $6,000. What is Andrew's amount realized?
    a. $100,000
    b. $325,000
    c. $306,000
    d. $300,000

16. An asset used in a trade or business is damaged by a fire. The adjusted basis of the asset before the fire is $25,000 and the fair market value is $15,000 after the fire. No insurance proceeds are received. The amount of the casualty loss deduction is $10,000. What is the adjusted basis of the asset after the fire?
    a. -0-
    b. $10,000
    c. $15,000
    d. $25,000
    e. Some other amount.

17. Van purchases a rental house and land for $90,000 in a depressed real estate market. Appraisals place the value of the house at $70,000 and the land at $30,000 (a total of $100,000). What is Van's basis in the house?
    a. $63,000
    b. $70,000
    c. $90,000
    d. $100,000
    e. Some other amount.

18. On March 1, 1999, Ming received a gift of stock having a donor's adjusted basis of $60,000 at the date of the gift. At the date of the gift, the fair market value (FMV) of the property was $50,000. Ming sold the property for $56,000 on August 1, 1999. If no gift tax was paid on the transfer, how much gain or loss should Ming report for 1999?
    a. No gain or loss
    b. $6,000 short-term capital gain
    c. $4,000 short-term capital loss
    d. $4,000 ordinary loss
    e. None of the above

19. Laura exchanged an old machine used in her business for a new machine to be used in her business. Laura is self-employed. Information on this transaction is as follows:

Original cost of old machine	$25,000
Adjusted basis of old machine	15,000
FMV of new machine	29,000

Cash payment by Laura	$12,000

What is the amount of ***gain or loss realized*** by Laura on this exchange?
a. $-0-
b. $2,000 gain
c. $2,000 loss
d. $9,000 gain
e. Some other amount

20. Edgar died this year leaving his entire estate to his son, Elmer. The executor of Edgar's estate elected to use the alternative valuation date. Edgar's estate contained stock in the Green Corporation that has a basis to Edgar of $300,000. The stock was distributed to Elmer four months after Edgar's death. The fair market value (FMV) of the stock on various dates was:

FMV on date of death	$425,000
FMV on date of distribution	$390,000
FMV on six months after death	$410,000

Elmer's basis in the distributed stock is:
a. $-0-
b. $300,000
c. $390,000
d. $410,000
e. $425,000

21. On March 1, 1999, Oscar learned that he was bequeathed 1,000 shares of Blue Corporation common stock under the will of his uncle. The uncle had paid $5,000 for the Blue stock in 1988. The fair market value of the Blue stock on March 1, 1999, the date of the uncle's death, was $8,000. Oscar sold the Blue stock for $9,000 on May 1, 1999, the date that the executor distributed the stock to him. Oscar's gain or loss on the sale of the Blue Company stock is:
a. $-0-
b. $1,000
c. $3,000
d. $4,000
e. Some other amount

22. Refer to question number 21. Oscar should treat the sale of the 1,000 shares of Blue stock as a:
a. Ordinary gain or loss
b. Sec. 1231 gain or loss
c. Short-term capital gain or loss
d. Long-term capital gain or loss
e. None of above.

23. Tim owns land with an adjusted basis of $100,000 (subject to a mortgage of $50,000). On May 1, 1999, Tim sells the land for $200,000 in cash, a note for $300,000, and property with a fair market value of $60,000. The $50,000 mortgage is assumed by the purchaser. What is the amount realized from this transaction?
a. $500,000
b. $550,000

c. $560,000
d. $610,000
e. Some other amount

24. The bank forecloses on Kay's office building. The property had been pledged as security on a nonrecourse mortgage, whose principal amount at the date of foreclosure is $600,000. The adjusted basis of the office building is $350,000 and the fair market value is $500,000. What is Kay's recognized gain or loss?
a. $-0-
b. $100,000
c. $250,000
d. $150,000
e. Some other amount

25. Lucy owns City of San Diego bonds with a face amount of $10,000. Lucy purchased the bonds on January 1, 1999, for $12,000. The maturity date is December 31, 2002, (five years later). Assuming annual amortization of the bond premium is $400 and the annual interest rate on the bonds is 8 percent, what is Lucy's adjusted basis in the bonds as of the end of 1999?
a. $10,000
b. $10,400
c. $11,600
d. $12,000
e. Some other amount

26. Ginny was given a residence in 1975 which she still owns. At the time of the gift, the residence had an adjusted basis to the donor of $100,000 and a fair market value of $250,000. The donor paid gift tax of $15,000 on the gift. What is Ginny's basis for gain in the residence?
a. $100,000
b. $109,000
c. $115,000
d. $250,000
e. Some other amount

27. Olga was given Black Company stock in 1999. At the time of the gift, the stock had an adjusted basis to the donor of $100,000 and a fair market value of $250,000. The donor paid gift tax of $15,000 on the gift. What is Olga's basis for gain in the Black Company stock?
a. $100,000
b. $109,000
c. $115,000
d. $250,000
e. Some other amount

Problem

Lisa purchased a new house three years ago. The purchase price and related items (all paid by Lisa) were as follows:

Purchase price (new house)	$180,000
Title fees	700

Recording fees	300
Survey fees	1,000
Appraisal fees	250
Escrow fees	$500

Two years ago, Lisa added a new room onto the house at a cost of $27,000. She also deducted $2,000 in depreciation on her home office and other home office expenses of $3,500. Her real estate taxes on the house to date are $9,500. What is Lisa's adjusted basis in the house?

SOLUTIONS TO CHAPTER 14

True or False

1.	False	"Recognized" is a term used for tax purposes only and refers to the amount of realized gain that is included in gross income or the amount of realized loss that is deductible for tax purposes. (p. 14-6)
2.	False	Trade-ins are dispositions. (p. 14-3)
3.	True	(p. 14-3)
4.	False	Liabilities are included in determining the amount realized. (p. 14-3)
5.	True	(p. 14-3)
6.	True	(p. 14-4)
7.	False	The adjusted basis is the original basis less capital recoveries, plus capital additions. (p. 14-4)
8.	True	(p. 14-5)
9.	True	(p. 14-6)
10.	True	(p. 14-7)
11.	False	Taxpayers are not taxed on the recovery of the cost or other basis of property. (p. 14-8)
12.	True	(p. 14-8)
13.	True	(p. 14-8)
14.	False	The basis of property acquired in a bargain purchase is FMV. (p. 14-9)
15.	False	The Regulations assume FIFO. (p. 14-9)
16.	True	(p. 14-9)
17.	True	(p. 14-12)
18.	True	(p. 14-12)
19.	False	The basis (for loss) of converted property is the lesser of the property's adjusted basis or FMV on the date of conversion. (p. 14-20)
20.	False	The wash sale provision only applies to losses. (p. 14-19)
21.	True	(p. 14-19)
22.	True	(p. 14-16)

Fill-in-the-Blanks

1. market (p. 14-12)
2. added (p. 14-14)
3. appreciation (p. 14-13)
4. death (p. 14-15)
5. added (p. 14-19)
6. basis, conversion (p. 14-20)

Multiple Choice

1.	B	(p. 14-15)
2.	A	(p. 14-17)
3.	B	The basis for depreciation is the lesser of the adjusted basis or FMV on the date of conversion. (p. 14-20)
4.	B	(p. 14-20)
5.	A	(p. 14-20)

6.	C	\$3,500 - 4,000 = (\$500), less 50% wash sale = (\$250) loss allowed. (p. 14-19)
7.	D	\$1,800 + 250 = \$2,050. (p. 14-19)
8.	A	(p. 14-17)
9.	C	\$9,000 - 6,000 = \$3,000, less (2,000) disallowed loss = 1,000 recognized gain. (p. 14-18)
10.	A	\$8,700 - 8,500 = \$200. (p. 14-12)
11.	B	\$7,500 - 8,000 = (\$500). (p. 14-12)
12.	A	(p. 14-12)
13.	D	\$50,000 + 60,000 - 40,000 = \$70,000. (p. 14-3)
14.	C	(p. 14-9)
15.	D	\$100,000 + \$225,000 - \$19,000 - \$6,000 = \$300,000. (p. 14-21)
16.	C	\$25,000 - 10,000 = \$15,000. (p. 14-5)
17.	A	(\$70,000 ÷ \$100,000) x \$90,000 = \$63,000. (p. 14-9)
18.	A	(p. 14-13)
19.	B	\$29,000 - (\$15,000 + \$12,000) = \$2,000 gain realized. (p. 14-3)
20.	C	The basis is the FMV six months after decedent's death unless the stock was distributed earlier, as in this question. (p. 14-15).
21.	B	(p. 14-15)
22.	D	(p. 14-17)

23. D

Cash received	\$200,000	
Note	300,000	
Property received	60,000	
Mortgage assumed by purchaser	50,000	
Total	\$610,000	(p. 14-3)

24. C

Amount realized (mortgage)	\$600,000
Less: Adjusted basis	-350,000
Realized gain	\$250,000
Recognized gain	\$250,000 (p. 14-3)

25. C

Cost of bonds	\$12,000	
Less: 1999 amortization	-400	
Basis at end of 1999	\$11,600	(p. 14-6)

26. C \$115,000 = \$100,000 + \$15,000. (p. 14-14)

27. B \$109,000 = \$100,000 + (\$150,000 ÷ 250,000 x \$15,000). (p. 14-13)

Problem

Purchase price (new house)	\$180,000
Title fees	+700
Recording fees	+300
Survey fees	+1,000
Appraisal fees	+250
Escrow fees	+500
New room	+27,000
Home office depreciation	-2,000
Adjusted basis	\$207,750

CHAPTER 15
PROPERTY TRANSACTIONS: NONTAXABLE EXCHANGES

CHAPTER HIGHLIGHTS

Realized gains and losses arising from certain exchanges are not recognized for tax purposes. In general, new property is viewed as a continuation of an old investment, so the taxpayer is in the same relative economic position. The recognition of gain or loss is postponed until the property received in the exchange is disposed of in a taxable transaction. This chapter discusses several major types of transactions that receive nontaxable exchange treatment. Chapter 20 covers nontaxable contributions for partnership or corporate formation.

I. LIKE-KIND EXCHANGES – Section 1031

Under Sec. 1031, gain or loss on a like-kind exchange will not be recognized if property held for investment or for productive use in a trade or business is exchanged for like-kind property. This provision is mandatory rather than elective.

A. Like-Kind Property. The term like-kind is intended to be interpreted broadly. However, the following three general limitations are placed on what qualifies as like-kind property:

1) livestock involved in an exchange must be of the same sex

2) realty must be exchanged for realty

3) personalty must be exchanged for personalty

Real property includes rental buildings, office and store buildings, manufacturing plants, and land. Personalty consists primarily of machines, equipment, trucks, automobiles, furniture, and fixtures. Exchanges of real property located in the United States and foreign real property is not considered like-kind property.

If the exchange involves a multiple asset business (e.g., a car dealership for a car dealership) the determination of whether assets qualify as like-kind will not be made at business level, instead the underlying assets must be evaluated.

Also, depreciable personalty used in a business must be exchanged for property within the same *general business class* or the *same product class*. Examples of general business classes are:

1) Office furniture, fixtures, and equipment

2) Information systems (computers and peripheral equipment)

3) Airplanes

4) Automobiles and taxis

5) Buses

6) Light general-purpose trucks

7) Heavy general-purpose trucks

B. Exchange Requirement. To qualify for the like-kind treatment, property must be part of an exchange not a sale and repurchase. In certain situations, taxpayers may want to avoid Sec. 1031 in order to receive a higher basis for depreciation purposes, to recognize a realized loss, or to recognize a gain that will receive favorable capital gain treatment or be available to offset passive activity losses.

C. Boot. On a like-kind exchange, gain realized will be recognized to the extent of boot received. However, the receipt of boot will not trigger the recognition of a realized loss. If boot is given, gain or loss is recognized only if the boot is appreciated or depreciated property.

D. Basis of Property Received. The basis of like-kind property received is equal to the fair market value of the like-kind property reduced by any postponed gain or increased by any postponed loss. Alternatively the basis may be determined by the following formula.

Adjusted basis of like-kind property surrendered
+Adjusted basis of boot given
+Gain recognized
–Fair market value of boot received
–Loss recognized
=Basis of like-kind property received

The holding period of the property surrendered in the exchange carries over and "tacks on" to the holding period of the like-kind property received. Depreciation recapture potential also carries over to the property received.

The amount of any liability assumed by the transferee is treated as boot received by the transferor and boot given by the transferee.

II. INVOLUNTARY CONVERSIONS- Section 1033

A. General Scheme. Under Sec. 1033, a taxpayer who suffers an involuntary conversion may postpone the recognition of *gain* realized from the conversion if certain conditions are met. In general, gain is recognized to the extent that the amount realized is not reinvested in replacement property.

B. Involuntary Conversion Defined. An involuntary conversion is the result of destruction (complete or partial), theft, seizure, requisition, condemnation, or the sale or exchange under threat or imminence of requisition or condemnation of the taxpayer's property. Most involuntary conversions are casualties or condemnations.

C. Computing the Amount Realized. The amount realized from a condemnation of property usually includes only the amount received as compensation for the property. It does not generally include amounts designated as severance damages that usually occur when only part of the property is condemned.

D. Replacement Property. The replacement property for an involuntary conversion must be similar or related in service or use to the property involuntarily converted. To qualify, owner-investors must meet the taxpayer use test and owner-users must pass the functional use test for replacement property. Business or investment real property that is condemned is subject to the broader replacement rules for like-kind exchanges, which means that the taxpayer has more flexibility in selecting replacement property.

E. Time Limitation on Replacement. A taxpayer normally has two years after the close of the tax year in which any gain is realized to replace the property. For condemnations of trade or investment real property the taxpayer has three years instead of two.

F. Nonrecognition of Gain. If the conversion is directly into replacement property then the nonrecognition of gain is mandatory. The taxpayer's basis in the converted property carries over to the new property.

If the conversion is into money, a taxpayer may elect to postpone the gain or the gain may be recognized. If the election to postpone gain is made by the taxpayer, gain still must be recognized to the extent the amount realized exceeds the cost of replacement property. The basis of the replacement property purchased is its cost less any postponed gain. The holding period includes that of the converted property if postponement of the gain is elected.

Sec. 1033 does not modify the general rules for loss recognition. Therefore losses from involuntary conversions of business or income producing property are recognized, whereas conversion losses (other than casualty losses) related to personal use assets are not recognized.

G. Involuntary Conversion of a Personal Residence. An involuntary conversion of a personal residence can have several tax treatments. In a loss situation, if the conversion is a condemnation, the loss realized is not recognized. If the conversion is a casualty, the taxpayer may recognize the loss subject to the personal casualty loss limitations. In a gain situation, if the conversion is a casualty, theft, or condemnation, the gain can be postponed under Sec. 1033 or excluded under Sec. 121.

H. Reporting Considerations. Supporting details should be included with the taxpayer's return in the year a gain is realized and in the year the property is replaced. If the property is not replaced within the time allotted, or it is replaced at a lower cost than anticipated, an amended return must be filed for the year the gain was realized.

III. SALE OF A RESIDENCE

Under Sec. 121, there are special rules for the taxation of gains on the sale of a personal residence. In general, the first $250,000 ($500,000 on a joint return) of gain realized is not recognized. Also, since a residence is a personal use asset, any realized loss is not recognized.

A. Requirements for Exclusion. In order to get the exclusion, the residence must have been owned and used by the taxpayer as a principal residence for at least two years of the five-year period ending on the date of sale. Note that the residence does not have to be the taxpayer's personal residence on the date of sale. Taxpayers are allowed this exclusion once each two years. The two-year requirement is waived if:

1) There is a change in place of employment of the taxpayer

2) The personal residence is sold for health reasons

3) There are unforeseen circumstances as prescribed by the Regulations.

B. Calculation of the Exclusion. The exclusion is available for up to $250,000 of realized gain. Realized gain is calculated in the normal manner (i.e., amount realized less adjusted basis). The amount realized (sales proceeds) is net of such items as advertising the property for sale, real estate commissions, legal fees, loan placement fees, and closing costs. Repairs and maintenance made by the seller as an aid to selling the property are not treated as selling expenses or as an adjustment to the adjusted basis of the residence.

If a married couple files a joint return, the $250,000 is increased to $500,000 if the following requirements are met:

1) One spouse meets the at-least-two-year ownership requirement.

2) Both spouses meet the at-least-two-year use requirement

3) Neither spouse is ineligible for the exclusion because of the sale of another principal residence within the prior two years.

The basis of the new residence is the cost of the new residence since this provision is an exclusion and not a deferral of the gain.

If a taxpayer uses one of the relief provisions (e.g., an employment location change) the gain exclusion is treated on a prorated basis for the number of months the property qualified for the exclusion.

C. Principal Residence. A principal residence does not have to be a house. It can be a house trailer, houseboat, condo, etc.

IV. OTHER NONRECOGNITION PROVISIONS

A. Exchanges of Stock for Property - Sec. 1032. No gain or loss is recognized by a corporation dealing in its own stock, including treasury stock.

B. Certain Exchanges of Insurance Policies - Sec. 1035. Under Sec. 1035 of the Code certain insurance contracts qualify for nonrecognition of gain or loss when exchanged.

C. Exchange of Stock for Stock of the Same Corporation - Sec. 1036. No gain or loss is recognized by a shareholder from the exchange of common stock for common stock, or preferred stock for preferred stock of the same corporation. An exchange of common stock for preferred stock is generally a taxable event.

D. Certain Reacquisitions of Real Property - Sec. 1038. When property sold on the installment basis is repossessed only limited gain may be recognized and no loss is recognized.

E. Transfers of Property Between Spouses Incident to Divorce - Sec. 1041. Transfers of property between spouses or former spouses incident to divorce or between spouses during marriage are nontaxable events. The basis of the property is carried over to the recipient.

F. Rollover of Publicly Traded Securities Gain into Specialized Small Business Investment Companies - Sec. 1044. Gain on the sale of securities is not recognized if the amount realized is invested in a specialized small business investment company (SSBIC). The proceeds must be reinvested within 30 days in order to qualify for nonrecognition treatment. The basis of the SSBIC stock must be reduced by the gain not recognized.

G. Rollover of Gain from Qualified Small Business Stock into another Qualified Small Business Stock- Sec. 1045. Realized gain from qualified small business stock held more than six months may be postponed if the taxpayers acquires other qualified small business stock within 60 days.

KEY TERMS:

Boot

Like-Kind Exchanges

Involuntary Conversions

Nontaxable Exchange

Replacement Period

Section 121 Exclusion on Sale of a Residence

Transfers Pursuant to Divorce

TEST FOR SELF-EVALUATION

True or False

Indicate which of the following statements are true or false by circling the correct answer.

T F 1. Raw land held for investment does not qualify for a Sec. 1031 like-kind exchange.

T F 2. A store building could be exchanged for a delivery truck and qualify for a like-kind exchange.

T F 3. In a like-kind exchange, gain realized will be recognized to the extent boot is received.

T F 4. The Sec. 1031 like-kind exchange provision is elective, not mandatory.

T F 5. If a liability is assumed in a like-kind exchange, it will be treated as boot given by the party assuming the liability.

T F 6. The holding period of like-kind property received begins on the day the exchange takes place.

T F 7. The involuntary conversion provisions under Sec. 1033 apply to gains and not to losses.

T F 8. The Sec. 1033 involuntary conversion provision is always elective.

T F 9. In an involuntary conversion, realized gain is recognized to the extent that the proceeds are not reinvested in property that is similar or related in service or use.

T F 10. Sec. 1033 applies to condemnation payments if they are designated as severance damages.

T F 11. Owner-investors must conform to the functional use test to postpone gain under Sec. 1033.

T F 12. To qualify for nonrecognition of gain under Sec. 1033, taxpayers have two years from the date property is involuntarily converted to replace it.

T F 13. Under Sec. 121 a principal residence does not have to be a house.

T F 14. A loss on the sale of a personal residence is recognized as a capital loss to the taxpayer if the residence was used for as a principal residence for two of the five prior years.

T F 15. The amount realized on the sale of a personal residence would include real estate commission, but not legal fees.

T F 16. The exclusion is $500,000 for a married couple filing a joint return, if they meet certain ownership and use requirements.

T F 17. If a taxpayer and spouse each own a qualifying principal residence, they can separately qualify for the $250,000 exclusion on the sale of their own residence, even if they file a joint return.

T F 18. In order to qualify for the $250,000 exclusion on the sale of a principal residence, the taxpayer must live in the residence on the date of sale.

T F 19. If Sec. 1031 does not apply to a transaction, the end result of an exchange may be the recognition of capital gain in exchange for a lower basis in a newly acquired asset.

T F 20. Taxpayers should try to avoid Sec. 1031 treatment when the adjusted basis of the property being disposed of exceeds the fair market value.

Fill-in-the-Blanks

Complete the following statements with the appropriate word(s) or amount(s).

1. In order to get the exclusion, the residence must have been owned and used by the taxpayer as a principal residence for at least ________ years of the five-year period ending on the date of sale.

2. The basis of like-kind property received in an exchange is the property's fair market value less the postponed _________ .

3. Under Sec. 1033 the replacement property must be _________ or _________ in service or use to the involuntarily converted property.

4. For involuntary conversions, the taxpayer normally has a _______ year period after the close of the tax year in which any gain is realized to replace the property.

5. In a Sec. 1031 exchange, if a taxpayer assumes a liability or takes property subject to a liability, the amount of the liability is treated as _______ given.

Multiple Choice

Choose the best answer for each of the following questions.

1. During the current year, Tim and Xavier exchange real estate investments. Tim gives up property with an adjusted basis of $250,000 (fair market value of $300,000) which is subject to a mortgage of $50,000 (assumed by Xavier). In return for this property, Tim receives property with a fair market value of $225,000 and $25,000 cash. What is Tim's realized gain?
   a. $-0-
   b. $50,000
   c. $75,000
   d. $100,000
   e. Some other amount

2. Assuming the same situation as in Question 1, what is Tim's recognized gain on the exchange?

a. $-0-
b. $50,000
c. $75,000
d. $100,000
e. Some other amount

3. Assuming the same situation as in Question 1, what is Tim's basis in the new property?
a. $225,000
b. $250,000
c. $275,000
d. Some other amount

4. Tom's building, which has an adjusted basis of $100,000, is destroyed by fire in 1999. During 1999, Tom receives $250,000 of insurance proceeds for the loss. Tom invests $160,000 in a qualified replacement building. By what date must Tom make a new investment to come within the nonrecognition provision of Sec. 1033?
a. December 31, 1999
b. December 31, 2000
c. December 31, 2001
d. December 31, 2002
e. None of the above

5. Assuming the same situation as in Question 5 and assuming the replacement building is acquired within the required period, what is Tom's realized gain on the involuntary conversion?
a. $-0-
b. $90,000
c. $60,000
d. $150,000
e. Some other amount

6. Assuming the same situation as in Question 5 and assuming the replacement building is acquired within the required period, what is Tom's recognized gain on the involuntary conversion providing Tom elects to be covered by Sec. 1033?
a. $-0-
b. $150,000
c. $90,000
d. $60,000
e. Some other amount

7. Teri is 60 years old and sells her personal residence for $180,000 (adjusted basis of $50,000). Under Sec. 121, she would have a recognized gain of:
a. $-0-
b. $5,000
c. $130,000
d. $55,000
e. Some other amount

8. Tom is 40 years old and sells his personal residence for $380,000 (adjusted basis of $50,000). Under Sec. 121, he would have a recognized gain of:

a. $-0-
b. $80,000
c. $330,000
d. $380,000
e. Some other amount

9. Which of the following exchanges would not qualify for like-kind exchange treatment under Sec. 1031?
a. Land held as an investment is exchanged for a rental house
b. A light-duty Ford business truck is exchanged for a light-duty Dodge business truck
c. A personal automobile is exchanged for a business automobile
d. A computer is exchanged for a laser printer, both are used in a business
e. All of the above would qualify

10. Three years ago Ted acquired a capital asset for $10,000. The asset is worth $20,000 today. This property was exchanged for another capital asset worth $20,000 in a qualified Sec. 1031 exchange. Five months later the new property was sold for $28,000. On this latest sale Ted should report:
a. $10,000 long-term capital gain
b. $10,000 short-term capital gain
c. $18,000 long-term capital gain
d. $8,000 short-term capital gain
e. None of the above

11. Sec. 1031, the like-kind exchange provision, applies to both gains and losses, and the Sec. 1033 involuntary conversion provision applies to:
a. Gains only
b. Losses only
c. Gains and losses
d. Capital gains only
e. None of the above

12. Indicate which of the following would not qualify for involuntary conversion treatment under Sec. 1033:
a. A personal residence burns down
b. Inventory damaged by a flood
c. A taxpayer sells his house because it is on a flood plain
d. None of the above

13. The Sec. 1033 involuntary conversion provision is:
a. Always elective
b. Never elective
c. Mandatory for direct conversions
d. Mandatory for conversions into money
e. None of the above

14. Which of the following does not qualify as a selling expense under Sec. 121?
a. Title transfer fees
b. Painting a house to make it ready for sale
c. Real estate commissions
d. Advertising the property for sale
e. All of the above qualify

15. Audrey sold her personal residence this year for $275,000. The residence was purchased ten years ago for $175,000. The following expenses relating to the sale were:

Advertising for sale	$3,000
Broker commissions	6,000
Title fees	2,000
Painting inside of house	3,000
Wallpaper bathrooms	1,000
New hot tub	$7,000

The painting, wallpaper and new hot tub expenses were incurred (and paid for) four weeks prior to the contract for sale. Audrey bought a new residence for $255,000. What is Audrey's realized gain?

a. $-0-
b. $275,000
c. $100,000
d. $82,000
e. Some other amount

16. In 1999, John, who is single, sells his personal residence (adjusted basis of $150,000) for $310,000. He has lived in the residence for four years. John's selling expenses are $20,000 and three weeks prior to sale he paid a carpenter and a painter $3,000 to make repairs and paint the bathrooms. What is John's recognized gain?

a. $-0-
b. $137,000
c. $140,000
d. $290,000
e. Some other amount

17. Ray transfers stock to his ex-wife in a divorce settlement. The stock has a basis to Ray of $70,000 and a fair market value of $120,000 on the date of the transfer. From this transaction Ray should recognize a gain of:

a. $-0-
b. $50,000
c. $70,000
d. $120,000
e. Some other amount.

18. In the current year, Ron exchanged an office building having a fair market value of $400,000, for cash of $100,000 plus another office building having a fair market value of $300,000. Ron's adjusted basis for the office building given up in the exchange was $230,000. How much gain should Ron recognize on his income tax return?

a. $-0-
b. $100,000
c. $170,000
d. $330,000
e. Some other amount

19. Under IRS Regulations, in order for depreciable tangible property to qualify for like-kind exchange treatment under Sec. 1031, the property must be:
   a. in the same general business asset class or the same product class
   b. held for at least five years prior to the exchange
   c. similar in service or use
   d. functionally similar
   e. None of the above

20. Part of a taxpayer's land (basis $50,000, FMV $90,000) is condemned to build a new state building. Another part of the land is rendered useless by the condemnation. The taxpayer receives $15,000 in *severance damages* for the condemnation. What is the taxpayer's basis in the land?
   a. $-0-
   b. $35,000
   c. $50,000
   d. $75,000
   e. Some other amount

21. During 1999, Brown Corporation sold 2,000 ($10 par value) shares of its treasury stock for $50,000. The stock was acquired five years ago for $30,000. The stock was originally issued for $20 per share. How much is Brown Corporation's recognized gain from this sale of stock?
   a. $-0-
   b. $10,000
   c. $20,000
   d. $30,000
   e. Some other amount

22. Hom exchanges a rental cottage at the beach with an adjusted basis of $90,000 and a FMV of $80,000 for a rental condo in the mountains with a FMV of $60,000 plus cash of $20,000. What (if any) is Hom's recognized gain or loss on this like-kind exchange?
   a. $-0-
   b. $10,000
   c. ($10,000)
   d. ($20,000)
   e. Some other amount

23. Joey sells his Ford Motor Company stock for $20,000. His basis in the Ford stock was $14,000. If Joey reinvests (within 60 days) the $20,000 in specialized small business investment company (SSBIC) stock, his taxable gain on the sale would be?
   a. $-0-
   b. $6,000
   c. $4,500
   d. $3,000
   e. Some other amount

24. Bob lives in Houston and sells his personal residence on September 1, 1998 with a realized gain of $200,000 which is excluded under Sec. 121. He purchased a new (second) residence on September 2, 1998 for $275,000. Bob's employer transfers him to San Diego, in July 1999. Bob sells the second Houston residence on July 2, 1999 and has a realized gain of $60,000. He purchases a third residence

in San Diego for $325,000. How much of the Sec. 121 exclusion is Bob allowed on the sale of the second residence within a two-year period?
a. $-0-
b. $25,000
c. $50,000
d. $60,000
e. Some other amount

25. Devona sells her personal residence for a realized gain of $450,000. She has owned and lived in the residence for six years. Devona is married to Norval who has lived in the residence since they were married one year ago. Norval sold his principal residence in order to move in with Devona on the date of their marriage. He used a $150,000 Sec. 121 exclusion when he sold his residence. How much is Devona's taxable gain on the sale of her principal residence if she files a joint return with Norval?
a. $-0-
b. $200,000
c. $250,000
d. $450,000
e. Some other amount

26. In the current year, Paula sells her principle residence, which qualifies for the Sec. 121 exclusion. Her realized gain is $100,000. For the last nine years, she rented a room to a college in the house. The total MACRS cost recovery Paula claimed on the room rental was $15,000. What is Paula's recognized gain on the sale of her personal residence?
a. $-0-
b. $15,000
c. $85,000
d. $100,000
e. Some other amount

SOLUTIONS TO CHAPTER 15

True or False

1. False Realty held for investment would qualify for a like-kind exchange. (p.15-4)
2. False Real estate cannot be exchanged for personal property. (p. 15-4)
3. True (p. 15-6)
4. False Sec. 1031 is not elective. (p. 15-3)
5. True (p. 15-8)
6. False The holding period of the newly acquired property begins on the date the original property was acquired. (p. 15-7)
7. True (p. 15-9)
8. False For direct conversions into replacement property, Sec. 1033 is mandatory. (p. 15-13)
9. True (p. 15-9)
10. False Sec. 1033 does not apply to amounts designated as severance damages. (p. 15-10)
11. False Owner-investors must conform to the taxpayer use test. (p. 15-12)
12. False Taxpayers have until two years after the close of the tax year in which gain was realized. (p. 15-12)
13. True (p.15-20)
14. False Losses are not recognized on the sale of a personal residence. (p. 15-15)
15. False Both real estate commissions and legal fees would be included. (p. 15-17)
16. True (p. 15-18)
17. True (p. 15-18)
18. False The taxpayer does not have to live in the residence on the date of sale. (p. 15-16)
19. False There will be a higher (not lower) basis. (p. 15-24)
20. True (p. 15-24)

Fill-in-the-Blanks

1. two (p. 15-16)
2. gain (p. 15-7)
3. similar, related (p. 15-12)
4. two (p. 15-13)
5. boot (p. 15-8)

Multiple Choice

1. B $225,000 + 25,000 + 50,000 - 250,000 = $50,000. (p. 15-6)
2. B Lesser of gain realized, $50,000, or boot received, $75,000. (p. 15-6)
3. A $250,000 + zero + 50,000 - 75,000 = $225,000. (p. 15-7)
4. C (p. 15-12)
5. D $250,000 - 100,000 = $150,000. (p. 15-11)
6. C $250,000 - 160,000 = $90,000. (p. 15-11)
7. A The is no gain recognized under $250,000. (p. 15-15)
8. B $380,000 - $50,000 - $250,000 = $80,000 (p. 15-15)
9. C (p. 15-3)
10. C $28,000 - 10,000 = $18,000 LTCG. (p. 15-7)

11.	A	(p. 15-9)		
12.	C	(p. 15-9)		
13.	C	(p. 15-13)		
14.	B	(p. 15-17)		
15.	D	Selling Price	$275,000	
		Selling Expenses	-11,000	
		Amount Realized	264,000	
		Adjusted Basis	-182,000	
		Gain Realized	82,000	(P. 15-17)
16.	A	Amount realized ($310,000 -$20,000)	$290,000	
		Adjusted Basis	-150,000	
		Realized Gain	140,000	
		Exclusion	-$140,000	
		Recognized gain	$-0-	(p. 15-17)

17. A The transfer is nontaxable. (p. 15-22)
18. B Gain is recognized to the extent of boot received. (p. 15-6)
19. A (p. 15-5)
20. B $50,000 - 15,000 = $35,000; (p. 15-10)
21. A See Sec. 1032. (p. 15-21)
22. A $80,000 - 90,000 = ($10,000); Losses are not recognized under Sec. 1031. (p. 15-3)
23. A No gain is recognized under Sec. 1044. (p. 15-22)
24. B $60,000 x (10 months/24 months) = $25,000 exclusion. (p. 15-19)
25. B $450,000 - $250,000 = $200,000. Because Norval has used the exclusion within the last two years, it is not increased to $500,000 on their joint return. (p. 15-18)
26. B The rental portion is not covered by Sec. 121. (p. 15-25)

CHAPTER 16
PROPERTY TRANSACTIONS:
CAPITAL GAINS AND LOSSES

CHAPTER HIGHLIGHTS

This chapter discusses the tax treatment of capital assets, including the special reporting requirements applicable to capital gains and losses. Historically, except for the years 1988 through 1990, long-term capital gains have received favorable tax treatment. Even in 1988 through 1990 when long-term capital gains were not granted favorable tax treatment, gains and losses from capital assets were required to be separately reported. The separate reporting of capital gains and losses is also necessary to apply certain limitations applicable to the deduction of capital losses.

I. GENERAL CONSIDERATIONS

A. Capital gain or loss reporting arises from the sale or exchange of a capital asset. Since capital gains and losses are subject to special tax treatment, they must be separated from other gains and losses. The reason for the separate reporting requirement is that taxable income may vary significantly when both ordinary and capital gains and losses are present. For example, after reducing capital losses by capital gains, any remaining capital losses of noncorporate taxpayers may be deducted only to the extent of $3,000 annually.

B. General Scheme of Taxation. Gains and losses that are recognized must be properly classified. The following three characteristics determine proper classification:

1) Tax status of the property (capital asset, Sec. 1231 asset, or ordinary asset).

2) Manner of the property's disposition (sale, exchange, casualty, theft, or condemnation).

3) Holding period of the property (short-term or long-term).

II. CAPITAL ASSETS

A. The definition of a capital asset is a definition by exception. Sec. 1221 defines what is *not* a capital asset. A capital asset is all property held by the taxpayer (whether or not connected with his or her trade or business) other than:

1) inventory or property held primarily for sale to customers in the ordinary course of business

2) accounts and notes receivable

3) depreciable property or real estate used in a business

4) certain copyrights, literary, musical, or artistic compositions, letters or memoranda

5) certain U.S. government publications

The most common capital assets held by an individual are items such as a personal residence, automobile, or investment property (land, stock, bonds, etc.). Since losses on the sale or exchange of personal use property are not recognized, the taxpayer need only be concerned with the capital gain treatment of such property.

B. Effect of Judicial Action. The courts have held that motive must be determined to distinguish a capital from an ordinary asset. Capital asset determination by the courts hinges on whether the asset is held for investment purposes (capital asset) or business purposes (ordinary asset).

C. Statutory Expansions. There are several provisions in the Code that expand the definition of capital assets found in Sec. 1221.

Dealers in securities must identify which securities are held for investment purposes; otherwise, the securities are presumed to be inventory. To receive capital gain treatment on a sale, securities held for investment must be identified as such on the date of acquisition. Losses are considered capital losses if at any time the securities have been identified as held for investment.

Under Sec. 1237, if certain rules are met, real estate investors with limited development activity can avoid dealer status; thereby having any gain treated as capital gain rather than ordinary gain. See text for requirements and limitations.

Lump-sum distributions of an employee's pension or profit-sharing plan are taxed in the current year. Under certain circumstances part of the gain may be taxed as a capital gain. See Chapter 19.

Nonbusiness bad debts are always treated as short-term capital losses.

III. SALE OR EXCHANGE

A. The recognition of a capital gain or loss requires a sale or exchange of a capital asset. The term "sale or exchange" is used in the Code but is not defined. A sale usually involves the receipt of money or the assumption of liabilities for property, and an exchange involves the transfer of property for other property.

B. Worthless securities that are capital assets are deemed to have become worthless on the last day of the taxable year. Under Sec. 1244, losses on certain corporate stock is an ordinary deduction. See chapter 7 for details.

C. Special Rule: Retirement of Corporate Obligations. As a rule, collection of a debt does not constitute a sale or exchange, so it does not qualify for capital gain treatment for tax purposes. However, under Sec. 1271, the retirement of corporate and certain governmental obligations are considered to be an exchange and therefore usually qualifies for capital gain or loss treatment.

D. Original Issue Discount. Bonds that are issued at less than maturity value may have an "original issue discount" (OID). If OID exists, it must generally be amortized over the life of the bond. As the OID is amortized, the basis of the bond to which the OID relates is increased by the amount of the amortization. Once the OID is fully amortized, the bond-holder's basis in the bond will be its face value, thus there will be no gain on the redemption of the bond by the issuer.

E. Options. The sale or exchange of an option to buy or sell property will generally produce a capital gain or loss if the property is (or would be) a capital asset in the hands of the option holder.

If an option holder fails to exercise an option, the lapse is considered a sale or exchange on the option expiration date. If the option is exercised, the amount paid for the option is added to the purchase price of the property. The grantee then has a larger basis and the grantor has a larger gain.

F. Patents. Under Sec. 1235, inventors are given long-term capital gain treatment on patents. To qualify for this provision, a holder must transfer all substantial rights to a patent. A holder is the creator, inventor, or anyone who purchases the patent rights from the creator, except the creator's employer and certain related parties. To constitute all "substantial rights," the patent rights must not be limited geographically or in duration.

G. Franchises, Trademarks, and Trade Names. Under Sec. 1253, the transfer of a franchise, trademark, or trade name is not considered a sale or exchange of a capital asset if the transferor retains any significant power, right, or continuing interest concerning the subject matter of the franchise, trade mark, or trade name.

1) A noncontingent lump-sum payment is capitalized and amortized by the franchisee. The amortization is subject to Sec. 1245 recapture.

2) Contingent payments are ordinary income for the franchisor and an ordinary deduction for the franchisee.
This section does not apply to professional sports franchises.

H. Lease Cancellation Payments. Payments received by a lessee for cancellation of a lease are treated as capital gains if the lease is a capital asset. Generally, a lease would be a capital asset if the property is used for personal use and an ordinary asset if the property is used in a trade or business. Payments received by a lessor for lease cancellation are always ordinary income because they are deemed to be in lieu of rental payments.

IV. HOLDING PERIODS

A. There are two holding periods for capital gains and losses: short-term and long-term. The short-term is one-year or less and the long-term holding period is more than 12 months.

B. Special Holding Period Rules.

The holding period of property received in a nontaxable exchange includes the holding period of the asset exchanged if such property is a capital or Sec. 1231 asset.

The holding period of an asset received in a nontaxable transaction (e.g., a gift) where the basis carries over will generally include the holding period of the former owner. The holding period for inherited property is treated as long-term no matter how long the property is actually held. Taxpayers who acquire property in a disallowed loss transaction do not carry over the holding period or the basis.

C. Short Sales.

A short sale is a form of speculation where a taxpayer sells borrowed property (usually stock) and later repays the lender with substantially identical property. See text for operational rules.

V. CAPITAL GAINS AND LOSSES OF NONCORPORATE TAXPAYERS

A. Capital Gain and Loss Netting Process.

Net long-term capital gain can be subject to a 28%, 25%, or 10%/20% maximum tax rate. The 28% rate applies to gains on collectibles (e.g., stamps and coins). The 25% rate applies to deprecation recapture on the disposition of certain Sec. 1250 assets. The 10%/20% rate applies to all other net long-term gains.

If the net short-term capital gain exceeds the net long-term capital loss, the amount receives no special tax treatment and is included with other ordinary income.

The ordering procedure for netting capital gains and losses is as follows.

1) Group all gains and losses into short-term, 28%, 25%, 10%/20%, and long-term.

2) Net the gains and losses within each group.

3) Offset the net 28% and net 25% amounts if they are of opposite sign.

4) Offset the result in step 3 against the 10%/20% amount is they are of the opposite sign. If the 20%/10 amount is a loss, offset it against the highest taxed gain first. After this step, the net amount is a net long-term capital gain or loss

5) Offset the net short-term amount against the results of step 4 if they are of opposite sign. The netting rules offset net short-term capital loss against the highest taxed gain first. Consequently, if there is net short-term capital loss and a net gain from step 4, the short-term capital loss offsets first the 28% gain, then the 25% gain, and finally the 10%/20% gain components resulting from step 4.

B. Alternative Tax on Net Capital Gains. The alternative net capital gains tax is applied in layers. Each portion and type of the net long-term capital gain is taxed at various rates. The layers are taxed in the following order: 25% gain, 28% gain, 10% gain, and then 20% gain.

C. Capital Losses. For individual taxpayers, net capital losses are deductible from gross income to the extent of $3,000 per tax year. Excess losses carry forward indefinitely.

VI. CAPITAL GAINS AND LOSSES OF CORPORATE TAXPAYERS

The treatment of capital gains and losses for corporations differs from that of individuals in the following areas.

A. An alternative tax rate of 35 percent is allowed in computing the tax on capital gains. Since the maximum corporate rate is 35 percent for ordinary income, there is nothing to be gained from the alternative capital gain tax rate.

B. Capital losses offset capital gains only. Capital losses may not be deducted against ordinary income.

C. There is a five-year carryover and a three-year carryback period for net capital losses. Corporate carryovers and carrybacks are always short-term, regardless of whether they start out as long-term or short-term capital losses.

KEY TERMS:

Capital Assets

Sale or Exchange

Capital Gains

Capital Losses

TEST FOR SELF-EVALUATION

True or False

Indicate which of the following statements are true or false by circling the correct answer.

T F 1. Inventory or stock used in a trade or business is not a capital asset as defined in Sec. 1221.

T F 2. A depreciable building used in a taxpayer's trade or business is not a capital asset.

T F 3. Accounts and notes receivable acquired in the ordinary course of a trade or business or from the sale of inventory are not capital assets.

T F 4. The taxpayer's use of property is important in determining whether the property is an ordinary or capital asset.

T F 5. Dealers in securities will always have ordinary gains and losses on the sale of securities.

T F 6. Under Sec. 1237, investors in real estate who engage in limited development activities may be allowed capital gain treatment.

T F 7. Taxable lump-sum distributions from qualified pension and profit-sharing plans are generally ordinary income (subject to certain transition rules).

T F 8. Nonbusiness bad debts are treated as long-term capital losses.

T F 9. The term "sale or exchange" is defined in the Internal Revenue Code.

T F 10. Losses on worthless securities that are capital assets are treated as arising from the sale or exchange of a capital asset on the last day of the taxable year.

T F 11. The retirement of a corporate bond is considered an exchange and therefore is usually subject to capital gain or loss treatment.

T F 12. If an option lapses, it is considered a sale or exchange on the last day of the taxable year.

T F 13. If an option is exercised, the amount paid for the option is added to the basis of the property subject to the option.

T F 14. The holder of a patent is entitled to long-term capital gain treatment if he or she transfers all substantial rights to the patent.

T F 15. The sale of a franchise always generates long-term capital gain under Sec. 1253.

T F 16. Lease cancellation payments received by a lessee are capital gains if the lease is a capital asset.

T F 17. Lease cancellation payments received by a lessor are always long-term capital gains.

T F 18. Unused capital losses of noncorporate taxpayers can be carried forward indefinitely.

T F 19. Capital losses for corporate taxpayers are deductible against ordinary income, subject to the annual limitation.

T F 20. For 1999, an individual taxpayer's maximum deduction against ordinary income for a capital loss is $3,000.

T F 21. A truck used in a taxpayer's trade or business is a capital asset.

T F 22. The long-term holding period is more than 12 months.

T F 23. Generally, the holding period of property "sold short" is determined by the length of time the seller held the property used to close the short sale.

T F 24. Corporate capital losses carry back three years and forward five years and all carryovers are treated as short-term, despite the original nature of the loss.

T F 25. Contingent franchise payments are ordinary income to the franchisor and an ordinary deduction to the franchisee.

T F 26. A mode of operation, a widely recognized brand name, and a widely known business symbol are commonly called patents.

T F 27. A noncontingent franchise fee is capitalized and amortized over 15 years (subject to Sec.1245 recapture if sold) by a franchisee.

T F 28. The alternative net capital gains tax is applied in layers. The layers are taxed in the following order: 28% gain, 25% gain, 20% gain, and then 10% gain.

Fill-in-the-Blanks

Complete the following statements with the appropriate word(s) or amount(s).

1. The required holding period for a gain to be a long-term capital gain is more than __________ months.

2. The holding period of property received in a nontaxable exchange generally ________ the holding period of the former asset.

3. In a short sale, the holding period of the property sold short is generally determined by the length of time the seller held the property used to __________ the lender when closing the short sale.

4. Net gains from short-term capital transactions are taxed as ordinary______________.

5. The maximum capital loss that can be deducted against other income by a noncorporate taxpayer is_______________.

6. Unused capital losses of individuals can be carried forward for an __________ time period.

Multiple Choice

Choose the best answer for each of the following questions.

1. In 1999 Tom incurs a short-term capital loss of $5,000. Tom's gross income for 1999 (not including the loss) is $20,000. If Tom is single, his adjusted gross income for 1999 is:
   a. $20,000
   b. $19,000
   c. $18,000
   d. $17,000
   e. Some other amount

2. Assuming the same situation as in Question 1, what is Tom's short-term capital loss carryover to 1999?
   a. $1,000
   b. $2,000
   c. $3,000
   d. $4,000
   e. Some other amount

3. Tasty Taco sells franchises to independent operators. In 1999 it sold a franchise with an 8-year life to Wilson for $70,000 plus 3 percent of sales. Tasty Taco retains significant rights to control management. If Wilson's 1999 sales amounted to $100,000, Tasty Taco would include in its computation of 1999 taxable income:
   a. Long-term capital gain of $73,000
   b. Long-term capital gain of $70,000, ordinary income of $3,000
   c. Ordinary income of $73,000
   d. Ordinary income of $70,000, long-term capital gain of $3,000
   e. Some other amount

4. Which of the following is a capital asset?
   a. Inventory
   b. Texaco stock owned by an investor
   c. Accounts receivable
   d. Land used in a trade or business
   e. None of the above

5. Teri owns a tract of land and subdivides it for sale. In 1999 she sells five lots for $10,000 each with a basis of $6,000 in each lot. Her total selling expenses are $2,000 and she meets the requirements of Sec. 1237. Teri should report for 1999:
   a. Capital gain of $18,000
   b. Capital gain of $500, ordinary income of $17,500
   c. Capital gain of $17,500, ordinary income of $500
   d. Ordinary income of $18,000
   e. Some other amount

6. Tim invents a machine that he patents. The patent is assigned to a manufacturer in 1999 for $100,000, plus a $5 per machine royalty. During 1999 1,000 machines are sold. Assuming Tim transferred all substantial rights and has a zero basis in the patent, he should report for 1999:
   a. Long-term capital gain of $105,000
   b. Long-term capital gain of $100,000, ordinary income of $5,000
   c. Long-term capital gain of $5,000, ordinary income of $100,000
   d. Ordinary income of $105,000
   e. Some other amount

7. To receive long-term capital gain treatment an asset acquired must be held a minimum of:
   a. Two years or more
   b. Nine months or more
   c. More than twelve months
   d. More than six months
   e. None of the above

8. During 1999, Todd has net long-term capital gains of $12,000 and a net short-term capital loss carryover of $8,000. On his 1999 tax return, Todd should report:
   a. $12,000 net capital gain
   b. $9,000 net capital gain
   c. $8,000 net capital gain
   d. $4,000 net capital gain
   e. None of the above

9. During 1999, Ted, an individual, sells his personal automobile for $2,000. He purchased the automobile six years ago for $14,000. In addition, Ted has a $7,000 long-term capital gain from the sale of stock that he held as an investment. What amount should Ted report on his 1999 individual income tax return related to these transactions?
   a. $7,000 net capital gain
   b. $4,000 net capital gain
   c. $3,000 net capital loss
   d. $5,000 net capital loss
   e. Some other amount

10. Sue purchased stock on November 30, 1996 for $5,000. Due to a series of unfortunate events, Sue is notified on July 1, 1999 that the stock is totally worthless. Assuming Sue has no other capital transactions, what amount of loss should Sue report on her tax return for 1999?
   a. $5,000 long-term capital loss
   b. $5,000 short-term capital loss
   c. $3,000 long-term capital loss
   d. $3,000 short-term capital loss
   e. Some other amount

11. For 1999 Earl has net long-term capital gains of $20,000 and net short-term capital losses of $8,000. What is Earl's "net long-term capital gain?"
   a. $20,000
   b. $17,000
   c. $12,000
   d. $8,000

e. Some other amount

12. In December 1999, Tony receives a lump-sum distribution of $52,000 from a qualified pension plan. Tony contributed $12,000 to the plan and the employer contributed the rest. If Tony was a participant in the plan for a total of eight years, he should report:
a. Long-term capital gain of $24,000, ordinary income of $16,000
b. Long-term capital gain of $10,000, ordinary income of $30,000
c. Long-term capital gain of $40,000
d. Ordinary income of $40,000
e. Some other amount

13. Blue Corporation issues bonds at 95 percent of the face amount. The bonds are due in ten years. Which of the following is true?
a. The bonds are not issued with original issue discount
b. The bonds are issued with original issue discount
c. These bonds are capital assets to T Corporation
d. The bond-holders can only be individuals
e. None of the above

14. Max buys an option on vacant land. He pays $4,000 for a three-year option to purchase land for $100,000. After six months Max sells the option for $9,000. From this transaction, Max would recognize:
a. Long-term capital gain of $5,000
b. Short-term capital gain of $5,000
c. Short-term capital gain of $9,000
d. Short-term capital gain of $109,000
e. Some other amount.

15. Same as number 14, except Max fails to exercise the option after the three-year period. What is Max's recognized gain or loss?
a. Long-term capital gain of $4,000
b. Short-term capital gain of $4,000
c. Long-term capital loss of $4,000
d. Short-term capital loss of $4,000
e. Some other amount

16. Yolonda had the following items of income, gains, losses, and deductions in 1999.

Salary	$30,000
Nonbusiness bad debt	-2,500
Gain on stock held eight months	5,000
Loss on stock held three years	-2,000
Home mortgage interest	12,000

What is Yolonda's AGI for the year?
a. $30,500
b. $32,500
c. $33,000
d. $37,500

e. Some other amount

17. Rose Corporation has ordinary income from operations of $60,000, net long-term capital gain of $20,000, and net short-term capital loss of $30,000. What is Rose Corporation's taxable income for 1999?
   a. $50,000
   b. $60,000
   c. $80,000
   d. $90,000
   e. Some other amount

18. Quincy, a cash basis individual taxpayer, executed a sale of stock on December 29, 1998. The sale was settled on January 4, 1999. The stock has a basis to Quincy of $20,000 and was acquired on December 27, 1993. The stock was sold for $25,000. What is Quincy's tax result from the sale?
   a. Long-term capital gain of $5,000 in 1999
   b. Short-term capital gain of $5,000 in 1999
   c. Long-term capital gain of $5,000 in 1998
   d. Short-term capital gain of $5,000 in 1998
   e. None of the above

19. When a taxpayer has a short sale of a capital asset it may be treated as:
   a. Ordinary income or short-term capital gain
   b. Capital gain or short-term capital gain
   c. Short-term capital gain or ordinary income
   d. Short-term capital gain only
   e. None of the above

20. Corporations may carry unused capital losses to what other tax years?
   a. Forward indefinitely
   b. Back three and forward fifteen years
   c. Back three and forward five years
   d. Back three and forward seven years
   e. None of the above

21. Mac buys an expensive painting, "St. Monroe," for $20,000. The painting is used to decorate Mac's office and is of *investment quality*. The painting is seven year class property (14.29% in the first year). How does Mac treat the painting for tax purposes?
   a. $20,000 is deducted in the first year.
   b. $2,858 is deducted in the first year.
   c. The cost of the painting cannot be deducted.
   d. The Sec. 179 election applies to the painting.
   e. None of the above.

22. For 1999, Nick, a single taxpayer, has taxable income of $75,000 including net long-term capital gain of $40,000. His regular tax calculation for 1999 is $18,029 [(15% x $25,750) + 28% ($62,450 - $25,750) + 31% ($75,000 - $62,450]. What is Nick's tax using the alternative tax on net long-term capital gains calculation?
   a. $14,453
   b. $6,453

c. $8,000
d. $18,029
e. Some other amount

23. In the current year, Floyd had the following capital transactions:

Long-term gain	$6,000
Short-term gain	10,000
Long-term loss	8,000
Short-term loss	$13,000

Before the above capital transactions, Floyd had taxable income of $15,000. Calculate Floyd's current year taxable income or loss after the capital transactions and the capital loss carryover to the next tax year.
a. $12,000, $2,000 long-term carryover
b. $10,000, $-0- carryover
c. $15,000, $5,000 long-term carryover
d. $15,000, $2,000 long-term carryover and $3,000 short-term carryover
e. Some other amounts

24. Helen had the following capital transaction during 1999:

Long-term gain	$17,000
Long-term loss	7,000
Short-term gain	24,000
Short-term loss	$7,000

What is Helen's net long-term and net short-term capital gain for 1999?
a. $10,000 Long-term gain; $17,000 Short-term gain
b. $17,000 Long-term gain; $24,000 Short-term gain
c. $24,000 Long-term gain; $31,000 Short-term gain
d. $10,000 Long-term gain; $24,000 Short-term gain
e. Some other amounts

25. Bluegill Corporation has $18,400 of long-term capital loss for 1999 and $20,000 of other taxable income. What is Bluegill's taxable income for 1999?
a. $-0-
b. $1,600
c. $17,000
d. $20,000
e. Some other amount

26. Same as number 25. What is Bluegill's capital loss carryover (if any)?
a. $-0-
b. $15,400 Short-term
c. $15,400 Long-term
d. $18,400 Short-term
e. Some other amount

27. Tim is in the 31 percent regular tax bracket. In 1999, he has a $10,000 gain on a coin collection that he has owned for 10 years. What is the alternative net long-term capital gains tax on the gain on the coin collection?
    a. $3,100
    b. $2,800
    c. $2,500
    d. $2,000
    e. Some other amount.

28. Linda had the following capital transaction during 1999:

10%/20% gain	$5,000
28% loss	-8,000
Short-term gain	12,000

    What is the nature and amount of Linda's net capital gains or losses for 1999?
    a. $9,000 short-term gain
    b. $12,000 short-term gain; $3,000 10%/20% loss
    c. $4,000 short-term gain; $5,000 10%/20% gain
    d. $17,000 short-term gain; $8,000 28% loss
    e. Some other amounts

29. Cindy had the following capital transaction during 1999:

10%/20% loss	-$6,000
25% gain	5,000
28% gain	10,000
Short-term loss	-3,000

    What is the nature and amount of Cindy's net capital gains or losses for 1999?
    a. $3,000 short-term loss; $9,000 28% gain
    b. $12,000 25% gain; $6,000 10%/20% loss
    c. $1,000 28% gain; $5,000 25% gain
    d. $3,000 short-term loss; $5,000 25% gain; $4,000 28% gain
    e. Some other amounts

30. Joyce had the following capital transaction during 1999:

10%/20% loss	-$11,000
25% gain	5,000
28% gain	10,000
Short-term loss	-3,000

    What is the nature and amount of Joyce's net capital gains or losses for 1999?
    a. $3,000 short-term loss; $4,000 28% gain
    b. $1,000 25% gain
    c. $1,000 28% gain
    d. $3,000 short-term loss; $1,000 28% loss; $5,000 25% gain;
    e. Some other amounts

Problem

1. During 1999 Pat had the following stock transactions:

Description	Acquired	Sold	Sales Price	Basis
100 shs Exxon	8/01/98	11/05/99	$6,000	$2,500
100 shs ATT	6/11/99	10/03/99	$4,000	$4,500
100 shs IBM	3/12/99	08/22/99	$6,000	$5,200
100 shs GM	5/12/91	09/15/99	$8,000	$5,000
100 shs Ford	9/15/88	12/01/99	$6,000	$7,000

Calculate the following amounts to arrive at Pat's net amount included in or deducted from gross income for 1999.

Net short-term capital gain or loss _______

Net long-term capital gain or loss _______

SOLUTIONS TO CHAPTER 16

True or False

1. True (p. 16-4)
2. True (p. 16-4)
3. True (p. 16-4)
4. True (p. 16-6)
5. False Dealers may designate securities as held for investment. (p. 16-6)
6. True (p. 16-7)
7. True (p. 16-8)
8. False Nonbusiness bad debts are treated as short-term capital losses. (p. 16-8)
9. False The term is not defined in the Code. (p. 16-8)
10. True (p. 16-9)
11. True (p. 16-9)
12. False It is a sale or exchange on the day it lapses. (p. 16-10)
13. True (p. 16-11)
14. True (p. 16-12)
15. False Franchises usually produce ordinary income on their sale. (p. 16-13)
16. True (p. 16-15)
17. False Lease cancellation payments received by a lessor are ordinary income. (p. 16-15)
18. True (p. 16-26)
19. False Corporations are not permitted to deduct capital losses against ordinary income. (p. 16-29)
20. True (p. 16-26)
21. False Depreciable assets used in a trade or business are excluded from the definition of a capital asset. (p. 16-4)
22. True (p. 16-20)
23. True (p. 16-17)
24. True (p. 16-29)
25. True (p. 16-13)
26. False They are called franchises. (p. 16-13)
27. True (p. 16-13)
28. False The layers are taxed in the following order: 25% gain, 28% gain, 10% gain, and then 20% gain. (p. 16-24)

Fill-in-the-Blanks

1. 12 (p. 16-20)
2. includes (p. 16-16)
3. repay (p. 16-17)
4. income (p. 16-21)
5. $3,000 (p. 16-20)
6. indefinite (p. 16-26)

Multiple Choice

1. D $20,000 - 3,000 (maximum) = $17,000. (p. 16-26)

2.	B	\$5,000 - 3,000 = \$2,000. (p. 16-26)
3.	C	\$70,000 + 3% (100,000) = \$73,000 ordinary income. (p. 16-13)
4.	B	(p. 16-4)
5.	A	5 x \$10,000 = \$50,000 - 2,000 - (5 x \$6,000) = \$18,000. (p. 16-7)
6.	A	\$100,000 + (\$5 x 1,000) = \$105,000. (p. 16-12)
7.	C	(p. 16-20)
8.	D	(p. 16-26)
9.	A	The loss on the sale of the personal automobile is not deductible. (p. 16-4)
10.	C	(pp. 16-9, 26)
11.	C	\$20,000 - 8,000 = \$12,000. (p. 16-21)
12.	D	\$52,000 - 12,000 = \$40,000 ordinary income. (p. 16-8)
13.	B	¼% x 10 Years = 2½%, the maximum discount is exceeded. (p. 16-9)
14.	B	\$9,000 - 4,000 = \$5,000 Short-term capital gain. (p. 16-10)
15.	C	(p. 16-10)

16. A

Salary	\$30,000
Net capital gain (\$5,000 - \$2,500 - \$2,000))	\$500
Adjusted gross income	\$30,500(p. 16-21)

17.	B	Net Short-term capital loss are not allowed for corporations. (p. 16-29)
18.	C	The date of sale is the date of execution. (p. 16-33)
19.	B	(p. 16-18)
20.	C	(p. 16-29)
21.	C	(p. 16-4)

22. A

Regular tax: (15% x \$25,750) + 28%(\$35,000 - \$25,750) =		\$6,453
Alternative tax on long-term capital gain: 20% (\$40,000) =		\$8,000
Total	\$14,453	

[1999] (p. 16-21)

23. A — \$15,000 - \$3,000 ST loss = \$12,000 TI. In offsetting taxable income, the net short-term loss always goes first, then any net long-term loss. Since the net short-term capital loss is \$3,000 (the maximum annual limit) all the long-term capital loss carries over. (p. 16-21)

24. A — Long-term capital gain: \$17,000 - 7,000 = \$10,000; Short-term capital gain: \$24,000 - 7,000 = \$17,000 (p. 16-21)

25. D — Corporation's cannot use capital losses against other income. (p. 16-29)

26. D — All corporate capital loss carryovers are short-term. (p. 16-29)

27. B — Collectibles are always taxed at a 28% rate. (p. 16-23)

28. A — a) Offset \$5,000 of the 28% loss against the 10%/20% gain, reducing it to zero.
b) Offset the remaining \$3,000 of the \$28% loss against the \$3,000 short-term gain, reducing it to \$9,000. (p. 16-21)

29. C — a) Offset the \$6,000 10%/20% loss against the \$10,000 28% gain, reducing it to \$4,000.
b) Offset the\$3,000 short-term loss against the \$4,000 28% gain, reducing it to \$1,000.
c) Since the 28% gain absorbed the short-term loss there is no offset against the 25% gain. (p. 16-21).

30. B — a) Offset the \$11,000 10%/20% loss against the \$10,000 28% gain, reducing it to zero.
b) Offset the remaining \$1,000 of 10%/20% loss against the \$5,000 25% gain, reducing it to \$4,000.

c) Then offset the $3,000 short-term loss against the $4,000 25% gain, reducing it to $1,000. (p. 16-21).

Problem

1. Net short-term capital gain:

IBM	$800
ATT	-500
	$300

Net long-term capital gain:

Exxon	3,500
GM	3,000
Ford	-1,000
	$5,600

(p. 16-21)

CHAPTER 17
PROPERTY TRANSACTIONS:
SECTION 1231 AND
RECAPTURE PROVISIONS

CHAPTER HIGHLIGHTS

This chapter summarizes Code Sec. 1231 that grants favorable long-term capital gain treatment on the sale or exchange of business properties or involuntary conversions. Also discussed are the recapture provisions that provide that certain gains, which would otherwise qualify for capital gain treatment, are to be treated as ordinary income. These provisions are Secs. 1245 and 1250 of the Code. Any amounts converted to ordinary income under these provisions are generally referred to as Sec. 1245 and Sec. 1250 recapture.

I. SECTION 1231 ASSETS

A. Relationship to Capital Assets. Sec. 1231 assets are not capital assets because they are excluded under Sec. 1221(2). The concept of Sec. 1231 assets was enacted by Congress in 1942 to ease the burden of taxation on the sale of business assets and to help the war effort.

Sec. 1231 provides that a net gain on Sec. 1231 property is treated as a long-term capital gain, and a net loss is treated as an ordinary loss.

B. Property Included. What is included in the definition of Section 1231 property is:

1) Depreciable or real property used in a business or for the production of income

2) Timber, coal, or domestic iron ore to which Sec. 631 applies

3) Livestock held for draft, breeding, dairy, or sporting purposes

4) Unharvested crops on land used in a business

5) Certain purchased intangible assets that are eligible for amortization (e.g., patents and goodwill).

Note that depreciable or real estate used in a *trade or business* qualifies as Section 1231 property.

C. Property Excluded. The property shown below is not Sec. 1231 property:

1) Property held less than the long-term holding period (the long-term holding period is greater than one year)

2) Property where casualty losses exceed casualty gains for the taxable year

3) Inventory and property held primarily for sale to customers

4) Copyrights; literary, musical, or artistic compositions; certain U.S. government publications

5) Intangible assets such as accounts and notes receivable

D. Special Rules for Certain Sec. 1231 Assets. The difference between the basis of timber and the fair market value on the first day of the year during which the timber is cut may be treated as Sec. 1231 gain, provided the timber is held for sale or use in a business and has been held for the required long-term holding period.

Special holding period rules apply to the classification of gains and losses on livestock as Sec. 1231 gain or loss. Cattle and horses must be held for at least 24 months while other livestock must be held for at least 12 months. Poultry is excluded from Sec. 1231 treatment.

Certain business and investment properties may be subject to Sec. 1231 treatment if the gain or loss is the result of a casualty or theft.

E. General Procedure for Sec. 1231 Computation. The general procedure for calculating Sec. 1231 gains and losses is as follows:

Net all long-term casualty gains and losses from nonpersonal use property.

1) If the casualty gains exceed the casualty losses, combine the excess with other Sec. 1231 gains.

2) If the casualty losses exceed casualty gains, exclude all losses and gains from further Sec. 1231 computations. All casualty gains are then considered ordinary income and casualty losses are deductible for AGI if business related and from AGI (subject to the 2 percent of adjusted gross income limitation), if not.

Net all Sec. 1231 gains (including any net casualty gains) and losses.

1) if the gains exceed the losses, net Sec. 1231 gains are offset by nonrecaptured Sec. 1231 losses for the previous five years; the excess is treated as long-term capital gain. Any offset amount is ordinary income.

2) If the losses exceed the gains, all gains are ordinary income and business losses are fully deductible. Other casualty losses (arising from income-producing property) are deductions from adjusted gross income.

II. SECTION 1245 RECAPTURE

Congress enacted Sec. 1245 to prevent taxpayers from receiving the dual benefits of depreciation deductions that offset ordinary income and Sec. 1231 long-term capital gain treatment when the property is sold. Under Sec. 1245, gain on the disposition is treated as ordinary income to the extent of depreciation taken. Any excess gain is either Sec. 1231 gain or casualty gain if the property was disposed of in a casualty event. Sec. 1245 does not apply where the taxpayer has a realized loss on the disposition of an asset.

A. Section 1245 Property. Sec. 1245 property includes all depreciable personal property, including livestock. Nonresidential buildings acquired after 1980 and before 1987 are subject to Sec. 1245 if accelerated cost recovery (ACRS) is used. The following special property is subject to Sec. 1245 treatment:

1) Amortizable personal property such as patents, copyrights, leaseholds, and professional sports contracts;

2) Amortization of reforestation expenditures and costs to remove handicap barriers;

3) Amounts expensed under Sec. 179;

4) Elevators and escalators acquired before January 1, 1987;

5) Certain depreciable tangible real property;

6) Amortization taken on pollution control facilities, railroad grading and tunnel boring equipment, on-the-job training, and child care facilities;

7) Agricultural and horticultural structures and petroleum storage facilities;

8) Nonresidential realty placed in service after 1980 and before 1987 (15-year, 18-year, or 19-year property) on which ACRS was taken.

B. Observations on Sec. 1245.

1) In most cases the gain on Sec. 1245 property results in ordinary income.

2) Recapture applies no matter what method of depreciation is used.

3) Recapture applies no matter what the holding periods is.

4) Section 1245 does not apply to losses.

5) Section 1245 gains may also be passive activity gains.

III. SECTION 1250 RECAPTURE

Section 1250 property includes depreciable real property that is not subject to Sec. 1245. Sec. 1250 is similar to Sec. 1245, but under Sec. 1250 only "additional depreciation" is subject to recapture. This additional amount is the accelerated depreciation taken in excess of straight-line depreciation that would have been allowed. Unless property is disposed of during the first year, Sec. 1250 does not apply to real property placed in service after 1986 because the straight-line method of depreciation is required.

A. Computing Recapture on Nonresidential Real Property. For Sec. 1250 property, other than residential rental property, the following general rules apply:

1) Post-1969 amount recaptured is depreciation taken in excess of straight-line after 1969.

2) If property is held one year or less, all depreciation taken is recaptured.

B. Computing Recapture on Residential Rental Housing. Recapture on residential rental housing is computed in the same manner as other Sec. 1250 property except that only additional depreciation attributable to periods after 1975 is recaptured in full. Depreciation prior to 1976 and after 1969 may be partially recaptured depending on the taxpayer's holding period.

C. Section 1250 Recapture Situations. The Sec. 1250 recapture rules apply to the following property if accelerated depreciation was used:

1) Residential rental real estate acquired before 1987.

2) Nonresidential real estate acquired before 1981.

3) Real property used outside the U.S.

4) Certain government-financed or low-income housing.

D. Unrecaptured Gain (25% Real Estate Gain).

Certain gain on real estate is eligible for the 25 percent tax rate on unrecaptured Sec. 1250 gain. Unrecaptured gain is all or some of the Sec. 1231 gain that is taxed as long-term capital gain and related to the sale of depreciable real estate.

The maximum amount of 25% gain is the deprecation taken on real property sold at a gain. This gain is limited in several ways such as when the gain is less than the deprecation taken. See text for all the 25% gain limitations.

IV. CONSIDERATIONS COMMON TO SECTION 1245 AND SECTION 1250

A. Exceptions. Recapture under Sec. 1245 and Sec. 1250 does not apply in the following situations:

1) For a gift of property, the recapture potential carries over to the donee.

2) If property is transferred by death the recapture does not carry to the heir.

3) For a charitable transfer, the recapture potential reduces the amount of the charitable deduction under Sec. 170.

4) For tax-free transactions in which the adjusted basis of the property carries over to the transferee, recapture potential also carries over. Sec. 351 tax-free incorporations fall into this category.

5) Gains recognized under the like-kind exchange or involuntary conversion provisions are subject to recapture as ordinary income under Secs. 1245 and 1250.

B. Other Applications. Special rules apply in the following situations:

1) For installment sales, recapture gain is recognized in full in the year of sale. Furthermore, all gain is ordinary income until recapture potential is fully absorbed.

2) For a distribution of property subject to recapture, gain must be recognized by the distributing corporation to the extent of the recapture.

V. SPECIAL RECAPTURE PROVISIONS

A. Special Recapture for Corporations. Corporations selling depreciable realty will be subject to an "ordinary gain adjustment."

B. Gain from Sale of Depreciable Property Between Certain Related Parties. In a sale or exchange of depreciable property between an individual and a controlled corporation or partnership or between certain other related parties, any gain recognized is ordinary income. In this case, depreciable means subject to depreciation in the hands of the transferee. Recapture under Secs.1245 and 1250 is applied before recapture under the related party provisions.

C. Intangible Drilling Costs and Depletion. Intangible drilling and development costs are recaptured on the sale or disposition of such property, if such costs were expensed instead of capitalized.

VI. REPORTING PROCEDURES

Form 4797 is used to report noncapital gains and losses, including Sec. 1231 gains and losses, and Secs. 1245 and 1250 gains. Form 4684, which is used for reporting casualties and thefts, should be completed first since a resulting net gain will impact the computation of Sec. 1231 gains and losses.

KEY TERMS:

Sec. 1231 Asset

Sec. 1245 Recapture

Sec. 1250 Recapture

Holding Period

Casualty Gains

TEST FOR SELF-EVALUATION

True or False

Indicate which of the following statements are true or false by circling the correct answer.

T F 1. Sec. 1231 assets are the same as capital assets under Sec. 1221.

T F 2. A contract to cut timber owned more than one year is a Sec. 1231 asset.

T F 3. The primary tax advantage of a Sec. 1231 asset is that gains are ordinary income and losses are capital losses.

T F 4. All livestock must be held for at least 24 months to qualify as a Sec. 1231 asset.

T F 5. Inventory is not a Sec. 1231 asset.

T F 6. Net gains from other than personal use property disposed of by casualty or theft are Sec. 1231 gains.

T F 7. Section 1245 applies to depreciable personalty and requires that all depreciation be recaptured if the gain realized exceeds the potential recapture amount.

T F 8. Depreciation on elevators and escalators acquired before 1987 is recaptured under Sec. 1245.

T F 9. Professional baseball and football players' contracts are not Sec. 1245 property.

T F 10. All depreciation on pre-1987 residential Sec. 1250 property is recaptured to the extent of gain on disposition.

T F 11. Any net gain from the disposal of Sec. 1245 property that is not recaptured is either Sec. 1231 gain or casualty gain.

T F 12. For gifts of property subject to depreciation recapture, the donor must recapture the depreciation, not the donee.

T F 13. For a charitable transfer, the recapture potential reduces the amount of the charitable contribution deduction under Sec. 170.

T F 14. Generally, if the adjusted basis in a transaction carries over to the transferee, the recapture potential also carries over.

T F 15. In an installment sale, capital gain treatment applies first, then recapture under Sec. 1245 or Sec. 1250.

T F 16. Intangible drilling costs that are expensed are recaptured to the extent of the lesser of the gain realized or the IDC expensed.

T F 17. The net Sec. 1231 gain is offset by nonrecaptured Sec. 1231 losses from the previous six years.

T F 18. All depreciation on post-1986 nonresidential rental property is recaptured.

T F 19. A gift transaction triggers recapture under Sec. 1245, but not under Sec. 1250.

T F 20. Chickens that are held for 12 months are Sec. 1231 assets.

T F 21. For real property acquired after 1986 there usually will be no Sec. 1250 recapture because depreciation is limited to straight-line.

T F 22. Sec. 1245 recapture is often referred to as partial recapture while Sec. 1250 recapture is referred to as full recapture.

T F 23. For Sec. 1245 recapture it does not matter which method of depreciation is used.

T F 24. The Sec. 1245 recapture rules apply before there is any casualty gain.

T F 25. A taxpayer can elect to treat the cutting of timber held for sale or use in business as a sale or exchange under Sec. 631.

T F 26. The maximum tax rate is 25 percent on unrecaptured Sec. 1250 gain on real estate held over 18 months.

Fill-in-the-Blanks

Complete the following statements with the appropriate word(s) or amount(s).

1. Sec. 1245 and 1250 recapture rules normally __________ all other Code sections.

2. Restrictions (under Sec. 1239) are imposed on sales or exchanges between an individual and his or her ____________ corporation.

3. Intangible drilling and development costs that are paid or incurred are recaptured if such costs were ____________ instead of capitalized.

4. For an individual taxpayer, a business Sec. 1231 loss is deductible ____________ adjusted gross income.

5. Any Sec. 1231 gain remaining after the required netting, depreciation recapture, and applying the lookback rule, is treated as ____________ gain.

Multiple Choice

Choose the best answer for each of the following questions.

1. On December 31 of the current year, Roberto owned the following assets:

A delivery truck used in his business	$20,000

A rental house	110,000
Texaco stock	25,000
Inventory used in his business	150,000
Accounts receivable	10,000
Racehorses	$50,000

What is the amount of Roberto's Sec. 1231 assets?
a. $180,000
b. $205,000
c. $130,000
d. $45,000
e. Some other amount

2. Assume the same situation as in Question 1. What is the amount of Roberto's Sec. 1250 assets?
a. $-0-
b. $25,000
c. $45,000
d. $110,000
e. $130,000

3. Mr. I.C. Ewe sold Exxon stock (owned 10 years) for a $25,000 gain in 1999. In addition, he had a loss of $10,000 on the sale of one acre of land used in his business. The land was purchased five years ago. Mr. Ewe's net gain from the sale or exchange of capital assets for 1999 will be:
a. -0-
b. $5,000
c. $10,000
d. $25,000
e. Some other amount

4. On January 6, 1999, Isadora Xena sold Sec. 1245 business equipment. She had purchased this equipment for $5,000 three years ago and had claimed straight-line ACRS depreciation of $2,500 on it. If the selling price was $4,000, Ms. Xena should recognize:
a. Sec. 1231 gain of $1,500
b. Sec. 1245 gain of $1,500
c. Sec. 1231 loss of $500
d. Sec. 1245 loss of $500
e. Some other amount

5. Assume the same situation as in Question 4, except that the selling price was $2,000. Ms. Xena should recognize:
a. Sec. 1245 loss of $500
b. Sec. 1231 loss of $500
c. Sec. 1245 loss of $2,000
d. Sec. 1231 loss of $2,000
e. Some other amount

6. Assume the same situation as in Question 4, except that the selling price was $5,500. Ms. Xena should report:
a. Sec. 1245 gain of $3,000

b. Sec. 1231 gain of $3,000
c. Sec. 1245 gain of $2,500, Sec. 1231 gain of $500
d. Sec. 1245 gain of $500, Sec. 1231 gain of $2,500
e. Some other amount

7. Becky acquired residential rental property on January 1, 1986 at a cost of $200,000. She used the accelerated method of cost recovery under ACRS. The asset is sold on January 1, 1999 for $250,000. Total cost recovery allowed during the period the asset was held by Becky was $64,000. Straight-line depreciation would have yielded a $42,000 total. What is Becky's recapture under Sec. 1250?
a. -0-
b. $22,000
c. $42,000
d. $64,000
e. Some other amount

8. Black owns 100 percent of Black Corporation. In 1999 Black sells a truck (basis of $6,000) to Black Corporation for $7,500. Black Corporation will use the truck in its business. Black should report:
a. A capital gain of $1,500
b. A capital loss of $1,500
c. Ordinary income of $1,500
d. No gain or loss
e. Some other amount

9. In the current year, Seth donates to Goodwill Industries Sec. 1245 property acquired three years ago. The property has a fair market value of $20,000 and an adjusted basis of $12,000. If the property is subject to $4,000 of Sec. 1245 recapture potential, what is Seth's charitable contribution deduction?
a. $20,000
b. $12,000
c. $8,000
d. $16,000
e. Some other amount

10. Coyote Corporation distributes, as a dividend, property subject to recapture potential. If the recapture potential is $500 and the property's fair market value exceeds the adjusted basis by $800, Coyote Corporation should recognize:
a. $500 ordinary income, $300 Sec. 1231 gain
b. $800 ordinary income
c. $300 ordinary income, $500 Sec. 1231 gain
d. No recognized gain or loss
e. Some other amount

11. In 1999, Jim has a Sec. 1231 gain of $12,000 on property that he sold. During 1995, Jim reported a Sec. 1231 loss of $7,000, which has not been recaptured. Jim did not have any other Sec. 1231 gains or losses during the past five years. What is Jim's ordinary income for 1999 because of the above transactions?
a. $-0-
b. $12,000
c. $7,000
d. $5,000

e. Some other amount

12. Ross acquired nonresidential realty in 1985 for $200,000. His total ACRS deductions claimed on the realty (assuming a straight-line election was not made), totaled $90,000, which gives him an adjusted basis of $110,000. In 1999, Ross sells the property for $230,000, for a gain of $120,000. Ross should report:
   a. $120,000 Sec. 1231 gain.
   b. $120,000 ordinary income.
   c. $30,000 Sec. 1231 gain and $90,000 ordinary income.
   d. $30,000 ordinary income and $90,000 Sec. 1231 gain.
   e. Some other amount.

13. Several years ago, Herb purchased a tract of land with timber on it. The land cost $50,000 and the timber cost $100,000. On the first day of 1999, the timber was appraised at $175,000. In September 1999, the timber was cut and sold for $195,000. If Herb elects Sec. 1231 what is his Sec. 1231 gain on the sale of the timber?
   a. $-0-
   b. $20,000
   c. $75,000
   d. $95,000
   e. Some other amount

14. On January 1, 1999, Gwen sells nineteen-year nonresidential realty with accumulated depreciation of $200,000. The property was depreciated under an accelerated method. Straight-line depreciation would have been $110,000. The property was sold on January 1, 1999 with a recognized gain of $245,000. What is the depreciation recapture on this realty?
   a. $-0-
   b. $200,000
   c. $90,000
   d. $45,000
   e. Some other amount

15. Purple Corporation sold equipment for $37,000 on December 31, 1999. The equipment had been purchased on January 4, 1993 for $40,000 and the equipment had an adjusted basis of $32,000 on the date of sale. From this transaction Purple should report?
   a. No gain or loss
   b. $8,000 ordinary income
   c. $5,000 ordinary income
   d. $5,000 Sec. 1231 gain
   e. $3,000 Sec. 1231 loss

16. During 1999, Pat recognized Sec. 1231 gains of $15,000 and Sec. 1231 losses of $11,000. Pat's AGI before Sec. 1231 gains and losses is $50,000. After accounting for Sec. 1231 transaction, what is Pat's AGI?
   a. $50,000
   b. $65,000
   c. $39,000
   d. $54,000
   e. Some other amount

17. Sec. 1231 property includes all of the following except:
   a. Stock held for investment
   b. Timber, coal, and domestic iron ore
   c. Real property used in a trade or business
   d. Livestock (other than poultry) held for breeding purposes
   e. Depreciable property used in a trade or business

18. During 1999, Sheng has a net Sec. 1231 gain of $50,000. Last year, Sheng had a net Sec. 1231 loss of $15,000. In 1999, Sheng should report:
   a. $50,000 long-term capital gain
   b. $50,000 ordinary income
   c. $15,000 ordinary income and $35,000 long-term capital gain
   d. $15,000 long-term capital gain and $35,000 ordinary gain
   e. None of the above

19. Ross owns business equipment with a $50,000 adjusted basis. He paid $90,000 for the equipment. Ross dies suddenly and his son, Sean, inherits the property. Sean sells the equipment for $67,000. What is the amount of Sec. 1245 recapture Sean must report as ordinary income?
   a. $-0-
   b. $17,000
   c. $23,000
   d. $40,000
   e. $90,000

20. Drew owns a truck with an adjusted basis of $12,000. The truck originally cost $30,000 and it is currently worth $18,000 as a used truck. Drew transfers the truck to Green Corporation in a tax-free Sec. 351 transaction in exchange for Green Corporation stock. What is the amount of gain Drew must report because of any Sec. 1245 recapture on this transaction?
   a. $-0-
   b. $8,000
   c. $12,000
   d. $18,000
   e. $30,000

21. In order for cattle and horse to qualify for Sec. 1231 treatment, they must be held for more than how many months?
   a. 6 months
   b. 12 months
   c. 15 months
   d. 18 months
   e. 24 months

22. Generally, which of the following are not subject to Sec. 1245 treatment?
   a. Amortization of reforestation expenses.
   b. Property expensed under Sec. 179
   c. Residential Realty
   d. Expenses for the removal of handicapped barrier
   e. All of the above are subject to Sec. 1245

23. Luke exchanges Sec. 1245 property with an adjusted basis of $1,000 for Sec. 1245 property with a fair market value of $8,000. The exchange qualifies as a like-kind exchange under Sec. 1031. Luke also receives $1,500 cash (boot). The property exchanged by Luke has Sec. 1245 recapture potential of $4,000. What is Luke's recognized Sec. 1245 gain on this exchange?
    a. $-0-
    b. $500
    c. $1,500
    d. $4,000
    e. $7,000

24. Jed sold real estate in 1999 (acquired in 1985) for an $80,000 gain recognized. Depreciation taken on the property totaled $100,000. Of the gain, $18,000 was recaptured under Sec. 1250. What is Jed's potential 25 percent gain amount on this sale?
    a. $-0-
    b. $18,000
    c. $62,000
    d. $80,000
    e, Some other amount

25. In 1999, Martha, a single taxpayer, has $62,450 in ordinary taxable income. In addition, she has a net capital gain of $18,000, consisting of unrecaptured Sec. 1250 gain of $10,000 and adjusted net capital gain of $8,000. What is Martha's total tax liability?
    a. $18,239
    b. $18,939
    c. $19,719
    d. $17,739
    e. Some other amount

26. Teddy, sells Sec. 1245 property for $40,000, to be paid in 10 annual installments of $4,000 each, plus interest at 8%. Teddy has a realized gain of $12,000 from the sale of which $8,000 is attributable to depreciation taken. Teddy elects to use the installment method to report the sale. How much of Teddy's gain is ordinary income in the year of sale?
    a. $-0-
    b. $4,000
    c. $8,000
    d. $12,000
    e. Some other amount

27. Same as number 26. How much Sec. 1231 will be recognized each year for the 10-year collection period?
    a. $-0-
    b. $400
    c. $1,200
    d. $4,000
    e. Some other amount

28. Offshore Oil Co. has intangible drilling cost (IDC) of $1,000,000 on an oil property. The property has a basis to Offshore of $10,000,000 and it is sold to the Dryhole Oil Co. for $15,000,000 for a $5,000,000 realized gain. What is Offshore's Sec. 1254 recapture on this sale?
   a. $-0-
   b. $500,000
   c. $1,000,000
   d. $4,000,000
   e. Some other amount

SOLUTIONS TO CHAPTER 17

True or False

1. False Capital assets and Sec. 1231 assets are different. (p. 17-2)
2. True (p. 17-5)
3. False Gains are capital gains and losses are ordinary. (p. 17-3)
4. False Livestock other than cattle and horses only has to be held 12 months or more. (p. 17-6)
5. True (p. 17-5)
6. True (p. 17-6)
7. True (p. 17-13)
8. True (p. 17-14)
9. False Player contracts are Sec. 1245 property. (p. 17-14)
10. False Only the excess over straight-line is recaptured. (p. 17-15)
11. True (p. 17-13)
12. False Recapture potential passes to the donee. (p. 17-20)
13. True (p. 17-21)
14. True (p. 17-21)
15. False In an installment sale, recapture gain is recognized in full in the year of sale. (p. 17-22)
16. True (p. 17-24)
17. False The previous five years, not six years (p. 17-9)
18. False There is no recapture because only straight-line depreciation can be used (unless the property is disposed of within the first year). (p. 17-18)
19. False A transfer of property by gift does not cause recapture under Sec. 1250 or Sec. 1245. (p. 17-20)
20. False Poultry is excluded from the definition of Sec. 1231 assets. (p. 17-6)
21. True (p. 17-16)
22. False Sec. 1245 recapture is called full recapture, while Sec. 1250 recapture is referred to as partial recapture. (p. 17-13)
23. True (p. 17-13)
24. True (p. 17-13)
25. True (p. 17-5)
26. True (p. 17-19)

Fill-in-the-Blanks

1. override (p. 17-22)
2. controlled (p. 17-23)
3. expensed (p. 17-24)
4. for (p. 17-3)
5. long-term capital (p. 17-19)

Multiple Choice

1. A $20,000 + $110,000 + $50,000 = $180,000 (p. 17-5)
2. D The rental house is both Sec. 1231 and Sec. 1250 property. (p. 17-15)
3. D (p. 17-3)

4. B $5,000 - 2,500 = $2,500 adjusted basis. $4,000 - 2,500 = $1,500 gain realized, which is less than the depreciation recapture potential. Therefore, the realized gain is all Sec. 1245 gain. (p. 17-13)
5. B $2,000 - 2,500 = ($500) Sec. 1231 loss. (p. 17-13)
6. C $5,500 - 2,500 = $3,000 gain realized, of which $2,500 is Sec. 1245 gain and $500 is Sec. 1231 gain. (p. 17-13)
7. B $250,000 - 136,000 (basis) = $114,000 gain realized
$64,000 - 42,000 = $22,000 Sec. 1250 recapture. (p. 17-15)
8. C $7,500 - 6,000 = $1,500 ordinary income because of Sec. 1239. (p. 17-23)
9. D $20,000 - 4,000 = $16,000. (p. 17-21)
10. A (p. 17-22)
11. C (p. 17-9)
12. C All of the depreciation claimed is recaptured for ACRS nonresidential real property depreciated under the accelerated method. (p. 17-15)
13. C $175,000 - 100,000 = $75,000. (p. 17-5)
14. B The recapture is under Sec.1245, therefore all the deprecation is recaptured as ordinary income. (p. 17-15)
15. C $37,000 - 32,000 = $5,000 ordinary income. (p. 17-13)
16. D $50,000 + ($15,000 - 11,000) = $54,000. (p. 17-9)
17. A (p. 17-5)
18. C Sec. 1231 "lookback" treats $15,000 as ordinary income, with the balance being a long-term capital gain. (p. 17-9)
19. A Recapture potential disappears at the death of the owner of the property. (p. 17-21)
20. A The is no recapture on a tax-free reorganization including a Sec. 351 transaction. (p. 17-21)
21. E (p. 17-6)
22. C (p. 17-14)
23. C Gain ($8,000 - $1,000) is recognized to the extent of boot received ($1,500). (p. 17-22).
24. C $80,000 - $16,000 = $62,000. (p. 17-18)
25. A $14,139 (tax on ordinary income of $62,450 from schedule X) + ($10,000 x 25%) + ($8,000 x 20%) = $18,239. [1999] (p. 17-19)
26. C In the year of sale, any gain realized is recognized as ordinary income to the extent of depreciation. (p. 17-22)
27. B ($12,000 - $8,000)/10 years = $400 per year. (p. 17-22)
28. C (p.17-24)

CHAPTER 18
ACCOUNTING PERIODS AND METHODS

CHAPTER HIGHLIGHTS

This chapter discusses some of the options available to taxpayers in choosing accounting methods and periods. The cash, accrual, and hybrid accounting methods are covered along with the special accounting methods available for long-term construction contracts, installment sales, and inventory valuation.

I. ACCOUNTING PERIODS

A. In General. Taxpayers may be entitled to use a calendar year or a fiscal year in filing a tax return. Most individual taxpayers use a calendar year. However, certain other taxpayers may be eligible to use a fiscal year ending on the last day of any month. If certain conditions are met, taxpayers may use a 52-53 week year so that their year always ends on the same day of the week.

The tax year of a partnership is dependent on the tax year of the majority partners. If the majority partners do not have the same tax year, the tax year of the principal partners must be adopted. If the principal partners do not have the same tax year, the tax year that results in the least deferral of income must be used.

B. Partnerships, S Corporations, and Personal Service Corporations. Partnerships and S Corporations generally must use a calendar year. However, Partnerships and S corporations can elect an otherwise impermissible tax year if any one of the following conditions are met:

1) A business purpose for the tax year can be demonstrated

2) The deferral period is not more than three months and the entity agrees to make "required tax payments"

3) The entity retains the same tax year it had for its fiscal year ending in 1987 and agrees to make "required tax payments"

The required tax payments are computed by applying the highest individual tax rate plus 1 percent to an estimate of the deferral period income.

Personal Service Corporations (PSCs) generally use the calendar year. A fiscal year may be retained or used if one of the following applies:

1) A business purpose can be demonstrated

2) The deferral period is not more than three months and a proportionate part of the annual salaries of shareholder-employees is paid to the shareholders during the deferral period

3) The same fiscal year is retained that was used for its fiscal year ending in 1987 and the required minimum salary payments are made

See the text for the calculation of the required minimum salary payments for a personal service corporation (PSC).

B. Making the Election. The election to use a calendar or fiscal year by the timely filing of the initial tax return.

C. Changes in the Accounting Period. To change an accounting period a taxpayer must have the consent of the IRS. The IRS will not usually grant a change unless the taxpayer can establish a substantial business purpose for the change. If the taxpayer has an NOL for the short period, the IRS may require that the loss be carried forward for six years.

D. Taxable Periods of Less Than One Year. A short year is a period of less than 12 months. A taxpayer may have a short year for the first tax reporting period, the final income tax return, or because of a change in the tax year. Due to the progressive tax rate structure, the short period tax must be "annualized" if the short year is due to a change in the tax year. Special calculations are required for the annualization of an individual taxpayer's taxable income.

The tax is computed on the amount of the annualized income and then converted to a short period tax. The conversion is made using the following formula.

$$\frac{\text{\# of months in short period}}{12} \times \text{Tax on annualized income} = \text{Short period tax}$$

E. Mitigation of the Annual Accounting Period Concept. There are several provisions in the tax law designed to give taxpayers relief from the bunching of income because of arbitrary accounting periods. An example of such relief is the net operating loss carryover provision.

Under the "claim of right" doctrine an amount is includible in income on actual or constructive receipt if the taxpayer has an unrestricted claim to the amount, even if the taxpayer's right to the income is disputed. If the taxpayer is later required to repay such income, a deduction is allowed in the year of repayment, or in the case of amounts exceeding $3,000, the year in which the income was included if the tax benefit is greater.

II. ACCOUNTING METHODS

A. Permissible Methods. The Code requires taxpayers to report taxable income under the method of accounting regularly used by the taxpayer in keeping his or her books, provided the method is consistently employed and clearly reflects income. The tax law recognizes three methods: (1) cash receipts and disbursements, (2) accrual, and (3) hybrid (a combination of cash and accrual).

Taxpayers for whom inventories are a significant income producing factor must use the accrual method in computing sales and cost of goods sold. Special accounting methods, which are discussed later in this chapter, are permitted for installment sales and long-term contracts.

B. Cash Receipts and Disbursements Method - Cash Basis. Under the cash method, income is recognized when the taxpayer actually or constructively receives cash and deductions are taken in the year of payment. There are exceptions to these rules for cash basis taxpayers. For example, capital expenditures and prepaid items such as interest cannot be deducted in the current period. Certain taxpayers cannot use the cash method. These include corporations other than S Corporations, partnerships with a corporate partner, and tax shelters. Farming businesses, qualified personal service corporations, and certain entities with $5,000,000 or less of average gross receipts are allowed to use the cash method.

C. Accrual Method. The accrual method of accounting requires that income be recognized when: (1) all events have occurred which fix the right to receive such income and (2) the amount can be determined with reasonable accuracy. An accrual basis taxpayer who receives prepaid income (e.g., rent) in advance must usually recognize the income on a cash basis. An expense is deductible for the year in which all events have occurred which determine the fact of liability and the amount of the liability can be determined with reasonable accuracy, and then only if "economic performance" has occurred. In the case of services or property to be provided, economic performance occurs in the year the services or property are actually provided. Certain liabilities, such as for taxes and worker's compensation, are not deductible until paid. There are several exceptions to the economic performance test such as for bad debt reserves of small banks, etc. See text for details.

D. Hybrid Method. A hybrid method involves the use of both cash and accrual accounting concepts. It is common for a taxpayer to report sales and cost of goods sold on the accrual method and other items of income and deductions on the cash method.

E. Change of Method. Taxpayers make an election to use an accounting method when they file an initial tax return and use a particular method. Taxpayers who later want to change a method of accounting must obtain the permission of the IRS.

A correction of errors such as incorrect postings, omissions of income or deductions, or an incorrect calculation of tax liability does not constitute a change in accounting method. An error may be corrected by filing an amended return.

Permission from the IRS is necessary to change an erroneous method of accounting to a correct method.

If the IRS requires a taxpayer to change accounting methods to clearly reflect income and the amount of a required positive adjustment exceeds $3,000, certain averaging techniques are available to prevent the bunching of income.

To *voluntarily* change accounting methods, the taxpayer must generally file a request for a change during the taxable year of the desired change. An adjustment due to a change in method initiated by the taxpayer is normally required to be spread over a four-year period, starting with the year of the change.

III. SPECIAL ACCOUNTING METHODS

A. Installment Method. The installment method applies to gains but not losses. Under the installment method, gains are recognized from the sale of property when installments are collected.

The installment method may not be used for any of the following:

1) Gains on property held in the ordinary course of business

2) Depreciation recapture under Sec. 1245 or Sec. 1250

3) Gains on stocks or securities traded on an established market

Exceptions to the first item generally include the following:

1) Timeshare units

2) Residential lots

3) Any property used or produced by a farming business

As a rule, those sales that are eligible must be reported using the installment method. Conditions for electing out of the installment method are discussed later.

The recognized gain for installment sales is computed by using the following formula.

$$\frac{\textit{Total gain}}{\textit{Contact price}} \times \textit{Collections} = \textit{Recognized gain}$$

Total gain is the selling price reduced by selling expenses and the adjusted basis of the property. The selling price is the amount received by the seller, including receivables from the buyer and liabilities assumed by the buyer. Contract price is generally the amount the seller will receive, other than interest, from the buyer (selling price less the seller's liabilities assumed by the purchaser). Collections are payments received in the tax year less any interest income.

If the installment sale contract does not provide for interest of an amount at least equal to the Federal rate, then interest will be imputed at the Federal rate. The Federal rate is the rate the Federal government pays to borrow money and is published monthly by the IRS. The imputed interest reduces the selling price and as a result, increases the percentage relationship of the payment in the year of sale to the total selling price.

Sales between related parties may be subject to the special provisions of Sec. 453(e) of the Code. This provision separates transactions regarding related parties into a "first" and "second" disposition. If the second disposition takes place within two years of the first disposition, then the gain on the first disposition may be recognized. See text for example.

The Code prohibits use of the installment method for sales of depreciable property between certain related taxpayers.

B. Disposition of Installment Obligations. If installment notes are disposed of, gain that was previously deferred, must be recognized. The gain recognized is equal to the difference between the amount realized or the fair market value of the obligation and the basis of the obligation. Exceptions to this rule include transfers to controlled corporations, contributions to partnerships, and transfers due to the death of the taxpayer. Borrowing against installment notes causes recognition of the gain in most cases. Occasionally taxpayers may be required to make interest payments on amounts of taxes deferred by using the installment method. See text for rules.

C. Interest on Deferred Taxes. In some situations taxpayers may be required to pay interest on the taxes deferred in some installment sales.

D. Electing Out of the Installment Method. An election not to use the installment method is made by reporting the gain under the taxpayer's usual accounting method on a timely filed return. A cash basis taxpayer cannot realize less than the value of the property sold. This allows a cash basis taxpayer to report gain or loss as an accrual basis taxpayer.

If the taxpayer elects out of the installment method, permission from the IRS is required to revoke the election.

E. Long-term Contracts. Generally a taxpayer must accumulate all of the direct and indirect costs incurred under a contract. Mixed service costs must be allocated to production. For example, fringe benefit costs would be allocated as follows.

$$\frac{\textit{Labor on the contract}}{\textit{Total salaries and labor}} \times \textit{Total cost of fringe benefits}$$

Taxpayers use one of the following two methods of accounting for long-term contracts:

1) The completed contract method

2) The percentage of completion method

The completed contract method can be used only on certain real estate construction contracts (see text). All other contractors must use the percentage of completion method.
Under the completed contract method revenue and expenses relating to the contract are recognized when the contract is completed. Under the percentage of completion method, a portion of the gross contract revenue, based on the ratio of the contract costs incurred for the period to the estimated total costs under the contract, is included in income each period.

IV. INVENTORIES

A. Determining Inventory Cost. The cost of inventory is the invoice price less any discounts, plus freight and other handling costs. The cost of goods manufactured must be determined using the uniform capitalization (UNICAP) rules. Inventory may be valued at the lower of cost or market except for LIFO inventories. Taxpayers using the LIFO method must value inventory at cost.

Taxpayers may use specific identification, FIFO, LIFO, or average cost methods of inventory valuation for tax purposes. A taxpayer may use any of these methods, but the method selected must be used consistently from year to year.

B. The LIFO Election. A taxpayer may adopt LIFO by using the method in the tax return for the year of change and attaching to the tax return the proper form for the change. Once the election is made, it cannot be revoked unless the IRS gives permission. The change will usually be granted if the request is filed timely.

KEY TERMS

Accounting Periods

Accounting Methods

Economic Performance

Installment Method

Inventories

Least Aggregate Deferral

Long-term Contracts

Short Taxable Years

UNICAP

TEST FOR SELF-EVALUATION

True or False

Indicate which of the following statements are true or false by circling the correct answer.

T F 1. If certain conditions are met, a taxpayer may adopt a 52-53 week fiscal year.

T F 2. For an accrual basis taxpayer to take a deduction, the "all events test" including economic performance must be met.

T F 3. If taxpayers do not keep adequate books and records, they are required to use a calendar tax year.

T F 4. The Internal Revenue Service will automatically grant requests for changes to fiscal years from calendar years.

T F 5. All short years must have the tax calculated on an annualized basis.

T F 6. The standard deduction will be allowed in calculating short-period income of an individual taxpayer.

T F 7. The Code requires that taxable income be computed under the method of accounting regularly used by a taxpayer in keeping books, provided the method clearly reflects income.

T F 8. Taxpayers who have more than one trade or business must use the same method of accounting for each trade or business.

T F 9. A cash basis taxpayer must include in income all amounts actually or constructively received as cash or its equivalent.

T F 10. Expenses for a cash basis taxpayer must usually be paid before they are allowed as a deduction for tax purposes.

T F 11. All cash expenses of a cash basis taxpayer are deductible when paid.

T F 12. An accrual basis taxpayer recognizes income when it is earned.

T F 13. Generally, reserves for expenses of an accrual basis taxpayer are allowed as a deduction.

T F 14. A hybrid accounting method uses elements of both cash and accrual methods.

T F 15. The correction of an error in a tax return is usually considered a change in accounting method.

T F 16. A taxpayer may file a request for a change in accounting method at any time during the tax year.

T F 17. A transfer at death causes deferred gain on installment notes to be recognized in full.

T F 18. Income from long-term contracts must always be recognized under the percentage of completion method.

T F 19. A taxpayer who has average annual gross receipts for the three prior years of $25,000,000 may use the completed contract method of accounting for long-term contracts.

T F 20. The installment method of reporting is not allowed for depreciation recapture under Sec. 1245 or Sec. 1250.

T F 21. Sales of real property must have a selling price of more than $1,000 to qualify for the installment method.

T F 22. Internal Revenue Service permission is required to adopt the LIFO inventory method for tax purposes.

T F 23. In periods of inflation, the use of the LIFO inventory method produces a lower tax liability than the use of the FIFO inventory method.

T F 24. Lower of cost or market inventory cannot be used for tax purposes.

T F 25. Direct costing is an acceptable method for calculating taxable income.

T F 26. The contract price in an installment sale is generally the total amount (except interest) the seller will collect from the purchaser.

T F 27. Partnerships, S Corporations, and Personal Service Corporations can never elect a fiscal year for tax years after 1986.

T F 28. The S Corporation required tax payment is due by April 15th (or later as prescribed by the IRS) of each tax year.

T F 29. The IRS applies an objective gross receipts test to determine if an entity has a natural business year. Under this test, 25% of the gross receipts must be realized in the final two months of the tax year for the prior three consecutive years.

T F 30. Taxpayers may be required to pay interest on deferred taxes from an installment sale if outstanding obligations exceed $5,000,000 at the close of the year.

T F 31. Secs. 483 and 1274 provide that if a deferred payment contract for the sale of property with a selling price greater than $2,000 does not contain a reasonable interest rate, a reasonable rate is imputed.

T F 32. Taxpayers are permitted to adjust ending inventory for estimate shrinkage that has occurred between a nonyear-end date of a physical inventory and the last day of the tax year.

Fill-in-the-Blanks

Complete the following statements with the appropriate word(s) or amount(s).

1. The IRS may require an NOL from a "short year" arising from a change in accounting period to be carried forward __________ years.

2. The contract price in an installment sale is generally the total amount (excluding interest) the seller will ultimately _________ from the purchaser.

3. In general, if an installment contract has a stated interest rate less than the Federal rate, the IRS will impute interest at the _____________ rate.

4. The cost of goods produced or manufactured by the taxpayer must be determined by using the uniform __________ rules of inventory costing.

5. Inventories may be valued at the lower of cost or market except for _________ inventories.

6. Taxpayers using LIFO must value inventory at ____________.

7. During a period of rising prices, LIFO will generally produce a lower ending inventory and a __________ cost of goods sold.

8. Once a LIFO election is made, it __________ be revoked without the permission of the IRS.

Multiple Choice

Choose the best answer for each of the following questions.

1. Red Corporation, a calendar year taxpayer, would like to switch to a fiscal year ending June 30, 1999. The last day that Red can file the election (Form 1128) is:
   a. July 15, 1999
   b. August 15, 1999
   c. September 15, 1999
   d. October 15, 1999
   e. None of the above

2. Gray Corporation obtained permission to change from a calendar year to a fiscal year ending March 31. For the short period (January 1 to March 31), the corporation had taxable income of $24,000. The annualized income for 1999 would be:
   a. $96,000
   b. $6,000
   c. $48,000
   d. -0-
   e. Some other amount

3. Imputed interest will not be calculated in which of the following examples:
   a. A deferred contract on real estate
   b. If the interest rate is less than the Federal rate
   c. A deferred contract with a selling price of $2,500
   d. Installment sales of personalty
   e. None of the above

4. The California Limited Publishing Company invests $60,000 in printing 20,000 copies of a book. Twelve thousand copies were sold in the first two years of operation, and none have been sold over the last four years. Regardless, the company expects the books will sell in the future and thus it leaves the price the same ($20 per copy). How much may the taxpayer write off (expense) in the current year?
   a. -0-
   b. $120,000
   c. $240,000
   d. $360,000
   e. Some other amount

5. Tammy is a small building contractor who agrees to construct a building for $200,000. In 1999 she incurs costs of $90,000 and in 2000 costs of $70,000. An architect estimates the building is 60 percent complete in 1999 and the building is completed in 2000. If Tammy uses the *completed contract method* for 1999, she should report income of:
   a. -0-
   b. $30,000
   c. $10,000
   d. $40,000
   e. Some other amount

6. In January 1999, a husband sells stock to his wife for $100,000, its fair market value. The husband's basis in the stock was $45,000. Under terms of the sale, his wife pays $25,000 down and issues notes for the balance, payable over ten years plus interest at 10 percent. Four months later the wife sells the stock for $105,000. If the husband elects installment sale treatment, how much gain should the husband report in 1999?
   a. -0-
   b. $13,750
   c. $14,250
   d. $55,000
   e. Some other amount

7. Tim sells a parcel of real estate (basis of $40,000) for $100,000, receiving $20,000 as a down payment and the buyer's note for the balance, payable over a period of five years at the Federal rate of interest. The first payment on the note is due next year. If Tim uses the installment method under Sec. 453, how much gain should be reported in the year of sale?
   a. $60,000
   b. $40,000
   c. $12,000
   d. -0-
   e. Some other amount

8. Assume the same situation as in Question 8. How much gain (excluding interest) should Tim report in each of the next five years?
   a. $9,600
   b. $16,000
   c. $80,000
   d. $48,000
   e. Some other amount

9. Yoshi sold a ranch she owned as an investment on June 1 of the current year. Pertinent information on Yoshi's transaction is as follows:

Date of Acquisition	1984
Adjusted Basis	$20,000
Mortgage, assumed by buyer	30,000
Cash down payment	25,000
10-year note, payable to Yoshi	100,000

The interest rate stated in the note exceeds the appropriate federal rate. The note payments are $10,000 per year and are due in annual installments. What is the contract price for the above sale?
a. $100,000
b. $125,000
c. $120,000
d. $135,000
e. Some other amount

10. Refer to the preceding problem. What amount of gain must be recognized in the year of sale?
a. $-0-
b. $10,000
c. $15,000
d. $35,000
e. Some other amount

11. Refer to the preceding problem. What amount must be recognized as income in the year the first installment payment is collected?
a. $-0-
b. $10,000
c. $15,000
d. $25,000
e. Some other amount

12. Green Corporation entered a $500,000 contract that will take two years to complete. Total costs of the project were estimated to be $450,000. Costs incurred during the first year were $315,000. If Green Corporation uses the percentage of completion method, how much revenue must be recognized in the first year of the contract?
a. $-0-
b. $250,000
c. $350,000
d. $500,000
e. Some other amount

13. The RGB Partnership is owned by R, G, and B. R owns 30 percent, G owns 30 percent, and B owns 40 percent. R and G close their tax years on September 30 while B uses the calendar year to report taxable income. The RGB Partnership's tax year must end on:
a. September 30
b. October 31
c. November 30
d. December 31
e. a date determined by the least aggregate deferral of income method

14. In 1999 Tom uses the lower of cost or market and FIFO inventory method. The FIFO cost of the ending inventory was $40,000 and its market value was $34,000. Therefore, the ending inventory for 1999 was $34,000. In 2000 Tom switched to the LIFO inventory method. How much income, if any, must Tom recognize for 2000?
    a. -0-
    b. $2,000 ordinary income
    c. $2,000 long-term capital gain
    d. $2,000 long-term capital loss
    e. Some other amount

15. Carol's corporation (a personal service corporation) paid her a salary of $132,000 during the fiscal year ended October 31, 1999. The corporation can continue to use its fiscal year, provided Carol receives a salary of how much during the period November 1 to December 31?
    a. $-0-
    b. $33,000
    c. $22,000
    d. $11,000
    e. Some other amount

16. The ABCD Partnership is owned by A Corporation, B Corporation, C Corporation, and individual D. The partners have the following tax years.

A (30%)	September 30
B (25%)	September 30
C (25%)	June 30
D (20%)	December 31

    On what date must the partnership's tax year end?
    a. June 30
    b. September 30
    c. December 31
    d. Any date the partnership chooses
    e. Some other date

17. In 1998 Amber Corporation, an accrual basis taxpayer, sold defective merchandise that caused injury to the purchaser. Amber admitted liability in 1999 and paid the customer claim in January 2000. What year is the purchaser's tort claim deductible?
    a. 1998
    b. 1999
    c. 2000
    d. The tort is not deductible

18. Silver Corporation, an accrual basis corporation, files its 1999 California state income tax return in April 2000. When the return was filed Silver had to pay an additional tax of $6,000. Due to an error in the original tax return, the corporation filed an amended California tax return in November 2000 and paid an additional $10,000 in tax. How much of the state taxes paid is deductible in 1999?
    a. $-0-
    b. $6,000
    c. $10,000
    d. $16,000

e. Some other amount

19. Julie owns a small coin shop. She values her inventory using the lower of cost or market method. What is Julie's ending inventory for 1999 based on the following information?

	Cost	Market
Gold coins	$10,000	$ 8,000
Silver coins	12,000	14,000
Rare silver dollars	4,000	9,000
Rare dimes	2,000	1,000
Total	$28,000	$32,000

a. $25,000
b. $28,000
c. $31,000
d. $32,000
e. Some other amount

20. Brown Corporation was to switch from the FIFO to the LIFO inventory method for tax purposes. In order to make this change Brown Corporation:
a. Must spread the adjustment over six years
b. Request permission from the IRS within 90 days of the change
c. Must have a "business purpose" for making the change
d. Must file a tax return using the LIFO method
e. None of the above

21. In 1999, Acme Contractors, Inc. entered into a contract to build a building for a local university for $12,000,000. The estimated time to complete the building was two years and the estimated cost is $10,000,000. At the end of 1999 the accumulated costs on the project are $4,000,000. Acme uses the percentage of completion method on the contract. At the end of 1999, the chief engineer estimates the building is 50 percent complete. Acme must recognize what amount of profit from this contract for 1999?
a. $-0-
b. $800,000
c. $1,000,000
d. $1,200,000
e. Some other amount

22. Gold Corporation, an accrual basis taxpayer, sold defective merchandise that injured a customer. Gold was held liable for $100,000 in 1999. After an appeal, Gold Corporation pays the customer $75,000 in 2000. How does Gold Corporation treat this liability for tax purposes?
a. Nothing is deductible because economic performance has not occurred.
b. Gold can deduct $100,000 in 1999
c. Gold can deduct $75,000 in 2000.
d. Gold deducts $100,000 in 1999 and then reports $25,000 as income in 2000.
e. None of the above.

23. Sam, a cash basis taxpayer, sold land on January 3, 1999, for $5,000,000. He received $500,000 cash down payment and the buyer's 5% note for $4,500,000. At the time of the sale, the Federal rate was 9%. At what rate (if any) will interest be imputed on this installment sale?

a. 6%
b. 7½%
c. 8½%
d. 9%
e. There will no imputed interest.

24. Susan, a cash basis taxpayer, sold land on January 3, 1999, for $450,000 to her son. She received $50,000 cash down payment and a $400,000 note from her son paying 5% interest. At the time of the sale, the Federal rate was 9%. At what rate (if any) will interest be imputed on this installment sale?
a. 6%
b. 7½%
c. 8½%
d. 9%
e. There will no imputed interest.

25. On January 1, 1999, Joan sold land to her son for $30,000 cash and a 9% installment note with a face amount of $180,000. In 1999, after paying Joan $40,000 on the principal of the note, the son sold the land to an unrelated party. In 1999, the son paid Joan and additional $50,000 on the note principal. Joan's basis in the land was $70,000. Assuming the son sold the land for $400,000. What is Joan's taxable gain in 1999?
a. $-0-
b. $10,000
c. $30,000
d. $70,000
e. $140,000

Problems

1. Jill acquired a duplex in 19X5 which she held as rental property. The original cost of the property was $80,000. During 19X5 Jill spent $14,500 for capital improvements on the property. For tax years 19X5 and 19X6, a total of $5,300 of depreciation was claimed on the property under the straight-line method. In the current year, 19X7, Jill sold the property for $120,000, receiving $20,000 on March 1st as a cash down payment and the buyer's note for $100,000 at the Federal rate of interest. The note is payable at $10,000 per year for ten years, with each payment due on December 1st, beginning in 19X7. Her selling expenses were $6,800. If Jill uses the Sec. 453 installment sale treatment on this transaction, calculate the amount of taxable gain that must be reported during 19X7. Use the following worksheet.

a.	Gross sales price	________
	Selling expenses	________
	Adjusted basis	________
	Net profit	________
b.	Gross profit percentage	________
c.	19X7 taxable gain	________

2. La Fonda Limited, a partnership, has a fiscal year ending on October 31. For the prior fiscal year ended October 31, 1999, La Fonda Limited had taxable income of $96,000. What is La Fonda's required tax payment that is due in 2000 (assuming there were no required tax payments in the prior year).

SOLUTIONS TO CHAPTER 18

True or False

1. True (p. 18-3)
2. True (p. 18-13)
3. True (p. 18-3)
4. False The IRS will grant requests where there is a substantial business purpose for the change. (p. 18-7)
5. False The tax for the first and last years does not have to be annualized. (p. 18-8)
6. False The standard deduction is not allowed. (p. 18-9)
7. True (p. 18-10)
8. False A different method of accounting may be used for each trade or business. (p. 18-11)
9. True (p. 18-11)
10. True (p. 18-11)
11. False Certain prepaid expenses must be capitalized and amortized. (p. 18-11)
12. True (p. 18-13)
13. False Reserves are usually not allowed as a deduction. (p. 18-15)
14. True (p. 18-15)
15. False A correction of an error is not a change in accounting method. (p. 18-16)
16. True (p. 18-16)
17. False A transfer due to a taxpayer's death does not cause deferred gain to be recognized. (p. 18-25)
18. False In certain cases, the completed contract method may be used for long-term contracts. (p. 18-27)
19. False The maximum is an average of $10,000,000. (p. 18-27)
20. True (p. 18-19)
21. False There is no minimum amount required for the selling price. (p. 18-19)
22. False IRS permission is not needed. (p. 18-35)
23. True (p. 18-34)
24. False Lower of cost or market can be used for tax purposes except where the LIFO method is used. (p. 18-33)
25. False Direct costing is not allowed for valuing inventories. (p. 18-31)
26. True (p. 18-20)
27. False They can elect a fiscal year if certain tests are met. (p. 18-4)
28. True (p. 18-5)
29. True (p. 18-7)
30. True (p. 18-26)
31. False The price has to be greater than $3,000. (p. 18-22)
32. True (p. 18-33)

Fill-in-the-Blanks

1. six (p. 18-8)
2. receive (p. 18-20)
3. Federal (p. 18-22)
4. capitalization (p. 18-32)
5. LIFO (p. 18-33)
6. cost (p. 18-33)
7. larger (p. 18-34)

8. cannot (p. 18-35)

Multiple Choice

1.	B	(p. 18-7)
2.	A	$24,000 x (12 ÷ 3) = $96,000. (p. 18-8)
3.	C	(p. 18-22)
4.	A	(p. 18-33)
5.	A	(p. 18-28)
6.	D	$100,000 - 45,000 = $55,000 realized. Because the wife sold the stock four months later, the entire $55,000 realized gain must be recognized by the husband. (p. 18-23)
7.	C	[($100,000 - 40,000) ÷ $100,000] x $20,000 = $12,000. (p. 18-20)
8.	A	[($100,000 - 40,000) ÷ $100,000] x $16,000 = $9,600. (p. 18-20)

9. D

Selling price	$155,000
Mortgage assumed	-30,000
Excess of mortgage over basis	+10,000
Contract price	$135,000

(p. 18-21)

10.	D	[$135,000/$135,000] x $35,000 = $35,000 (p. 18-21)
11.	B	[$135,000/$135,000] x $10,000 = $10,000 (p. 18-21)
12.	C	[$315,000/$450,000] x $500,000 = $350,000 (p. 18-29)
13.	A	(p. 18-4)
14.	B	($40,000 - 34,000) ÷ 3 years = $2,000 ordinary income. (p. 18-36)
15.	C	(2÷12) x $132,000 = $22,000. (p. 18-6)
16.	B	The year end must be the same as the majority interest partners. (p. 18-4)
17.	C	The tort is deductible in the year paid. (p. 18-14)
18.	B	Recurring payments within 8.5 months meet the economic performance test. (p. 18-14)
19.	A	$8,000 + 12,000 + 4,000 + 1,000 = $25,000. (p. 18-33)
20.	D	Approval to change is not needed. (p. 18-35)
21.	B	($4,000,000 ÷ $10,000,000) x ($12,000,000 - 10,000,000) = $800,000. (p.18-29)
22.	C	(p. 18-14)
23.	D	(p. 18-22)
24.	A	(p. 18-23)
25.	E	If the land is sold to a family member and then resold within two years, the gain is taxable to the family member. $210,000 - $70,000 = $140,000. (p. 18-23)

Problems

1. a.

Gross sales price		$120,000
Selling expenses		-6,800
Adjusted basis:		
Original cost	$80,000	
Capital improvements	14,500	
Depreciation	-5,300	
		-89,200
Net Profit		$24,000

b. Gross profit percentage: $24,000÷$120,000 = 20 percent

c. Taxable gain:

Amount received in 19X7:		
Down payment	$20,000	
12/1/X7 payment	10,000	
Total received	$30,000	
Gross profit %	20%	
Taxable gain	$6,000	(p. 18-19)

2. $96,000 x (2/12) x 40.6% = $6,496. (p. 18-6)

CHAPTER 19
DEFERRED COMPENSATION

CHAPTER HIGHLIGHTS

This chapter covers various deferred compensation plans that are available to employees and self-employed taxpayers. Deferred compensation means that an employee receives compensation after the services are performed. Contributions to such plans and income on the contributions are generally not taxed to employees until the funds are actually received. Such favorable tax treatment is meant to encourage deferred compensation plans that supplement the Social Security system.

I. QUALIFIED PENSION, PROFIT SHARING, AND STOCK BONUS PLANS

A. Types of Plans. The tax law provides substantial benefits for retirement plans that meet certain qualifications. Three types of plans qualify under the law: (1) pension, (2) profit sharing, and (3) stock bonus.

A pension plan is a deferred compensation arrangement that provides for systematic payments of retirement benefits to employees who meet the requirements set forth in the plan. There are two basic types of pension plans, defined benefit plans and defined contribution plans.

A profit-sharing plan is an arrangement established and maintained by an employer to provide for employee participation in the company's profits, either current or accumulated.

A stock bonus plan is a plan established and maintained by an employer to provide contributions of the employer's stock to the plan. There is no requirement that contributions be dependent on profits.

An employee stock ownership plan (ESOP) is a stock bonus plan that qualifies as a tax-exempt employee trust under Sec. 401(a).

B. Qualification Requirements. To be "qualified," a plan must meet the following requirements:

1) Exclusive benefit requirement

2) Nondiscriminatory rules

3) Participation and coverage requirements

4) Vesting requirements

5) Distribution requirements

The plan must be created by an employer for the exclusive benefit of the employees or their beneficiaries. To meet the exclusive benefit requirement, the investment must be of the type that a "prudent person" would make.

The plan must not discriminate in favor of employees who are highly compensated. A plan is not considered discriminatory if contributions and benefits uniformly relate to compensation.

At a minimum, the plan must provide that all employees in the covered group who are 21 years of age are eligible to participate after completing one year of service. Furthermore, the plan must cover a reasonable percentage of the company's employees.

The plan must meet certain vesting requirements for both the employer and employee contributions. The employee must, from the date of contribution, have a nonforfeitable right to the accrued benefits from his own contributions. Benefits from employer contributions must be nonforfeitable according to one of two minimum vesting schedules.

Uniform minimum distribution rules exist for all qualified plans, IRAs, unfunded deferred compensation plans of state and local governments and tax-exempt employers, and tax-sheltered custodial accounts and annuities. Distributions must begin by April 1st of the calendar year following the calendar year in which the participant attains the age of 70½ or retires. A five percent owner or a traditional IRA owner must begin distributions no later than April 1st of the year following the year the owner reaches age 70½. This rule does not apply to Roth IRAs.

Early distributions are subject to an additional 10 percent penalty tax.

C. Tax Consequences to the Employee and Employer. The primary tax benefit of a qualified plan to the employee is that the employer's contributions to the plan are not subject to income taxation until such amounts are made available or distributed to the employee. In addition, earnings on the contributions are not taxable until withdrawn.

Employee contributions have been previously subject to taxation. Therefore, part of the payments from the plan are excluded from the employee's income under the annuity rules of Sec. 72.

An employee who receives a lump-sum distribution from a qualified plan is subject to various special rules on the distribution. See text for rules.

D. Limitations on Contributions to and Benefits from Qualified Plans. Under a defined contribution plan, the annual addition to an employee's account cannot exceed the smaller of $30,000 or 25 percent of the employee's compensation. If the plan is a defined benefit plan, the annual benefit payable to an employee is limited to the smaller of $130,000 (in 1999) or 100 percent of the employee's average compensation for the highest three years of employment. For collectively bargained plans with at least 100 participants, different annual limitations apply (see text).

The employer's contribution is deductible when paid into the pension trust. An employer's deduction for contributions to profit-sharing and stock bonus plans is limited to 15 percent of the compensation (up to a maximum of $160,000 per employee) of the plan participants. If there are two or more plans, the percentage limitation is increased to 25 percent. Any unused contributions can be used in later years as a carryover deduction, subject to certain limitations.

E. Top-heavy Plans. A top-heavy plan is generally one that provides more than 60% of the cumulative benefits to an employer's key employees. Key employees include officers, the ten employees owning the largest interest in an employer, a greater-than-five percent owner of an employer, or an employee who has annual compensation greater than $150,000 and who owns more than 1 percent of the employer.

F. Section 401(k) Plans. A Sec. 401(k) plan allows participants to elect either to receive up to $10,000 (in 1999) in cash or to have a contribution made on their behalf to a profit sharing or stock bonus plan. The plan may also be a salary reduction agreement. Any pretax amount elected as a contribution is not includible in the employee's gross income and is 100% vested. The employer's contributions and earnings on the contributions are tax deferred.

Employers with 100 or fewer employees who do not have a qualified retirement plan may establish a SIMPLE plan for employees. The plan can be a 401(k) plan or an IRA. Employees can make elective contribution of up to $6,000 (in 1999) per year. Employers generally are required to match up to 3 percent of the employee's compensation.

II. RETIREMENT PLANS FOR SELF-EMPLOYED INDIVIDUALS

Self-employed individuals and their employees are allowed to receive qualified retirement benefits under H.R. 10 (Keogh) plans.

A. Coverage Requirements. Contributions and benefits of a self-employed individual are subject to the general percentage, ratio, and average benefits tests applied to other qualified plans.

B. Contribution Limitations. The maximum annual contribution that may be made to a defined contribution Keogh plan is the smaller of $30,000 or 25 percent of earned income. Earned income is reduced by the Keogh contribution that means that the contribution is limited to 20 percent of income before the contribution. There is a 15 percent (instead of 25 percent) limit on contributions to profit-sharing Keogh plans. Under a defined benefit Keogh plan, the annual benefit payable to an employee is limited to the smaller of $130,000 (in 1999) or 100 percent of the employee's average compensation for the highest three years of employment.

If a Keogh Plan is considered top-heavy, the 25% limitation on employee contributions is on the first $160,000 (in 1999) of earned income.

III. INDIVIDUAL RETIREMENT ACCOUNTS (IRAs)

A. General Rules. All taxpayers may have an individual retirement account. The maximum contribution is the smaller of $2,000 ($4,000 for a spousal account) or 100 percent of compensation. In 1999, if the taxpayer is not covered by another plan, or if the taxpayer's AGI is not more than $31,000, the IRA contribution is fully deductible. If the taxpayer is covered by another qualified retirement plan, the deduction is phased out 20 cents on the dollar until it is no longer available once AGI reaches $41,000. For married taxpayers the 1999 phaseout is from $51,000 to $61,000.

Simplified employee pension (SEPs) plans are available to employers as an alternative to regular qualified plans. The employer may contribute to an IRA covering an employee the lesser of 15 percent of the employee's earned income or $30,000.

A taxpayer may make a contribution to an IRA any time before the original due date (April 15th) of his or her tax return and still claim the amount as a deduction for the year.

B. Roth IRAs. Starting in 1999, taxpayers may contribute to a Roth IRA. Contributions to a Roth IRA are not deductible, however, the earnings and withdrawals after age 59 ½ are tax free (if held for over five years). If the Roth IRA does not meet these tests, the part of the distribution that is in excess of a return of capital will be taxable. The maximum annual contribution to a Roth IRA is phased-out starting at $95,000 for single taxpayers and $150,000 for married couples filing jointly.

C. Education IRAs. The maximum that can be contributed to an Education IRA is $500 per year for each beneficiary. The contributions are not deductible. The maximum annual contribution to an education IRA is phased-out starting at $95,000 for single taxpayers and $150,000 for married couples filing jointly. The education IRA exclusion is not available in any year which the beneficiary claims the HOPE credit or the Lifetime Learning Credit.

Starting in 1999, education IRA distributions to pay for qualified higher education expenses are tax-free. Qualified education expenses are: tuition, fees, books, supplies, and related equipment. Room and board qualify if the student is at least a half-time student. Any excess distributions are taxable.

Distributions from noneducation IRAs for qualified education expenses are not subject to the 10 percent penalty on early withdrawals.

D. Penalty Taxes for Excess Contributions. There is a cumulative nondeductible 6 percent excise penalty tax imposed on the smaller of any excess contributions or the market value of the plan assets determined at the close of the tax year.

E. Taxation of Benefits. A participant has a zero basis in his or her deductible contributions to an IRA, and once retirement payments are received, they are included in ordinary income. Payments made to a participant before age 59½ are subject to a nondeductible 10 percent penalty tax on such actual or constructive payments. Penalty-free withdrawals prior to age 59½ are allowed for certain medical, educational, and first-time home buyer expenses.

IV. NONQUALIFIED DEFERRED COMPENSATION PLANS

A. Underlying Rationale for Tax Treatment. Nonqualified deferred compensation plans allow individuals to defer income taxes on income payments until they are possibly in a lower tax bracket. Unlike qualified plans, most deferred compensation plans do not have to meet the discrimination, funding, coverage, and other requirements.

B. Tax Treatment to the Employer and Employee. In an unfunded NQDC plan, the employee relies upon the company's promise to make the compensation payment in the future. In this case, the employee is taxed when the compensation is paid or made available and the employer is allowed a deduction when the employee recognizes income.

Golden Parachutes. Certain excessive severance payments to employees may be penalized. The tax law denies a deduction to an employer who makes a cash payment to an employee that satisfies both the following conditions:

1) The payment is contingent on a change of ownership of a corporation through a stock or assets acquisition, and

2) The aggregate present value of the payment equals or exceeds three times the employee's average annual compensation (for the past five years).

Golden parachute payments rules do not apply to payments made to qualified pension, profit sharing, stock bonus, annuity, or SEP plans.

Publicly-Held Companies' Compensation Limitation. For purposes of the regular and alternative income tax, the deductible compensation for the top five executives of publicly-traded companies is limited to $1 million for each executive. There are several exceptions to this limitation. See text for details.

V. RESTRICTED PROPERTY PLANS

A. General Provisions. A restricted property plan is an arrangement whereby an employer transfers property to an employee at no cost or at a bargain price. The fair market value of the transferred property is included in gross income of the employee the earlier of when the property is no longer subject to substantial risk of forfeiture or when the employee has the right to transfer property free of the substantial risk of forfeiture.

B. Substantial Risk of Forfeiture. A substantial risk of forfeiture exists if a person's rights to full enjoyment of such property are conditioned on the future performance, or refraining from the performance, of substantial services by the employee. An employee may elect within 30 days after the receipt of restricted property, to recognize immediately, as ordinary income the excess of fair market value over the amount paid for the property. Any future appreciation is considered capital gain instead of ordinary income.

C. Employer Deductions. An employer is allowed a tax deduction for restricted property for the same amount and at the same time that the employee is required to include the compensation in income.

VI. STOCK OPTIONS

A. In General. A stock option gives an individual the right to purchase a stated number of shares of stock from a corporation at a certain price within a specified period.

B. Incentive Stock Options. Incentive stock options (ISO) are designed to help corporations attract management. To qualify for incentive stock option treatment the option holder must be an employee of the corporation from the date the option is granted until three months before the date of exercise. Under this plan there are no tax consequences when an option is granted or exercised. Once the option is exercised and the stock is sold, any gain is long-term capital gain to the employee provided the employee holds the stock for a certain period.

The excess of the fair market value of the stock at the date of exercise over the option price is a tax preference item for the alternative minimum tax.

C. Nonqualified Stock Options. The fair market value of nonqualified stock options must be included in the employee's income at the date the stock options are granted.

If the fair market value is not ascertainable, then the difference between the fair market value of the stock at the exercise date and the option price is ordinary income in the year of exercise.

The corporation will receive a deduction at the same time and in the same amount as the income recognized by the employee.

KEY TERMS:

Qualified Plan

Keogh Plan

IRAs

Nonqualified Plans

Restricted Property Plan

Section 401(k) Plans

SIMPLE Plans

Stock Options

Top Heavy Plans

TEST FOR SELF-EVALUATION

True or False

Indicate which of the following statements are true or false by circling the correct answer.

T F 1. The three basic types of qualified plans are pension plans, profit-sharing plans, and stock bonus plans.

T F 2. Profit-sharing plans maintain separate accounts for each participant in the plan.

T F 3. A stock bonus plan is a deferred compensation arrangement established to provide contributions to the plan of stock other than the employer's stock.

T F 4. The two types of qualified pension plans are defined contribution plans and defined benefit plans.

T F 5. A defined contribution plan provides a formula that defines the benefits employees are to receive.

T F 6. An ESOP is a defined contribution plan that is either a qualified stock bonus plan or a stock bonus plan and a money purchase plan, each of which qualify under Sec. 401(a).

T F 7. A qualified plan does not have to be for the exclusive benefit of employees or their beneficiaries.

T F 8. The contributions or benefits of a qualified plan may discriminate in favor of employees who are officers, stockholders, or highly compensated.

T F 9. In all qualified plans, employer contributions must vest immediately.

T F 10. Employer contributions to qualified plans are not subject to taxation until such amounts are made available or distributed to the employees.

T F 11. It is possible for a taxpayer to be covered by a qualified retirement plan and have a Keogh plan to which contributions are made in the current year.

T F 12. All lump-sum distributions qualify for the special ten-year averaging rule.

T F 13. For 1999, the maximum contribution to a defined contribution plan is the smaller of $30,000 or 25 percent of the employee's compensation.

T F 14. For <u>all</u> defined benefit plans, the maximum contribution for 1999 is the smaller of $130,000 or 100 percent of the employee's average compensation for the three highest paid years of employment.

T F 15. The maximum deduction permitted each year for contributions to profit sharing and stock bonus plans is 15 percent of the compensation paid or accrued with respect to the participants in the plan.

T F 16. All employees of a company must be covered under its Keogh plan in order for the plan to be qualified.

T F 17. All individual taxpayers with earned income can qualify for an individual retirement account, to which contributions may or may not be deductible.

T F 18. The maximum deductible IRA contribution for an unmarried taxpayer with AGI of $25,000 or less is $2,000, regardless of how many accounts the taxpayer has.

T F 19. Employee benefits under a qualified plan must vest under one of two alternative schedules.

T F 20. Unless special circumstances apply, the earliest age to withdraw funds without penalty from a deductible IRA is 59½ years old.

T F 21. All IRA contributions of an individual are deductible.

T F 22. An employer with 125 employees can establish a SIMPLE plan for those employees as long as the employer matches any employee contributions to the plan to a maximum of 3 percent.

T F 23. Bea receives $35,000 in alimony in the current year, her only income. She may contribute $2,000 to an IRA.

T F 24. The maximum annual contribution to a Roth IRA is phased-out at $95,000 for single taxpayers and $150,000 for married couples filing jointly.

T F 25. For 1999, distributions from noneducation IRAs for qualified education expenses are not subject to the 10 percent penalty on early withdrawals.

Fill-in-the-Blanks

Complete the following statements with the appropriate word(s) or amount(s).

1. The deduction for an IRA is limited to the smaller of _________ or the individual's taxable compensation from personal services.

2. In an IRA, a participant has a basis of _________ in his or her deductible contributions.

3. The doctrine of __________ receipt is an important concept relating to the taxability of nonqualified deferred compensation.

4. In a restricted property plan, if an employee performs services and receives property, the fair market value of the property in excess of any amount paid is _________ in the gross income of the employee.

5. If a person's rights to full enjoyment of property are conditioned on future performance, or the refraining from the performance of substantial services there is said to be a substantial _________ of forfeiture.

6. An employee may elect within ___________ days after the receipt of restricted property to recognize immediately as ordinary income the excess of fair market value over the amount paid for the property.

7. In a restricted property plan, the employer is allowed a deduction for the same amount and at the same time the employee is required to __________ the compensation in income.

8. If a nonqualified stock option has a readily ascertainable fair market value, the value of the option must be included in the employee's __________ at the date of the grant.

9. If a nonqualified stock option does not have a readily ascertainable price, the employee's recognized income in the year of __________ is the amount equal to the difference between the fair market value of the stock at the exercise date and the option price.

Multiple Choice

Choose the best answer for each of the following questions.

1. The qualified pension plan of Grossmont Corporation calls for both the employer and employee to contribute 6% of the employee's compensation to the plan. This plan is a:
   a. Defined benefit plan
   b. Defined contribution plan
   c. Profit-sharing plan
   d. Stock bonus plan
   e. None of the above

2. Dee has completed six years of service with her employer. If her pension plan uses "graded vesting," what is Dee's nonforfeitable percentage?
   a. 10%
   b. 40%
   c. 60%
   d. 80%
   e. Some other amount

3. Assume the same situation as in Question 2 If the plan vests under "cliff vesting," what percentage of the employer's contributions must be vested?
   a. 100%
   b. 55%
   c. 50%
   d. 45%
   e. Some other amount

4. Karen, receives a $500,000 payment under a golden parachute agreement entered into in 1999. Karen's statutory base amount is $360,000. What amount of this payment is not deductible to the corporation under Sec. 280G?
   a. -0-
   b. $120,000
   c. $360,000
   d. $140,000

e. Some other amount

5. Sue is single and self-employed. During the current year, her adjusted gross income was $14,000, including interest of $12,500 and salary of $1,500. The maximum amount that could be contributed to an IRA and deducted by Sue is:
a. -0-
b. $1,500
c. $2,000
d. $2,100
e. Some other amount

6. Assume the same situation as in Question 5 except that Sue's adjusted gross income is all from salary. The maximum amount that could be contributed by Sue to an IRA is:
a. -0-
b. $1,500
c. $1,200
d. $2,000
e. Some other amount

7. I. Shade, C.P.A., is self-employed and has established a *defined contribution* Keogh (H.R. 10) plan. The plan states that he will contribute the maximum percentage of earned income to the plan. Shade has no employees. His self-employment income before any Keogh deduction for 1999 is $190,000. Shade's deduction for this plan is:
a. $47,500
b. $38,000
c. $30,000
d. $90,000
e. Some other amount

8. Currently, the basic required minimum coverage for a qualified plan for all employees is:
a. 25 years old and three years of service
b. 21 years old and one year of service
c. 18 years old and three years of service
d. 21 years old and three years of service

9. Tim was employed by Purple Corporation at a salary of $70,000. Purple Corporation contributes to a retirement plan for Tim that allows extra voluntary Sec. 401(k) contributions. For 1999, what is the maximum additional amount that Tim may contribute to this plan?
a. $6,000
b. $10,000
c. $10,500
d. $2,000
e. Some other amount

10. Pink Corporation and Tom (a cash basis employee) enter into an employment agreement which provides for an annual salary of $140,000. Of this amount, $120,000 is to be paid currently and $20,000 is to be paid in 10 installments on Tom's retirement. How much would be taxable to Tom in the current year?
a. -0-
b. $100,000

c. $120,000
d. $140,000
e. Some other amount

11. In the current year, Toni is granted a nonqualified stock option to purchase 200 shares of stock from his employer at $9 per share. On the date the options are issued, the stock was selling on the New York Stock Exchange for $14 per share. For the current year Toni should report:
a. $1,000 long-term capital gain
b. $1,000 ordinary income
c. $1,800 ordinary income
d. $1,800 long-term capital gain
e. Some other amount

12. On March 1, 1998, Ted is granted a nonqualified stock option for 100 shares of common stock at $12 per share. On that date, there is no readily ascertainable fair market value for the stock. Ted exercised the option on May 1, 1999, when the stock is selling for $20 per share. The stock is sold for $30 in 2000. For 1999, Ted should recognize:
a. No gain or loss
b. $800 ordinary income
c. $800 long-term capital gain
d. $1,200 ordinary income
e. Some other amount

13. Tina is a sole proprietor with six employees. She has offered her employees a SEP IRA, which all six have elected to participate in. William, an employee, has a salary of $18,000 for the current year. In 1998, what is the maximum contribution to William's IRA?
a. -0-
b. $2,000
c. $2,250
d. $2,700
e. Some other amount

14. On March 1, 1998, Tess is given a nonqualified option on 100 shares of her employer's stock. The option price and FMV are $75 per share on the date the option is granted. Tess exercises the option on April 1, 1998 when the price of the stock is $125 per share. She sells the stock on October 15, 1999 for $200 per share. What is Tess's reported gain in 1999?
a. -0-
b. $12,500 long-term capital gain
c. $12,500 ordinary income
d. $5,000 long-term capital gain
e. Some other amount

15. Trudy has $15,000 in a deductible IRA and $5,000 in a nondeductible IRA. In the current year, Trudy withdraws $1,000 from the nondeductible IRA. What portion of the withdrawal is included in Trudy's income?
a. $-0-
b. $250
c. $750
d. $1,000

e. Some other amount

16. In the current year, Nancy is over 70½ years old. As of December 31 of last year, her IRA account had a balance in it of $157,300. Her life expectancy multiple is 14.3 and she has taken out a total of $22,000 from the IRA in prior years. Her required minimum distribution from this IRA is:
a. $-0-
b. $11,000
c. $9,441
d. $135,300
e. $157,300

17. Gene has compensation (and AGI) for 1999 of $38,000 and Gene was an active participant in a qualified plan. What is the maximum amount that he may deduct for contributions to his regular IRA?
a. $-0-
b. $600
c. $1,400
d. $2,000
e. None of the above

18. Zoe is a new employee in a qualified retirement plan in 1999. Zoe would be considered a highly compensated employee if:
a. she owns 6.0 percent of the stock of the company.
b. she is an officer or member of the top-paid group in the company and her salary is $75,000.
c. she is an officer in the company and her salary is $60,000.
d. she is a union steward and her salary is $52,000.
e. None of the above

19. In order to be considered a "qualified" plan, a retirement plan must meet all these requirements except:
a. Certain vesting rules
b. Nondiscrimination rules
c. Exclusive benefit requirement
d. The *res judicata* requirement
e. All of the above must be met

20. In which type of qualified plan does an employer's contribution to the employee's plan have to vest immediately?
a. SIMPLE plan
b. Defined benefit plan
c. Profit-sharing plan
d. Defined contribution plan
e. All of the above must vest immediately

21. The compensation paid by Bass Corporation to the plan participants of a profit-sharing plan in 1999 was $120,000. During 1999, Bass Corporation contributed $30,000 to the plan. What is Bass Corporation's deductible amount for 1999?
a. $-0-
b. $12,000
c. $18,000
d. $30,000

e. Some other amount

22. Same as #21 What is Bass Corporation's contribution carryover (if any) from 1999 to 2000?
a. $-0-
b. $12,000
c. $18,000
d. $30,000
e. Some other amount

23. Jim is married to Jennifer. Jim's salary for 1999 is $75,000 and Jennifer is not employed outside the home. If Jim is covered by pension plan at work, what is the maximum amount Jim and Jennifer can contribute to an IRA?
a. Jim $2,000 and Jennifer $2,000
b. Jim $2,000 and Jennifer $-0-
c. Jim $-0- and Jennifer $2,000
d. Some other amount

24. Bea has AGI of $103,000. What the maximum amount she can contribute to a Roth IRA?
a. $-0-
b. $933
c. $1,067
d. $2,000
e. Some other amount.

25. John establishes a Roth IRA at age 45 and contributes $2,000 per year for 20 years. The account is worth $100,000, consisting of $40,000 nondeductible contributions and $60,000 of accumulated earnings. If John (at age 65) withdraws $50,000, how much is taxable to him?
a. $-0-
b. $10,000
c. $50,000
d. $60,000
e. Some other amount.

26. Assume the same facts as #25 except that John started the Roth IRA when he was 35 years old and he is now 55 years old. How much is taxable to him?
a. $-0-
b. $10,000
c. $50,000
d. $60,000
e. Some other amount.

27. The maximum annual contribution to an education IRA for each beneficiary is?
a. $500
b. $1,000
c. $1,500
d. $2,000
e. Some other amount.

28. Ann receives a $3,000 distribution from her education IRA. She uses $2,000 to pay for qualified education expenses. On the date of the distribution her account balance is $8,000, of which $6,000 is her contributions. How much of the $3,000 distribution is a distribution of earnings (before any exclusion)?
a. $-0-
b. $750
c. $2,000
d. $2,250
e. Some other amount

29. Same as #28 What is the taxable amount after the exclusion?
a. $-0-
b. $250
c. $500
d. $750
e. Some other amount

SOLUTIONS TO CHAPTER 19

True or False

1. True (p. 19-5)
2. True (p. 19-6)
3. False A stock bonus plan uses the employer's stock. (p. 19-7)
4. True (p. 19-5)
5. False A defined contribution plan does not define benefits. (p. 19-5)
6. True (p. 19-7)
7. False The plan must be for the exclusive benefit of employees. (p. 19-8)
8. False Plans cannot discriminate. (p. 19-8)
9. False Vesting of employer contributions may occur over a period of time as prescribed by law. (p. 19-10)
10. True (p. 19-12)
11. True (p. 19-21)
12. False Ten-year averaging has been replaced with a 5-year forward averaging rule, to which certain limitations apply. (p. 19-13)
13. True (p. 19-16)
14. False For certain collectively bargained plans, lower limits may apply. (p. 19-16)
15. True (p. 19-17)
16. False Employee coverage must follow the corporate coverage rules. (p. 19-21)
17. True (p. 19-22)
18. True (p. 19-22)
19. True (p. 19-10)
20. True (p. 19-28)
21. False There are AGI limitations for taxpayers covered under other qualified plan(s) (p. 19-23)
22. False The maximum number of employees is 100. (p. 19-20)
23. True (p. 19-27)
24. True (p. 19-24)
25. True (p. 19-24)

Fill-in-the-Blanks

1. $2,000 (p. 19-22)
2. zero (p. 19-28)
3. constructive (p. 19-30)
4. includible (p. 19-34)
5. risk (p. 19-35)
6. thirty (p. 19-35)
7. include (p. 19-36)
8. income (p. 19-39)
9. exercise (p. 19-40)

Multiple Choice

1. B (p. 19-5)

2.	D	See table in text. (p. 19-10)
3.	A	After 5 years the benefits are 100% vested. (p. 19-10)
4.	D	$500,000 - 360,000 = $140,000. (p. 19-33)
5.	B	Lesser of $2,000 or $1,500. (p. 19-22)
6.	D	Lesser of $2,000 or $14,000. (p. 19-22)
7.	C	20% x $190,000 = $38,000, however the maximum is $30,000. (p. 19-21)
8.	B	(p. 19-9)
9.	B	The 1999 limit. (p. 19-18)
10.	C	(p. 19-31)
11.	B	($14 - $9) x $200 = $1,000. (p. 19-40)
12.	B	($20 - $12) x $100 = $800. (p. 19-39)
13.	D	$18,000 x 15% = $2,700. (p. 19-25)
14.	B	($200 - $75) x $100 = $12,500 LTCG. (p. 19-39)
15.	C	($15,000÷$20,000) x $1,000 = $750. (p. 19-28)
16.	B	$157,300÷14.3 = $11,000. (p. 19-11)
17.	B	$2,000 - [(($38,000-$31,000)÷$10,000) x $2,000] = $600. [1999] (p. 19-23)
18.	A	(p. 19-9)
19.	D	(p. 19-8)
20.	A	(p. 19-25)
21.	C	$120,000 x 15% = $18,000. (p. 19-17)
22.	B	$30,000 - $18,000 = $12,000. (p. 19-17)
23.	C	Jennifer can contribute to an IRA if their AGI is less than $150,000. (p. 19-22)
24.	B	$933 = $2,000 - [$2,000 x ($8,000/$15,000)]. (p. 19-24)
25.	A	Since John is over 59½, there is no taxable income. (p. 19-23).
26.	B	$50,000 - $40,000 = $10,000 (p. 19-24).
27.	A	(p.19-25)
28.	B	$750 = $3,000 x .25 [($8,000 - $6,000)/$8,000]. (p. 19-25)
29.	B	$250 = $750 x .333 [($3,000 - $2,000)/$3,000]. (p.19-25)

CHAPTER 20
CORPORATIONS AND PARTNERSHIPS

CHAPTER HIGHLIGHTS

This chapter provides a brief overview of the tax provisions applicable to the formation and operation of corporations, S corporations, and partnerships, as well as the tax consequences of corporate liquidations.

I. WHAT IS A CORPORATION?

A. Compliance with State Law. Although important, compliance with state law is not the only requirement to qualify for corporate tax status. The degree of business activity at the corporate level is the key consideration for corporate tax status.

B. Entity Classification Prior to 1997. Under the association approach, it is possible for an organization to be taxed as a corporation although it is not a legal corporation under state law. If an association has more corporate than noncorporate characteristics, then it will be taxed as a corporation. The corporate characteristics are:

1) Associates
2) Objective to carry on a business and divide the gains therefrom
3) Continuity of life
4) Centralized management
5) Limited liability
6) Free transferability of interests

According to the Regulations, if an organization has the first two characteristics and three of the last four, it is an association (corporation) for tax purposes.

C. Entity Classification after 1996. Under the IRS's "check-the-box" Regulations, unincorporated entities can elect to be taxed either as a partnership or as a corporation regardless of their corporate or noncorporate characteristics. Limited liability companies (LLCs) are treated as incorporated under state law, and they can elect to be taxed as a corporation or a partnership.

II. INCOME TAX CONSIDERATIONS

A. General Tax Consequences of Different Forms of Business Entities. A business may be conducted as a sole proprietorship, partnership, or corporation. Sole proprietorships and partnerships are not separate taxable entities, so all transactions are reported on the tax returns of the owners or partners. On the other hand, corporations (other than S corporations) are recognized under the tax law as separate taxpaying entities. S corporations are treated in a manner similar to partnerships.

B. Individuals and Corporations Compared. Individual and corporate tax rules vary in several situations. These situations include:

1) Capital gains and losses
2) carryback and carryover provisions
3) Charitable contribution limitations
4) Net operating losses
5) Special deductions for corporations

C. Specific Provisions Compared. Net capital gains of corporate taxpayers are included in ordinary income. Capital losses of corporations are deductible only against capital gains. Corporate capital losses carry back three years and forward five years. All capital loss carrybacks or carryovers become short-term capital losses.

Corporations selling depreciable realty may have ordinary income in addition to that under Sec. 1250. Under Sec. 291, the additional ordinary income element is 20 percent of the excess Sec. 1245 recapture potential over the Sec. 1250 recapture.

Corporate charitable contributions are limited to 10 percent of taxable income, computed without regard to the charitable contribution deduction, net operating loss carryback or capital loss carryback, and the dividends received deduction. Excess contributions are carried over to the succeeding five years.

The net operating loss deduction for a corporation is usually equal to taxable income including any dividends received deduction. The NOL is carried back two years and forward twenty years. An election may be made to forgo the carryback period.

D. Deductions Available Only to Corporations. A corporate taxpayer is allowed a deduction for dividends received from other corporations. The amount of the deduction depends on the amount of stock owned in the dividend paying corporation. If the ownership percentage is less than 20%, then the deduction is 70%; if the ownership percentage is 20% or more and less than 80%, then the deduction is 80%; and if the ownership percentage is 80% or more, then the deduction is 100%. The deduction is limited to the appropriate percentage of taxable income computed without regard to any net operating loss deduction, the dividends received deduction, and any capital loss carryback. However, there is no taxable income limit if a net operating loss results from the dividends received deduction.

Corporations are entitled to amortize organizational expenses over a period of 60 months or more. Organizational expenses include legal and accounting services incident to organization, expenses of temporary directors, expenses of organizational meetings, and fees paid to the state of incorporation.

E. Determination of Tax Liability. The current corporate tax rates are as follows:

Taxable Income	Rate
0 - $50,000	15%
$50,001 - $75,000	25%
$75,001 - $100,000	34%
$100,001 - $335,000	39%
$335,001 - $10,000,000	34%
$10,000,001 - $15,000,000	35%
$15,000,001 - $18,333,333	38%
Over $18,333,333	35%

Qualified personal service corporations (PSCs) are taxed at a flat 35 percent rate on all taxable income. They do not get any benefit from the graduated rate schedule.

Corporations are subject to an alternative minimum tax similar to individual taxpayers. See Chapter 12.

F. Filing Requirements. Generally, corporations file tax returns on Form 1120, however, certain small corporations may file the corporate short Form 1120A. S corporations use Form 1120S. The corporate income tax return must be filed by the fifteenth day of the third month following the close of the tax year. Corporations must file a tax return even when they do not have taxable income. Estimated payments must be made quarterly if the tax liability is expected to be $500 or more.

G. Reconciliation of Taxable Income and Accounting Income. Corporate taxpayers must reconcile taxable income to financial statement income since these amounts are rarely the same. The reconciliation is done on Schedule M-1 of Form 1120.

III. FORMING THE CORPORATION

A. Capital Contributions. The receipt of money or property in exchange for capital stock or as a capital contribution is not income to the corporation. Contributions by other than shareholders are not income to the corporation and a corporation has a zero basis in such contributions.

Debt financing is often more advantageous to a corporation than equity financing since interest payments are deductible and dividend payments are not. In certain instances, such as when a corporation issues debt with features similar to capital stock, the IRS may contend that the debt is really a form of stock and disallow the interest deduction.

B. Transfers to Controlled Corporations. If property is exchanged for stock in a corporation and the shareholders are in "control" of the corporation after the transfer, pursuant to Sec. 351, gain on the transfer is not recognized. Gain or loss is postponed by adjusting the basis of the stock and property. The basis of the stock received by the shareholder in a Sec. 351 transaction is equal to the basis of the property transferred plus any gain recognized by the shareholder, less the fair market value of any boot received by the shareholder. The basis of property received by the corporation is equal to the basis in the hands of the transferor plus any gain recognized to the transferor shareholder. Realized gain is recognized to the extent that the shareholder receives boot.

IV. OPERATING THE CORPORATION

A. Dividend Distributions. Corporate distributions of cash or property to shareholders are dividends to the extent the corporation has accumulated or current earnings and profits (E&P). Any distribution in excess of E&P is a nontaxable return of capital and reduces the basis of the stock held by the shareholder. If there is a distribution in excess of E&P and in excess of the shareholder's stock basis, the excess amount is treated as a capital gain assuming the stock is a capital asset. While E&P is similar to retained earnings, numerous differences may arise in its calculation. For example, nontaxable stock dividends do not affect E&P.

Distributions of property are valued at fair market value. The shareholder's basis in the property received is also the fair market value. The corporation must recognize gain on the distribution of appreciated property to the shareholder.

In closely-held corporations the IRS may contend that certain economic flows to a shareholder are constructive dividends. Therefore, the corporation and shareholder may lose certain tax benefits. Constructive dividends include:

1) Unreasonable compensation
2) Excessive rent paid to shareholders
3) Interest on certain debt to shareholders
4) Advances to shareholders
5) Interest-free or below-market loans
6) Certain shareholder use of corporate property
7) Absorption of personal expenses by the corporation
8) Bargain purchase of corporate property by shareholders

B. Stock Redemptions. Redemptions of stock in a corporation are treated as dividends under Sec. 301 unless the redemption can qualify as a sale or exchange under Sec. 302 or Sec. 303.

V. LIQUIDATING THE CORPORATION

A. General Rule of Sec. 331 and Exceptions. Under Sec. 331, shareholders recognize gain or loss (usually capital) in a corporate liquidation.

B. Exception to the General Rule. If the liquidating corporation is a subsidiary, then under Sec. 332 no gain or loss is recognized by the parent corporation on the liquidation.

C. Basis Determination. The shareholder's basis in property received in a liquidation is usually its fair market value. The basis of property received from a subsidiary under Sec. 332 is the basis of the property to the subsidiary, unless the basis rules of Sec. 338 apply. In such a case, the basis of the property to the parent is the parent's basis in the subsidiary's stock.

D. Effect of the Liquidation on the Corporation. Under the general rule of Sec. 336, the liquidating corporation recognizes any gain or loss, except in certain parent-subsidiary situations.

VI. THE S ELECTION

A. Justification for the Election. The S corporation election allows qualified small corporations to elect not to pay the corporate income tax and to pass the income through to shareholders. To qualify, a corporation must have the following characteristics:

1) Be a domestic corporation
2) Not be a member of an affiliated group
3) Have 75 or fewer shareholders
4) Have as its shareholders only individuals, estates, and certain trusts
5) Not have a nonresident alien shareholder
6) Have only one class of stock outstanding

B. Operational Rules. The S corporation is a tax-reporting entity, not a taxpaying entity. Taxable income and losses are reported by the shareholders.

Certain items pass through to the shareholders of a S corporation "as is." Examples of items that are passed from the S corporation to its shareholders without changing identity are:

1) Tax-exempt income
2) Capital gains and losses
3) Sec. 1231 gains and losses
4) Charitable contributions
5) Foreign tax credits
6) Depletion
6) Nonbusiness income and losses under Sec. 212
7) Intangible drilling costs
8) Investment interest and expenses under Sec. 163(d)
9) Certain portfolio income
10) Passive gains, losses, and credits under Sec. 469
11) Tax preference items and alternative minimum tax adjustments

Taxable income of the S corporation is equal to the net of all items that are not passed through "as is" to the shareholders. The dividends received deduction and net operating loss deduction are not allowed to the S corporation.

Taxable income and separately stated items are passed through to the shareholders as of the last day of the S corporation's tax year, allocated on a per share and per day of stock ownership basis.

The shareholder's basis in the S corporation's stock will be increased or decreased by the pass through of income or loss (including the separately stated items). Distributions will decrease the basis of the stock. Losses in excess of the basis are applied against the basis of loans that the shareholders may have made to the corporation, and any remaining loss is carried forward until there is basis against which to deduct the loss.

VII. PARTNERSHIPS

A. Nature of Partnership Taxation. Partnerships are not separate taxable entities. Instead partnership income is passed through to the partners. A partnership tax return is an information return only. It provides the necessary information to determine a partner's income and expenses.

B. Partnership Formation. Under Sec. 721 no gain or loss is recognized to a partnership or any of its partners on the transfer of property to a partnership in exchange for a capital interest in the partnership. If the partner receives money, an interest for services, or transfers property with a liability more than basis, gain may be recognized on the transfer.

The partner's basis in his or her partnership interest is the sum of money contributed plus the adjusted basis of other property transferred. A partner's basis is determined without regard to any amount on the partnership books such as the capital or equity account. The partner's basis will be increased or decreased by gains, losses, contributions, withdrawals, and changes in partnership liabilities.

The basis of property contributed to a partnership by a partner is equal to the adjusted basis of the property to the partner.

C. Partnership Operation. Reporting partnership income requires that certain transactions be segregated and reported separately. Such items as charitable contributions, capital gains and losses, dividends, etc., must be allocated separately to the partners. Otherwise the taxable income of a partnership is calculated like that of an individual without the following deductions: 1) Exemptions, 2) Deduction for foreign taxes paid, 3) Net operating losses, and 4) Itemized deductions.

Partnership losses pass through to partners and are deductible to the extent of the partner's basis in the partnership interest at the end of the tax year. Losses in excess of the basis carry forward and can be used against future income in a manner similar to S corporation losses.

A partner engaging in a transaction with a partnership is regarded as a nonpartner. If the partner's direct or indirect interest is more than 50 percent, or the transaction is between two partnerships in which the same persons own more than 50 percent, losses from the sale or exchange of property will be disallowed.

Payments made by a partnership to one of its partners for services rendered or for the use of capital, to the extent they are determined without regard to the partnership income, are called guaranteed payments. Such payments are generally deductible by the partnership and must be reported as income by the partner.

KEY TERMS:

Associations

Check-the-Box

Corporate Tax Rates

Corporate Formation

Earnings & Profits

Corporate Liquidations

S Corporations

Partnerships

TEST FOR SELF-EVALUATION

True or False

Indicate which of the following statements are true or false by circling the correct answer.

T F 1. All legal corporations will be taxed as corporations for Federal tax purposes.

T F 2. It is possible for an organization that is not a legal corporation under state law to be taxed as a corporation for Federal tax purposes.

T F 3. Sole proprietorships and partnerships are not separate taxable entities.

T F 4. A regular corporation is recognized as a taxable entity.

T F 5. A partner engaging in a transaction with his partnership is generally regarded as a nonpartner or as an outsider. However, a loss on a sale or exchange between a partnership and a 60 percent partner would be disallowed.

T F 6. Net capital losses of a corporation are deductible against ordinary income.

T F 7. When carried back or forward, a corporate long-term capital loss becomes a short-term capital loss.

T F 8. Corporate charitable contributions are limited to 10 percent of taxable income computed without regard to the charitable contribution deduction, NOL carrybacks or capital loss carrybacks, and the dividends received deduction.

T F 9. A net operating loss deduction is carried back three years and forward five years.

T F 10. The dividends received deduction is always equal to 80 percent of dividends received.

T F 11. The purpose of the dividends received deduction is to prevent triple taxation.

T F 12. In 1999, a corporation with taxable income of $25,000,000 would be taxed at a 35% tax rate on all its taxable income.

T F 13. Qualified organizational expenditures under Sec. 248 may be written off over 50 months or more.

T F 14. Expenses incident to the printing and sale of stock certificates will not qualify as Sec. 248 expenses.

T F 15. Each partner must include in income his or her share of partnership income and any guaranteed payments from the partnership whose tax year ends with or within the partner's tax year.

T F 16. A corporate tax return is due on the fifteenth day of the third month following the close of the tax year.

T F 17. The purpose of Schedule M-1 of Form 1120 is to reconcile retained earnings at the end of the year to the retained earnings at the beginning of the tax year.

T F 18. The receipt of money or property in exchange for stock produces recognized gain to the recipient corporation.

T F 19. If a corporation has excessive debt in its capital structure and a substantial portion of the debt is held by shareholders, the corporation may have thin capitalization problems.

T F 20. Control for purposes of nonrecognition of gain or loss under Sec. 351 means stock ownership of at least 80 percent of the total combined voting power of all classes of stock entitled to vote and at least 80 percent of the total number of shares of all other classes of stock.

T F 21. Gain will never be recognized on a Sec. 351 transfer to a controlled corporation.

T F 22. The term "earnings and profits" is defined in the Code.

T F 23. Earnings and profits and retained earnings will always be the same amount.

T F 24. Partnership losses reduce a partner's basis in his partnership interest, but not below zero and any excess is lost to the partner.

T F 25. Since a partnership is not a taxable entity, it does not have to file any type of tax return.

T F 26. A corporation with gross sales of $625,000 can file a Form 1120A (corporate short form) since its gross receipts are less than $1,000,000.

T F 27. In 1999, Tuna Corporation has taxable income of $60,000. Tuna's corporate income tax before credits is $10,000.

T F 28. Judy is a 40 percent partner is Salmon Partnership. During 1999, Salmon has income of $90,000 and Judy receives cash distributions of $31,000 from the partnership. Judy's taxable income from the partnership is $31,000.

T F 29. Marlin Corporation (a profitable closely-held corporation) owns stock in Ford Motor Corporation. The Ford stock paid Marlin dividends of $12,000 during 1999. Marlin Corporation's dividend received deduction is $9,600 for 1999.

T F 30. Sam transfers property with a basis of $25,000 and a fair market value of $20,000 to a new partnership for a 10 percent interest in the partnership. Sam's basis in the partnership interest is $25,000.

T F 31. Under the proposed "check-the-box" Regulations, an unincorporated business entity can elect to be taxed as a corporation or partnership.

Fill-in-the-Blanks

Complete the following statements with the appropriate word(s) or amount(s).

1. A distribution of property to a shareholder is measured by the __________ of the property on the date of distribution.

2. Under the general rule of Sec. 331, gain or loss is recognized to the shareholders of a corporation in a __________.

3. Under the general rule of Sec. 334, the basis of property received by shareholders in a liquidation is __________.

4. The maximum number of shareholders in an S corporation is __________.

5. Unlike corporations, partnerships are not considered separate taxable __________.

6. A partner's basis in his partnership interest is __________ by additional capital contributions.

7. Partnership taxable income and distributions are reported on Form __________.

8. Taxable income of a partnership is computed (with exceptions) in the same manner as the taxable income of an __________.

9. A partner's deductions for partnership losses may not exceed the partner's adjusted __________ of his or her partnership interest at the end of the partnership year in which the losses were incurred.

10. Payments made to partners for services or use of capital, computed without regard to partnership income, are called __________ payments.

Multiple Choice

Choose the best answer for each of the following questions.

1. Amber Corporation's taxable income for 1999 was $120,000, all from regular operations. Amber's tax liability before credits would be:
   a. $57,600
   b. $44,100
   c. $30,050
   d. $26,400
   e. Some other amount

2. Which of the following items do not pass through separately from an S corporation to its shareholders?
   a. Long-term capital gains
   b. Tax-exempt interest
   c. Wages of employees
   d. Short-term capital gains
   e. Sec. 1231 losses.

3. Which of the following could not be a shareholder in an S corporation?

a. Nonresident alien
b. Individual
c. Certain trusts
d. Estate

4. In 1999 Beige Corporation had gross income of $80,000, including $50,000 of dividends received from domestic corporations of which it owned less than 20 percent of the stock. Beige had business expenses of $33,000. What is the 1999 dividends received deduction?
a. -0-
b. $35,000
c. $50,000
d. $32,900
e. Some other amount

5. In 1999 Blue Corporation had a net long-term capital loss. If this loss is carried over to Blue's 1999 income tax return, it will be treated as a(n):
a. Ordinary loss
b. Sec. 1231 loss
c. Long-term capital loss
d. Short-term capital loss
e. None of the above

6. Gray Corporation is a closely-held corporation. Its sole shareholder is Philo Gray. The corporation currently pays Philo a salary of $600,000 per year. A reasonable salary for a person in Philo's position would be $200,000 per year. During an IRS audit, the government will probably contend that there is a constructive dividend of:
a. $-0-
b. $200,000
c. $400,000
d. $600,000
e. Some other amount

7. Black Corporation had taxable income of $100,000 before considering charitable contributions. If during the year the corporation gave $12,000 in cash to a qualified charitable organization, how much of the $12,000 contribution may the company deduct for the current year?
a. -0-
b. $12,000
c. $10,000
d. $9,500
e. Some other amount

8. Sharon contributes property with a basis of $15,000 and a fair market value of $18,000 to a partnership in exchange for a 25 percent interest therein. Her basis in the partnership interest is:
a. -0-
b. $15,000
c. $18,000
d. $33,000
e. Some other amount

9. Assume the same situation as in Question 8. What is the basis of the property to the partnership if Sharon recognized no gain on the transfer of the property to the partnership?
   a. -0-
   b. $15,000
   c. $18,000
   d. $33,000
   e. Some other amount

10. Brown Corporation, a calendar year S corporation, has taxable income for 1999 of $25,000. If there is one shareholder and she receives a cash distribution from Brown of $40,000 on July 1, 1999, how much ordinary income should she report on her 1999 individual income tax return, assuming her basis is sufficient to cover any dividend?
   a. $100,000
   b. $60,000
   c. $25,000
   d. $40,000
   e. Some other amount

11. White Corporation, an accrual basis calendar year taxpayer, was formed and became operational on July 1, 1999. The following expenses were incurred during its first year of operation:

Expenses of organizational meetings	$600
Fee for state charter	$300
Expenses for sale of stock	$300

   What is White Corporation's maximum organization expense deduction under Sec. 248 for 1999?
   a. $180
   b. $240
   c. $90
   d. $120
   e. Some other amount

12. Red and White form Red & White Corporation. Red contributes cash of $50,000 and White contributes property with a basis of $20,000 and a fair market value of $50,000. If Red and White own all the stock in Red & White Corporation immediately after the transfer, what is White's recognized gain on the transfer?
   a. $-0-
   b. $30,000
   c. $20,000
   d. $50,000
   e. Some other amount

13. Assume the same situation as in Question 12. What is White's basis in the stock he receives from White Corporation?
   a. $-0-
   b. $30,000
   c. $50,000
   d. $20,000
   e. Some other amount

14. Green Corporation has E&P of $25,000. In the current year the corporation makes a $60,000 distribution to its only shareholder. The shareholder's basis in his Green stock is $20,000. From this distribution the shareholder would have a capital gain of:
   a. $-0-
   b. $15,000
   c. $25,000
   d. $20,000
   e. $45,000

15. Diamond Corporation's only asset is raw land with an adjusted basis of $80,000 and a fair market value (net of tax on liquidation) of $135,000. Tony, an individual, owns all the stock (basis of $90,000) in Diamond. The corporation distributes the land to Tony in complete liquidation. How much gain or loss should Tony report?
   a. $10,000 loss
   b. $45,000 gain
   c. $55,000 gain
   d. $10,000 gain
   e. Some other amount

16. Green Medical Group is a qualified personal service corporation. For 1999 the company has taxable income of $42,000. What is the tax liability for the corporation?
   a. $6,300
   b. $10,500
   c. $14,700
   d. $16,400
   e. Some other amount

17. Quincy owns a 60% interest in the capital and profits of the QRS Partnership. On October 15, 1999, Quincy sells property to the partnership for its fair market value of $100,000. The property has a basis to Q of $120,000. On December 20, 1999, QRS sells the property to an outsider for $115,000. What is Quincy's recognized gain or loss in 1999 as a result of the sale of the property to the partnership?
   a. $-0-
   b. ($20,000)
   c. $5,000
   d. ($12,000)
   e. Some other amount

18. Drew contributes land (basis of $100,000 and fair market value of $150,000) to a partnership for a 40% interest in the partnership. The land is subject to a mortgage of $80,000 which is assumed by the partnership. What is Drew's basis in her partnership interest?
   a. $-0-
   b. $100,000
   c. $52,000
   d. $48,000
   e. Some other amount

19. A partnership is allowed which of the following deductions at the partnership level?
   a. Sec. 162 trade or business expenses

b. Sec. 170 charitable contributions
c. Sec. 172 net operating losses from prior years
d. Sec. 212 production of income expenses
e. None of the above are allowed at the partnership level

20. Chad is a 40% shareholder in an S corporation. On January 1, 1999, his basis in the S corporation stock is $25,000. During 1999, Chad loans the corporation $5,000. For 1999, the corporation has an operating loss of $90,000. What amount of loss may Chad deduct in 1999?
a. $-0-
b. $25,000
c. $30,000
d. $36,000
e. Some other amount

21. A regular (C) corporation has a deficit in accumulated earnings and profits of $20,000 at the beginning of the current year. Current earnings and profits are $7,000. During the year the corporation distributes $10,000 to its shareholders. How much of the distribution is taxable as a dividend to the shareholders?
a. $-0-
b. $3,000
c. $10,000
d. $7,000
e. Some other amount

22. In the current year, Yellow Inc. (a retail furniture store) donates unsold furniture to the Goodwill Army (a qualified charity for the care of the needy). The furniture is inventory and has a basis to B of $20,000 and a fair market value of $26,000. What is Yellow's charitable contribution deduction for this gift?
a. $-0-
b. $20,000
c. $23,000
d. $26,000
e. Some other amount

23. A limited liability company (LLC) is treated like which of the following for federal income tax purposes?
a. Regular corporation
b. S corporation
c. Trust
d. Partnership
e. Estate

24. A regular corporation with taxable income of $11,000,000 is taxed at a corporate tax rate of which of the following?
a. 34%
b. 35%
c. 38%
d. 39%
e. Some other rate

Problems

1. Three individuals (A, B, and C) form a closely-held corporation with the following investments:

		Basis to Transferor	FMV	Number of Shares
From A:	Cash	$20,000	$20,000	
	Equipment	$75,000	$80,000	100
From B:	Equipment	$10,000	$15,000	5
From C:	Land	$60,000	$50,000	50

In addition to the five shares of stock, B receives $10,000 in cash. The value of the stock is $1,000 per share. Based on the above information, complete the answers to the following questions.

	A	B	C
Realized gain (or loss)	______	______	______
Recognized gain (or loss)	______	______	______
Basis of the property to the corporation (excluding cash)	______	______	______
Stock basis to shareholder	______	______	______

2. Crown Corporation was formed and began operations on January 2, 1999. The adjusted trial balance as of December 31, 1999, is as follows:

Account	Debit	Credit
Cash	$35,000	
Accounts receivable	8,000	
Land	15,000	
Building	50,000	
Accumulated depreciation-building		3,000
Accounts payable		18,000
Common stock		10,000
Revenue		275,000
Interest on certificate of deposit		10,000
Cost of goods sold	95,000	
Compensation of officers	70,000	
Salaries and wages	25,000	
Repairs	6,000	
Depreciation expense	3,000	
State taxes	9,000	
Total	$316,000	$316,000

Based on the above information, calculate Crown Corporation's taxable income.

Revenue	__________
Cost of goods sold	__________
Gross profit	__________
Other income	__________
Total income	__________
Expenses	__________
Taxable income	__________

3. Violet Corporation reported taxable income, before special items, of $600,000. Selected information available from the corporate records is as follows:

Federal income tax expense	$204,000
Book depreciation	140,000
Tax depreciation	85,000
Life insurance proceeds on death of an officer	100,000

What is Violet's net income per books?

Net income per books	__________
Adjustments:	__________
	__________
	__________
	__________
Taxable income	__________

SOLUTIONS TO CHAPTER 20

True or False

1. False Some corporations may not be recognized as separate entities for tax purposes. (p. 20-3)
2. True (p. 20-3)
3. True (p. 20-5)
4. True (p. 20-5)
5. True (p. 20-33)
6. False Corporate capital losses can only offset capital gains. (p. 20-7)
7. True (p. 20-7)
8. True (p. 20-9)
9. False NOLs are carried back two years and forward 20 years. (p. 20-10)
10. False The dividends received deduction is equal to either 70%, 80%, or 100% of dividends received and may be subject to limitations based on taxable income. (p. 20-11)
11. True (p. 20-11)
12. True (p. 20-13)
13. False Sec. 248 expenses may be written off over 60 months or more. (p. 20-12)
14. True (p. 20-12)
15. True (p. 20-34)
16. True (p. 20-14)
17. False Schedule M-1 reconciles financial net income to taxable income. (p. 20-14)
18. False A corporation does not recognize a gain on the receipt of money or property in exchange for its stock. (p. 20-18)
19. True (p. 20-16)
20. True (p. 20-18)
21. False Realized gain is recognized to the extent of boot received. (p. 20-18)
22. False E&P is not defined in the Code. (p. 20-21)
23. False The calculation is not the same. (p. 20-21)
24. False The excess losses carry forward for each partner. (p. 20-33)
25. False Partnerships file an information return, the Form 1065. (p. 20-30)
26. False Gross sales have to be under $500,000. (p. 20-14)
27. True (15% x $50,000) + (25% x 10,000) = $10,000. (p. 20-13)
28. False Her income is 40% x $90,000 = $36,000. (p. 20-33)
29. False 70% x 12,000 = $8,400. (Assuming Marlin owns less than 20% of Ford). (p. 20-11)
30. True The basis carries over to the partnership interest. (p. 20-31)
31. True (p. 20-4)

Fill-in-the-Blanks

1. fair market value (p. 20-21)
2. liquidation (p. 20-23)
3. fair market value (p. 20-23)
4. 75 (p. 20-25)
5. entities (p. 20-30)
6. increased (p. 20-32)
7. 1065 (p. 20-30)
8. individual (p. 20-32)

9. basis (p. 20-33)
10. guaranteed (p. 20-34)

Multiple Choice

1. C 15%($50,000) + 25%($25,000) + 34%($25,000) + 39%($20,000) = $30,050. (p. 20-13)
2. C (p. 20-27)
3. A (p. 20-25)
4. D 70% x $50,000 = $35,000 general rule; 70% x $47,000 = $32,900 limitation. (p. 20-11)
5. D (p. 20-7)
6. C $600,000 less $200,000. (p. 20-21)
7. C 10% x $100,000 = $10,000 maximum. (p. 20-9)
8. B (p. 20-32)
9. B (p. 20-32)
10. C (p. 20-27)
11. C [($600 + 300)÷60 months] x 6 months = $90. (p. 20-12)
12. A (p. 20-18)
13. D (p. 20-18)

14. B

Distribution	$60,000	
Dividend	-25,000	
Return of Capital	-20,000	
Capital gain	$15,000	(p. 20-20)

15. B $135,000 - 90,000 = $45,000. (p. 20-23)
16. C 35% x $42,000 = $14,700. (p. 20-13)
17. A Q is a related party, therefore the loss is not recognized. (p. 20-33)
18. C $100,000 - ($80,000 x 60%) = $52,000. (p. 20-30)
19. A (p. 20-32)
20. C 40% x $90,000 = $36,000; however, the loss is limited to the basis in the S corporation stock plus the loan of $5,000, $30,000. (p. 20-29)
21. D The distribution is taxable to the extent of current E&P. (p. 20-20)
22. C $20,000 + 50%($26,000 - $20,000) = $23,000. (p. 20-9)
23. D (p. 20-4)
24. B (p. 20-13)

Problems

1.

	A	B	C
Realized gain (or loss)	$5,000	$5,000	-$10,000
Recognized gain (or loss)	-0-	5,000	-0-
Basis of the property to the corp. (ex. cash)	75,000	15,000	60,000
Stock basis (p. 20-19)	95,000	5,000	60,000

2.

Revenue	$275,000
Cost of goods sold	-95,000
Gross profit	$180,000
Other income	10,000
Total income	$190,000
Expenses	-113,000
Taxable income	$ 77,000

3.

Net income per books	$441,000
Federal income tax	204,000
Depreciation ($140,000 - $85,000)	55,000
Life insurance proceeds	-100,000
Taxable income	$600,000

(p. 20-15)